D1348760

SUPPLEMENTARY VOLUME LXXVIII
2004

THE
ARISTOTELIAN
SOCIETY

THE SYMPOSIA READ AT THE
JOINT SESSION OF THE
ARISTOTELIAN SOCIETY
AND THE MIND ASSOCIATION
AT UNIVERSITY OF KENT
JULY 2004

PUBLISHED BY

The Aristotelian Society

2004

First published 2004 by
The Aristotelian Society

© The Aristotelian Society 2004

ISBN 0 907111 50 5

ISSN 0309-7013

All rights reserved. No part of this publication may be reproduced, stored in a retrieval system, or transmitted, in any form or by any means, electronic, mechanical, photocopying, recording or otherwise, without prior permission of the Aristotelian Society. Requests for permission to reprint should be addressed to the Editor.

THE ARISTOTELIAN SOCIETY PUBLICATIONS

PROCEEDINGS: as a journal, three times a year, and as a bound volume annually in June.

SUPPLEMENTARY VOLUME: annually in June. This records the papers read at the annual Joint Session of the Aristotelian Society and the Mind Association.

BOOK SERIES (in co-operation with Blackwell Publishers): The Society has editorial responsibility for these books, which are published by Blackwells. They are available at less than half price to members of the Society. Currently available:

Barry Taylor	*Modes of Occurrence: Verbs, Adverbs and Events* (1985)
Jonathan Westphal	*Colour: Some Philosophical Problems from Wittgenstein* (1987)
Tim Maudlin	*Quantum Non-Locality and Relativity: Metaphysical Intimations of Modern Physics* (1994)
John Martin Fischer	*The Metaphysics of Free Will* (1994)
S. Lovibond & S. Williams (eds)	*Essays for David Wiggins: Identity, Truth and Value* (1996)
J. Corbi and J. Prades	*Minds, Causes and Mechanisms* (2000)
Tom Sorell	*Moral Theory and Anomaly* (2000)

LINES OF THOUGHT SERIES: These books are published by Oxford University Press, which offers them to members of the Society at a 25% discount. Already published:

Jerry A. Fodor	*Hume Variations* (2003)
David O. Brink	*Perfectionism and the Common Good: Themes in the Philosophy of T. H. Green* (2003)

ORDERS for past Proceedings and *Supplementary Volumes:* Single issues from the current and previous two volumes are available at the current single issue price from Blackwell Publishers Journals. Earlier issues may be obtained from Swets & Zeitlinger, Back Sets, Heereweg 347, PO Box 810, 2160 Lisse, The Netherlands. Email: backsets@swets.nl

All institutional enquiries should be addressed to the Distributors.

OTHER ENQUIRIES should be addressed to the Editor.

Printed in England by
J. W. Arrowsmith Ltd
Winterstoke Road
Bristol BS3 2NT

Journals Subscriptions Department
Marston Book Services
PO Box 87   Oxford OX2 0DT
Tel (01865) 791155
Fax (01865) 791927

Editor:
A. W. Price
Department of Philosophy
Birkbeck College
Malet Street
London WC1E 7HX

Assistant Editor:
Dr Jesse Norman
Department of Philosophy
University College
19 Gordon Square
London WC1E 6BT

Please check in most recent volume for current addresses

CONTENTS

PROGRAMME

JOINT SESSION OF THE ARISTOTELIAN SOCIETY AND THE MIND ASSOCIATION
UNIVERSITY OF KENT, JULY 9–11 2004

Friday
5.00 pm
The Inaugural Address: Dorothy Edgington
Two Kinds of Possibility
Chair: Sean Sayers

Saturday
9.00 am
Daniel Garber and Jean-Baptiste Rauzy
Leibniz on Body, Matter and Extension
Chair: David Wiggins

11.00 am
Justin Broackes and Peter Hacker
Substance
Chair: David Charles

2.00 pm
Graduate Papers

4.00 pm
Open sessions

8.00 pm
Sarah Broadie and Anthony Kenny
The Creation of the World
Chair: Richard Cross

Sunday
9.00 am
Michael Smith and Edward Harcourt
Instrumental Desires, Instrumental Rationality
Chair: Richard Norman

11.00 am
Andrew Williams and Michael Otsuka
Equality, Ambition and Insurance
Chair: Jonathan Wolff

4.30 pm
Open sessions

8.00 pm
Crispin Wright and Martin Davies
On Epistemic Entitlement
Chair: Michael Williams

The Inaugural Address

TWO KINDS OF POSSIBILITY

By Dorothy Edgington

ABSTRACT I defend a version of Kripke's claim that the metaphysically necessary and the knowable *a priori* are independent. On my version, there are two independent families of modal notions, metaphysical and epistemic, neither stronger than the other. Metaphysical possibility is constrained by the laws of nature. Logical validity, I suggest, is best understood in terms of epistemic necessity.

I

I *ntroduction.* I offer a way of thinking of the modal notions, and a way of classifying them, which is much indebted to Saul Kripke's *Naming and Necessity* (1980).[1] But it differs from how most philosophers who have been impressed by Kripke understand modality. My reading is not only compatible with but, I think, a natural reading of *almost* everything Kripke says in elucidation and defence of his claims about metaphysical possibility and necessity. (The incompatibility concerns a passage many find unconvincing, which I discuss later.)

What I take from Kripke, and what I consider to be a liberating release from a philosophical strait-jacket, is the two-way independence of the knowable *a priori* and the metaphysically necessary. But I take more seriously than he does the family of epistemic modal notions to which, I claim, the *a priori* belongs. It is the epistemic modal notions, I think, which we need to understand logic: so-called broadly logical necessity (by which I mean, not necessarily formal logical necessity) is an epistemic notion.

What, then, is metaphysical necessity? I argue that it derives from a modal concept we all use, in distinguishing things which can happen and things which can't, in virtue of their nature, which we discover empirically: the metaphysically possible, I claim, is constrained by the laws of nature. That this isn't totally

1. Page references to Kripke's work refer to this volume.

at odds with Kripke is indicated by the final remark in his book: 'The third lecture suggests that a good deal of what contemporary philosophy regards as mere physical necessity is actually necessity *tout court*. The question how far this can be pushed is one I leave for further work' (164).

Why not drop the 'meta' and just call these physical possibilities? 'Physical' would be too narrow a term. First, a theory of modality should not prejudge the question whether all laws of nature are reducible to laws of physics. Second, on a Platonist view of mathematics, there will be real necessities there which may not be epistemically necessary. In any case, I see this more as upgrading the notion of physical necessity than as downgrading metaphysical necessity, though it is perhaps a little of the latter as well—an attempt to make that notion, once separated from the knowable *a priori*, less mysterious. But physical necessity—better, natural necessity—will be a paradigm of metaphysical necessity. To use the narrower term to present my thesis as contentiously as possible: it is not uncommon, in explaining the allegedly important, philosophers' sense of the modal notions, to do so by contrast with 'mere' epistemic possibility, or with 'mere' physical possibility (or impossibility). I try to show, on the contrary, that we can get by with just these two families of modal notions, though there are important distinctions to be made within each family, according to whether they are relativized to a context—a time, and in the epistemic case, a person—or freed from such relativization.

II

First Motivation. I give three motivations for this view. First, laws of nature: there have always been temptations to assimilate these to necessary truths, and temptations to differentiate them from necessary truths, a dilemma which could not be resolved so long as the *a priori* and the metaphysically necessary were not separated. Very roughly, the prevalent philosophical view before Hume, correctly perceiving that such statements have the mark of necessity, was that we have to think of them as *somehow* deducible from self-evident truths about how the world must be—if we only knew how. Hume showed definitively that reason was not up to the task. The prevalent view since Hume, recognising that they can't be known *a priori*, concludes that they are contingent regularities, but has been hard put to explain how they differ from other, merely accidental, contingent regularities. Of course, anyone can *call* a statement physically necessary if and only if it is true in all possible situations in which the laws of nature of the actual world hold, thus making the actual laws themselves necessary by stipulative fiat, but throwing no light on the nature of laws. (An out-and-out Humean could speak according to this stipulation.) William Kneale (1949 Chapter 2, 1950) bravely tried to resuscitate the view that natural laws had to be treated as necessary in some serious sense. But at a time when the prevalent view was that necessity is analyticity if it is anything, his ideas met with little favour. Only with Kripke's separation of the *a priori* and the metaphysically necessary is there room for the view that the pre-Humeans were right in thinking that laws of nature are necessary but wrong in thinking they are knowable *a priori*, and the post-Humeans made exactly the opposite mistake. *If* Kripke has shown that there is a class of necessary truths which can only be known empirically, and *if* there are reasons for treating laws as necessary in some serious sense, why should this class not be the natural home for natural laws?

Why should we treat natural laws as necessary in some serious sense? First, the modal idiom is the natural one for distinguishing laws from accidental generalisations. Nothing *can* travel faster than light. These plants *can't* be grown at freezing temperatures. These other plants, merely, never are, in the history of the universe, grown at freezing temperatures, although they could have been. Second, all neo-Humean attempts to make this distinction, I think, fail. Here are some *prima facie* difficulties for the best neo-Humean theory of laws, the 'Mill–Ramsey–Lewis theory',[2] according to which laws are those true contingent generalisations which occur as axioms or theorems in the true deductive system which achieves the best combination of

---

2. This is really David Lewis's theory, with some affinity to Mill, *A System of Logic*, Book III, Chapter IV, Section 1, and inspired by remarks of F. P. Ramsey in 'Universals of Law and of Fact' (1928, in Ramsey 1990, 140–4), retracted by Ramsey a year later ('General Propositions and Causality' *op. cit.* 150). See Lewis (1973, 74–5, 1986, xi–xvi, 122–31, 1994).

simplicity and strength—by our standards of simplicity and strength.

While we may like better a world in which laws fit into nice systems, and we may have acquired reason to think we live in such a world, it is far from obvious that our concept of law precludes the possibility of relatively isolated laws governing the workings of their own subject matter, not clashing, of course, but not particularly cohering either. Conversely, might there not be highly informative and simple generalisations which are not laws? Bas van Fraassen (1989, 46–47) has suggested an example like this: consider a world which contains just two kinds of object, iron cubes and gold spheres, whizzing around according to Newtonian mechanics. It is hard to deny that 'All and only cubes are iron' and 'All and only spheres are golden' add a lot of informational content to the description of this world, at little loss of simplicity. But they are not laws. It just so happens that there were not, though there could have been, collisions which altered the shape of these objects.[3]

III

Second and Third Motivations. My second motivation comes from the relation between possibility and probability. Probability is weighted possibility—a measure on a space of possibilities. It is a widely-held view that there are two kinds of probability, one epistemic, one empirical.[4] One kind of probability is a measure of a person's degree of closeness to certainty that a proposition is true (epistemic use). But also, there are probabilities 'out there' for scientists to discover—about radioactive decay, about whether eating garlic reduces one's chance of getting heart disease, and so forth.

On objective probability, I agree with David Lewis's (1980) account—setting aside the last few pages, to which I return later.

3. For further criticism of Humean views, see D. M. Armstrong (1983, Part I). There has been a revival of necessitarian views of laws in the last twenty years or so, including Armstrong's work. (However, I do not myself see the need to postulate contingent relations of necessitation between universals.) See also Foster (1982), Bird (2001) and Leeds (2001).

4. See Ramsey (1990, 53): 'The conclusions we shall come to as to the meaning of probability in logic must not ... be taken as prejudging its meaning in physics'; and see Carnap (1945) and Lewis (1980).

It applies to single cases: there is such a thing as the present chance of a particular tritium atom's decaying within a year. In general, it varies with time. Lewis illustrates this with a man walking through a maze at constant speed, making each choice with a randomizing device of some sort—a die or coin or spinner. If we know the chances governing the functioning of this device, we can calculate the chance that he will be at the centre by noon. This can go up and down, as he takes lucky or unlucky turns, until noon, when it becomes 1 or 0, and remains 1 or 0 thereafter.

I can invoke Kripke's support for the connection between probability and possibility, from the example he gives in the Introduction to *Naming and Necessity* of the two dice, intended to allay doubts and misunderstandings about his use of possible worlds. He says 'An analogy from school—in fact it is not merely an analogy—will help to clarify my view. ... Now in doing these school exercises in probability, we were in fact introduced at a tender age to a set of (miniature) possible worlds' (16). We can add that a person's epistemic probability of an outcome will not in general equal the 'metaphysical' (real, objective) probability. Indeed, a person's epistemic probability can be non-zero while there is zero real chance of the proposition in question. And the converse is *prima facie* possible as well: of having zero epistemic probability for something which has a positive real chance of occurring, and even comes about. (For example, I assign epistemic probability 1 to my being in Oxford right now. Hence I give 0 to the scenario that in a moment I shall wake up surrounded by brain surgeons and a view of the Manhattan skyline. But occasionally one gets epistemic shocks of these proportions.)

Probabilities of both sorts are, typically, context dependent. Objective chance changes with time, epistemic probability with the state of information of the subject. This leads me to my third motivation, which is to try to take as basic our pre-philosophical use of modal concepts, and to derive the more rarefied philosophical use from these. The novice at philosophy has some catching on to do in coming to understand the philosopher's favourite sense, according to which e.g. 'It is possible that the Conservative Party won the last election' is true, and 'It is possible that a man lives for years unaided under water' is true. And I think there are two primitive modal notions, both context dependent, in terms of which we can define two more abstract notions. A primitive epistemic possibility is what you are considering when you are wondering whether something is the case. It is relative to an individual and a time. The other pre-philosophical notion is that certain things can happen, certain things can't; people and other objects can do certain things and can't do others. What can and can't happen, in this sense, is a matter of empirical discovery. This car can do a hundred miles per hour (though it never will), this other car can't—as they are presently constituted. Later, when the first has deteriorated and the second hotted up, the position may be reversed. Diseases which were once incurable no longer are.

These latter possibilities are constrained by two sorts of things, the way things are now, and the laws of nature. The laws of nature render some combinations of situations always impossible. Call something absolutely metaphysically impossible if it is metaphysically impossible at all times. Its negation is absolutely metaphysically necessary. What is not absolutely metaphysically impossible is absolutely metaphysically possible.

Relative epistemic possibilities are also constrained by two kinds of thing, one peculiar to the subject—what she already takes as known, the other not—what combinations of things can be recognised as impossible whatever state of information the subject is in. Call these things absolutely epistemically impossible, or *a priori* impossible. I leave unanswered the question of the source of *a priori* knowledge. But I do capture the core of the traditional notion: *a priori* knowledge is independent of the state of information of the subject. We are all, at all times, capable of ruling out that a thing be both round and square, and so on.[5]

As noted by Kripke, (34, 158–60), a 'can' is used in characterising the absolute epistemic modal notions. If this 'can' were epistemic, circularity would be involved. But I think we can show that this 'can' is metaphysical. Suppose Goldbach's Conjecture is true, but there is no way of proving it: it can't be known *a priori*, or indeed at all. Suppose further that the fact that there is no way of proving it, itself cannot be proved. So it is

---

5. Of course there are far more complex cases! We need to idealise our cognitive capacities, and suppose we are talking about ideally rational subjects, in specifying what is *a priori* impossible.

always *epistemically* possible that we will come up with a proof. But that doesn't show that we *can* come up with a proof: it is not an epistemic 'can' that is involved in 'can be known *a priori*'. So, epistemic modality needs metaphysical modality in its character-isation. This is no problem for the view that these are two, independent families of modal notions.

Philosophers take a professional interest in timeless, eternal, in some sense necessary truth. I have tried to explain these notions in terms of ordinary everyday tensed modal talk. When a philosopher says 'It is possible that ...' or 'There is a possible situation (or world) in which ...' she means 'There is or will be or was a possible situation in which ...' No great harm in that, but we are in danger of losing the very significant difference between a past and a present possibility, the difference between what may be true and what might have been true but no longer may be true, whether that is read epistemically or metaphysically.

IV

Independence. It can be epistemically possible that *p* without being metaphysically possible that *p*. Suppose the security men find, inside the tradesmen's entrance to 10 Downing Street, a large parcel. On closer inspection, they hear a ticking noise. They call the bomb squad. That parcel might shortly explode. It turns out that the parcel contains a handsome eighteenth century clock just back from repair. There was no metaphysical possibility that the parcel would explode, though there was an epistemic possibility.

Here is one of Kripke's examples of the converse (79). Leverrier, noticing some irregularities in the orbits of the planets, concludes that they must be caused by another, as yet unseen planet, and decides to call it 'Neptune'. Now, it was epistemically possible that his hypothesis was wrong—that there is no such planet. But if his hypothesis is right—if Neptune exists—it is the planet causing these perturbations. And this conditional is known *a priori*—at least by Leverrier: it follows from his stipulation about the use of 'Neptune'. There's no epistemic possibility that Neptune exists and has nothing to do with the perturbations. But such is a metaphysical possibility—at least in the timeless sense. Making it tensed: it was metaphysically possible that Neptune, which actually caused these perturbations, should have been knocked off course a million years ago and done no such thing.

The mechanism of the example is simple. An object comes into existence—a star (or planet) is born. There are many metaphysically possible histories it can have—many spatial paths it can follow, among other things. One of these is its actual history. This object gets given a name. However this is done, whether by pointing, using demonstratives, or as in this case, by description of some of its actual properties, it is in virtue of some part of its actual history, its being in some actual relation to us, the namers, that the object is the bearer of the name. And of course we can use the name to refer to the object in discussing the different histories it could have had, including those in which it would not have been in the relation to us in virtue of which it got its name— possible situations which we know *a priori* do not obtain.

Suppose an unconnected group of astronomers, in China, developed a new, more powerful telescope and detected this heavenly body, and decided to call it 'Buddha'. It is not knowable *a priori* that Neptune is Buddha. But, if the same object was named twice, any metaphysically possible thing which could have happened to Neptune could have happened to Buddha. There is no metaphysically possible situation in which they are different objects. Though, for anyone wondering whether Neptune is Buddha, it is epistemically possible that it is not.

What Kripke sometimes describes as an illusion of contingency I describe as a kind of contingency. We agree that a person can be competent in the use of two names, by normal standards of competence (indeed, far above the minimal standards that Kripke thinks are sufficient for competence), yet not have the information to know whether they designate the same object. I say, this is just what it is for it to be an epistemically contingent matter.

V

Validity. In the light of the above independence between the metaphysically necessary and the epistemically necessary, there is a decision to make about how to characterize valid arguments. (I do not mean only *formally* valid arguments: I include cases such as 'It's round; so it's not square'.) We were familiar with two thoughts: first, an argument is valid if and only if it is necessary that the conclusion is true if the premises are true; and second, if an argument is valid, and you accept that the premises are true, you need no further empirical information to enable you to recognise that the conclusion is true. The premises rationally commit you to the conclusion. Given Kripke's work, and taking 'necessary' in its metaphysical sense, these two thoughts are not equivalent. Consider 'Hesperus is larger than the moon; therefore, Phosphorus is larger than the moon'; or, marginally more complex, 'Hesperus is a planet smaller than the earth; Phosphorus is a planet larger than the moon; therefore, some planet is smaller than the earth and larger than the moon.' It is metaphysically impossible that the premise or premises are true and the conclusion false. But someone who accepts the premise(s) and rejects the conclusion is not making an error in reasoning. It is his astronomy that is at fault. A further piece of empirical information is needed to add to the premises in order for him to be able to deduce the conclusion, namely, the information that Hesperus is Phosphorus.

On the other hand, granted that Leverrier knows *a priori* that, if Neptune exists, it causes these perturbations, his argument from the premise that Neptune exists to the conclusion that it causes these perturbations is trivial, and needs no extra information, despite the fact that it is, or rather, was metaphysically possible that the premise be true and the conclusion false.

To take a marginally less trivial example, consider Evans's descriptive name, 'Julius' which rigidly designates the person who actually invented the zip-fastener. Consider the argument

> Julius was a mathematician.
> The person who invented the zip fastener emigrated to Tahiti.
> Therefore, some mathematician emigrated to Tahiti.

We know *a priori* that if the premises are true the conclusion is true. Yet, there are metaphysically possible situations in which the premises are true and the conclusion false, namely, ones in which Julius, the actual inventor of the zip fastener, did not do so and someone else, who emigrated to Tahiti, did, and no mathematician emigrated to Tahiti.

We have now perhaps four distinct possible notions of validity, that governed by metaphysical necessity, that governed by epistemic necessity, that governed by both—the conjunction of the first two, and that governed by either—the disjunction of the first two. In my view it is the least departure from traditional, pre-Kripkean thinking, and more consonant with the point of distinguishing valid from invalid arguments, to take validity to be governed by epistemic necessity, i.e., an argument is valid if and only if there is an *a priori* route from premises to conclusion.

The alternative interpretation of Kripke, to which I am opposed, goes something like this: Kripke is talking about strict necessity. (That I don't deny: he is talking about one kind of strict necessity.) We used to think of strict necessity as (broadly) logical necessity (as opposed, perhaps, to 'mere' physical necessity). Kripke has shown us that that notion applies to certain truths which can only be discovered empirically.[6]

This alternative interpretation tries to minimise the distance between metaphysical necessity and the knowable *a priori* by claiming that if it is metaphysically necessary that *p*, at least its modal status, if not its truth, is knowable *a priori*; that is, it is knowable *a priori* that if *p*, then necessarily *p*. This seems to me to be an over-generalisation from the case of identity statements, which is the only case where we have a purported proof. Take 'Water is composed of H_2O molecules' or 'Gold has atomic number 79'. It is empirical scientific investigation that discovers their truth; and it is also, arguably, scientific investigation that tells us that these properties are fundamental to being water, and to being gold.[7] Just as we could not have ruled out *a priori* that

6. See for example Graeme Forbes (1985), and Christopher Peacocke (1997, 1999 Chapter 4).

7. One cannot appeal to the necessity of identity for these examples without further ado. With identity statements involving people, planets, etc., we have a firm pre-theoretical grasp of the identity and difference between the entities in question: of what it would be for 'the man in the corner' to pick out a different man, and the like. (No doubt our pre-theoretical grasp becomes shaky in some problem cases, but they need not arise to get a firm handle on the sense in which, e.g. 'Benjamin Franklin' is a rigid designator while 'the inventor of bifocals' is not.) But the identity conditions of substances are a theoretical matter. Water = the substance composed of H_2O. Water = the substance which falls as rain. But the former description, not the latter, science tells us, specifies the essential nature of water.

future science would pronounce these statements false, so we could not have ruled out *a priori* that future science would preserve their truth but treat them as giving accidental properties: describe counterfactual situations in which there could have been water—that which has the true essential properties of water—which was not composed of H_2O molecules.

Timothy Williamson gave (in discussion) a very simple example which shows that one cannot hold in general that, if a proposition is metaphysically necessary, it is knowable *a priori* that if it is true it is necessarily true. Just consider the disjunction of an *a posteriori* identity statement, $a = b$, and an *a posteriori*, clearly contingent statement, c is F. We can't know *a priori* whether the disjunction is true. Nor can we know *a priori* that, if it's true, it's necessarily true; for it might be true in virtue of the first disjunct, or in virtue of the second.

And on my view that laws of nature are metaphysically necessary, there is little reason to think that we know *a priori* of a regularity that, if it is true, it is necessarily true. We might be agnostic about whether, if it is true, it is accidentally or necessarily true.

Ian McFetridge (1990, 137–40) argued against my aligning logical necessity with what is knowable *a priori*. He argued that logical necessity is the strongest kind of necessity: if the argument 'A, so B' is valid, there is no sense of 'possible' in which it is possible that A and not B. (Well, almost no sense. The exception is 'mere time- and person-relative epistemic possibility which may be asserted even when logical possibility cannot' (137)—the mere expression of ignorance about a proposition p, when p is clearly logically necessary or logically impossible: 'It may be prime', said of a ten-digit number, does not commit one to the logical possibility that it is prime. This kind of possibility he sets aside.) His argument rests on two assumptions: first, if the argument 'A, so B' is valid, so is the argument 'A & C, so B', for any C; second, a valid argument from A to B justifies any conditional, *indicative or subjunctive*, 'If A, then B' (his emphasis).

Suppose, then, that 'A, so B' is valid. But suppose that in some sense of 'possible', it is possible that A & $\neg B$. Let C be a circumstance in which this possibility is realised. Now consider the argument 'A & C, so B'. By the first assumption, it is valid, and by the second, we should be able to assert 'if A & C were the case, then B would be the case'. Yet C specifies a circumstance in which A & $\neg B$.

He illustrates with the Leverrier example. McFetridge agrees that Leverrier knows *a priori* that if Neptune exists it is a planet causing such-and-such perturbations. I say Leverrier's argument 'Neptune exists, so Neptune causes such-and-such perturbations' is valid. But there is (or was: 'is' in the timeless sense) a metaphysical possibility that the premise should have been true and the conclusion false, one in which Neptune was knocked off course long ago. What then of the argument 'Neptune exists and was knocked off course a million years ago, so Neptune is the cause of these perturbations'? If the original argument is valid, so is this one (by the first assumption). But if it is, then, by the second assumption, we ought to be entitled to assert 'If Neptune had existed and been knocked off course a million years ago, it would have caused these perturbations'. But we are not: if the antecedent had been true the consequent would have been false.

I first want to point out that an exactly parallel argument would rule out the alternative view that logical necessity is metaphysical necessity. Consider the argument: 'There is water in this glass, so there is H_2O in this glass.' Suppose it is logically valid. Then by McFetridge's assumptions so is 'There is water in this glass and our theory of the chemical structure of water is all wrong. Therefore, there is H_2O in this glass', and the conditional 'If our theory of the chemical structure of water is all wrong and there is water in this glass, then there is H_2O in this glass' is acceptable. But it is not.[8]

So given McFetridge's assumptions, it appears that the third option is the right one: logical necessity, the kind of necessity that governs valid arguments, is the conjunction of the two: metaphysically necessary *and* knowable *a priori*. Logical possi-

---

8. Someone who holds that it is logically necessary that water is H_2O might object that we are dealing with 'mere' epistemic possibility here, and this has been set aside. But in the context of the present dialectic, that would be question-begging. One may set aside cases of 'mere' epistemic possibility when it is agreed on all sides that they are compatible with logical impossibility, but not, without begging the question, cases where logical impossibility is in dispute.

bility is the disjunction: metaphysically possible or not knowable *a priori* to be false. An *a priori* route from premise(s) to conclusion is not sufficient for validity, nor is the metaphysical impossibility of true premises and a false conclusion.

Are McFetridge's assumptions unassailable? I shall not dispute the first, that if '*A*, so *B*' is valid, so is '*A* & *C*, so *B*', but we should distinguish the case where *A* and *C* are compossible from the case in which they are not: in the latter case, our premise is impossible, and, following classical logic, we shall say (perhaps reluctantly) that an argument from an impossible premise to any conclusion is valid. But in what sense of 'impossible'? That is what is at issue. Reconsider the argument 'Neptune exists and was knocked off course a million years ago, so Neptune is the cause of these perturbations.' Given Leverrier's stipulation, the premise is *a priori* impossible. There *is* no possibility that Neptune exists and was knocked off course a million years ago (so as to be elsewhere, or nowhere, at the time in question). So an argument from that premise to any conclusion is a degenerate case of a valid argument, despite the fact that there *was* a possibility, known *a priori* not to have come about, that Neptune should have existed and not been around to cause the perturbations. Conversely, for someone who wants to align logical possibility with metaphysical possibility, and who accepts present chemical theory, an argument from the premise 'Water is XYZ and there is water is the glass' to any conclusion is valid; but he will not accept the conditional 'If water *is* XYZ and there is water in the glass, there is H_2O in the glass.'

We are familiar with the fact that an indicative and a subjunctive 'If *A*, *B*' can disagree: if Oswald hadn't killed Kennedy, no one else would have; but if Oswald didn't kill Kennedy, someone else did. In the indicative the antecedent presents something as an epistemic possibility, while in the subjunctive the antecedent typically presents something as *not* an epistemic possibility, but as something which *was* a real possibility ('If you had come by train ... '). Each kind of conditional goes with a different kind of possibility. McFetridge's second assumption, that there is a unitary sense of 'possible' that governs both, is not obligatory. And it is tantamount to what was to be proved: that the sense of necessity relevant to logic governs absolutely every kind of possibility.[9]

VI

The Two-Dimensional Framework. Can we restore unity to this bipartite approach to modality by defining both notions in terms of a single set of possible worlds? This has become a popular strategy, due to David Chalmers (1996)[10] and Frank Jackson (1998). Take the set of metaphysically possible worlds. A proposition is metaphysically necessary if and only if it is true in all of them. Now one of these worlds is the actual world. Not being omniscient, there are many worlds which, for all we know, might be the actual world: one with rain tomorrow, and one without, for instance. We can define another notion of necessity, call it necessity$_2$: p is necessary$_2$ if and only if, whichever world we take to be the actual world, it is actually true that p. Define a sentence operator 'actually': 'Actually p' is true at a world w if and only if p is true at the actual world. We can show the independence of these two notions of necessity, and give a kind of model to illustrate Kripke's claims. Suppose the actual F is the actual G. Then in all possible worlds, the actual F is the actual G: it is metaphysically necessary. But it is not typically necessary$_2$: it's not true that whatever world we take to be the actual world, the actual F is the actual G. Conversely, consider 'It is actually raining if and only if it is raining' or '(If anyone is Prime Minister) the actual Prime Minister is the Prime Minister.' Whichever world we take to be actual, these are actually true. They are necessary$_2$. But it is not the case that they are true at all worlds: there are worlds at which the actual Prime Minister is not

9. Bob Hale (1996, 1997, 489–90) gives what he sees as a version of McFetridge's argument, without mentioning subjunctive conditionals. His crucial assumption is this: if A logically entails B, and it is in any sense possible that A, it is in that sense possible that B. But this assumption is question-begging. The opponent thinks that A & $\neg B$ is logically impossible, and so entails everything, yet A & $\neg B$ is possible in some other sense. But she does not accept that everything is possible in this other sense.

For an application of the idea that something can be logically necessary but not metaphysically necessary to the question of contingent existence, see Rumfitt (2003). Also, Putnam's (1981, 14–16) discussion of brains in vats involves the idea that what is physically possible may be logically impossible.

10. Chalmers's more recent work is not committed to deriving both notions from a single set of worlds. See the references to papers on his website.

the Prime Minister; and worlds at which it is not raining although it is raining at the actual world. Moreover, necessity$_2$ does seem to be an epistemic notion; and in our examples, what is necessary$_2$ is knowable *a priori*.

This is an elegant framework. But there are problems with the claim that necessity$_2$ coincides with what is knowable *a priori*. Necessity$_2$ comes into its own only with statements involving this rather artificial device, the actually operator, and it is a contentious claim (and against the spirit of Kripke's work on names) to suppose that much ordinary thought and talk should be analysed in terms of it. Secondly, once the metaphysically necessary has been separated from the knowable *a priori*, there may be all sorts of claims which are metaphysically necessary, *and* true whichever world we take to be actual (because they don't involve 'actually' in any way), yet not knowable *a priori*. Suppose it's metaphysically necessary that nothing travels faster than light. It is true in all metaphysically possible worlds. Whichever world we take to be actual, actually, nothing travels faster than light. But it is not knowable *a priori* that nothing travels faster than light. So, while it is elegant and has its place, I don't think this framework captures the knowable *a priori*, i.e. the epistemically necessary.

VII

Kripke on Metaphysical Possibility. To repeat, the penultimate sentence of *Naming and Necessity* reads 'The third lecture suggests that a good deal of what contemporary philosophy regards as mere physical necessity is actually necessity *tout court*.' Many of Kripke's remarks in defence of particular metaphysical possibilities are naturally read as though this were true. Some examples:

1. 'If Hesperus had been hit by a comet, it might have been at a different position at that time.' (58)
2. 'Surely Moses might have just decided to spend his days more pleasantly in the Egyptian courts ... and ... never gone into either politics or religion at all.' (58)
3. 'Nixon might have been a Democrat.' (52)

4. 'If heat had been applied to stick S at t_0, then at t_0 stick S would not have been one meter long.' (55)

All these are compatible with metaphysical possibility being constrained by the laws of nature. Now imagine things different in the following (far-fetched) ways, and ask whether the possibilities survive:

1. The astronomical situation into which Hesperus was born was such that there is nothing else around which could (given the laws of nature) interfere with its course. Add, if necessary, that these are the only circumstances in which Hesperus could have come into existence. Does the metaphysical possibility (as opposed to the *a priori* possibility) survive?
2. It is God's ineluctable will that Moses lead the Israelites out of Egypt.
3. Political propensities are genetically determined at least enough to rule out Nixon's being a Democrat.
4. Suppose we have a stick made of a very special kind of material such that nothing you can do to it or can happen to it can alter its length. And this manufacturing process only works for sticks of a certain length. Is it still true that this stick could have been a different length at t_0?

If metaphysical possibility is not constrained by the laws of nature, these changes do not affect the possibilities in question. But then, the manner of defending the original claims is potentially misleading. I suggest that what makes Kripke's cases so compelling is that we intuitively read them as natural possibilities. And the readiness with which we accept that there are metaphysical necessities which are not knowable *a priori* is partly explained by our reading these as natural necessities.

VIII

The Mind-Body Problem. Kripke's discussion of mind-brain identity (144–55) does conflict with my preferred reading. (It is also the part that many fans like least.)

Let 'A' name a particular pain sensation, and let 'B' name a corresponding brain state. It is alleged that $A = B$. But, says

Kripke 'It is at least logically possible that *B* should have existed without the presence of *A*' (146). On my view there is no conflict. The case is analogous to the metaphysical necessity but epistemic contingency of 'Hesperus is Phosphorus'. Kripke, however, points out a disanalogy: 'The difficulty can hardly be evaded by arguing that although *B* could not exist without *A*, *being a pain* is merely a contingent property of *A*, and that therefore the presence of *B* without pain does not imply the presence of *B* without *A*. Can any case of essence be more obvious than the fact that *being a pain* is a necessary property of each pain?' (146, italics original). And similarly for brain states: *being a brain state* is an essential property of each brain state. The disanalogy is that we are identifying the pain and the brain state in terms of essential properties, Hesperus and Phosphorus in terms of accidental properties. But the disanalogy does not settle the matter. An essential property of an object is a metaphysically necessary property of it. It is standardly a matter of empirical discovery what essential properties an object has. That one thing has these two essential properties is again a matter of empirical discovery.

Let us suppose, if we can, that for some reason there is only one metaphysically possible history for the planet Venus. The two portions of its actual history in terms of which we identify it as Hesperus and as Phosphorus respectively *are* essential to it. It would still not be knowable *a priori* that Hesperus is Phosphorus. There would still be what Kripke calls an illusion of contingency and what I call epistemic contingency. (One can get the same effect on the cheap by 'rigidifying' the bits of actual history which identify the planet for us, with 'actually'. But these are very artificial examples of essential properties.)

The point can be better made in terms of examples due to Kripke. It is an essential property of me that I have the genetic structure of a human being. It is an essential property of me, according to Kripke, that I was born of certain parents. But it is an empirical fact, not knowable *a priori*, that a creature identified by its origin has this genetic structure, and conversely, that a creature identified by its genetic structure has this origin, or that a creature, however identified, has these two essential properties. A sort of analogy with the pain case: a child is being born, and those present can be credited with direct epistemic access to the fact that this creature comes from this woman (analogy: direct access to the pain). It remains *a priori* possible (i.e. it is not ruled out *a priori*) that the child has any old genetic structure or none, even if it is metaphysically impossible that the child has any but this particular one (analogy: it is *a priori* possible that the pain is any old brain state or none, even if it is metaphysically impossible that it is any but this particular one).

One senses that Kripke would have liked to say 'Can any case of non-essence be more obvious than the fact that being a pain is *not* an essential property of this brain state, that being a brain state is *not* an essential property of this pain?' But this would be to state his convictions rather than to argue for them.

Of course it remains puzzling, in the pain/brain-state case, how one and the same thing can have these two different kinds of essential properties. That is the perennial problem about the relation between mind and matter. But nothing that Kripke has said rules out that they do.

IX

Lewis's Problem about Chance. Lewis recognises only one fundamental concept of possibility, though stronger notions can be defined by restricting quantification over possible worlds to a subset of worlds. His fundamental notion is, at least extensionally, much closer to what I call (absolute) epistemic possibility than to what I call metaphysical possibility: what is possible can be settled *a priori* if it can be settled at all. He does however accept a bipartite theory of probability: there is epistemic degree of belief, and there is objective chance. The former he does sometimes express as a measure on possible worlds—what I call, or nearly what I call, epistemic possible worlds. I see the latter as a measure on metaphysical possibilities (relative to a time). Lewis does not. Facts about chances are contingent facts about a given world. (I agree that they are epistemically contingent.)

At the end of a wonderful paper exploring the relation between epistemic probability and chance (1980), Lewis turns to metaphysics. Assume that a world is chancy and that there are laws (or other conditionals) about how chance depends on history at that world. Call the collection of these a theory of chance. What makes a theory of chance true at a world? The answer he would like to give, in line with his account of laws and general doctrine of supervenience on local matters of fact, is 'The complete theory of chance for a world is that one of all possible theories of chance that ... best fits the global pattern of outcomes and frequencies' (1986, 111). But, he concludes, this must be rejected: 'Consider a time long before the pattern is complete. At that time, the pattern ... has some chance of coming about and some chance of not coming about. There is some chance of a very different global pattern coming about; one which, according to the proposal under consideration, would make true some different complete theory of chance. But a complete theory of chance is not something that could have chance of coming about or not coming about' (111–2). And he proves, in a way that need not concern us, that the theory of chance must itself have chance 1 of being true. (Indeed he wisely adds to his theory of lawhood that 'No genuine law ever could have a chance of not holding' (1986, 124). For one prominent way in which a generalisation can be merely accidentally true is by being true by chance.)

To take a simple example, suppose we have a fair coin which is to be tossed a large finite number of times, and this is the only chance process of its kind, at a world. Our theory of chance tells us that there is a small chance that it will land heads every time, or nearly every time. But if it did so, some other theory of chance would fit the pattern of outcomes better, and hence be the true theory of chance for the coin at this world. If the true theory of chance is determined by pattern of outcomes, it does not allow that significant deviations from this pattern can come about. And yet it does allow this: it tells us that all these alternative patterns are possible, in that they have non-zero chance of occurring. If chance is determined by the actual pattern, it both does and does not allow significant deviations from this pattern.

Lewis considers another alternative: the only other way the theory of chance could supervene on the pattern of outcomes is the trivial way in which all necessary truths supervene on anything. 'Perhaps all worlds are alike in the dependence of chance on history' (1986, 112). But this has an equally unpalatable consequence for him: if the theory of chance is a necessary truth, it is knowable *a priori* if it is knowable at all. An extreme rationalism would ensue, about such matters as the half-life of radon—and about other laws of nature as well, as they are now specified in part in terms of the fact that they always have chance 1 of being true.

The way the rationalism surfaces for Lewis is this. Fundamental to understanding chance is understanding how beliefs about chance affect epistemically rational degrees of belief in the outcomes of chance processes. More often than not, we don't know the chance, but a crucial ingredient in our reasoning is our degree of belief in an outcome *on the assumption that* the chance is such-and-such. But if the theory of chance is a necessary truth, true at all worlds, it should get (epistemic) probability 1 in all probability distributions, and it drops out as redundant as a premise in our reasoning.

Neither horn of the above dilemma is tolerable. A theory of chance *tells* us that a great variety of patterns *can* come about, so can't be determined by the pattern that actually does come about. Yet a theory of chance is accepted on empirical, not *a priori* grounds.

Here, if anywhere, we do well to recognise metaphysically necessary truths which are not knowable *a priori*, which come to be accepted only on empirical grounds. On my view, the theory of chance is necessary in that it governs all metaphysically—really—possible worlds. That doesn't make it redundant as an empirically established premise, any more than 'Hesperus is Phosphorus' is redundant as a premise. We do have metaphysical supervenience in the trivial sense: no two metaphysically possible worlds differ in their laws of chance, without differing in other respects, because no two metaphysically possible worlds differ in their laws of chance, period. But epistemically possible worlds differ in their laws of chance. That is why the premise is not redundant.[11]

11. Lewis came to a new 'solution' to his problem (see Lewis 1994). But it is not a very happy one. Chances are contingent, i.e. vary between worlds, and the true theory of chance at a world is the one that combines with the laws to give the best fit to all actual outcomes. There really are no possible worlds in which the outcomes match badly the chances: in which a fair coin lands heads all the time, or almost all the time, say. This falsifies his fundamental Principle about the relation between chance and degree of belief. (This isn't just Lewis's principle, though he gave it a name, 'the Principal Principle'. It is integral to the orthodox way of arriving at epistemic probabilities in the presence of chances.) Yet the Principle remains the 'key to our

X

Conclusion. I do not mean to be mean-minded about what possibilities there are. We can let our imaginations rip and speak of all manner of weird and wonderful possibilities. They are (absolutely) epistemically possible. That is, they can't be ruled out *a priori*. We also need a more constrained notion: the possibilities for this world, and for the things that are in it, the various really possible histories they could have.[12]

In some respects, this is a rather old-fashioned view. There is conceptual necessity. And there is natural necessity. The Kripkean framework can be made sense of in these terms.[13]

REFERENCES

Armstrong, D. M. 1983, *What is a Law of Nature?* Cambridge: Cambridge University Press.

Bird, A. 2001, 'Necessarily, Salt Dissolves in Water', *Analysis* 61, 267–74.

Carnap, R. 1945. 'The Two Concepts of Probability'. *Philosophy and Phenomenological Research* 5, 513–32.

Chalmers, D. 1996, *The Conscious Mind*, Oxford: Oxford University Press.

———'The Nature of Epistemic Space'. http://www.u.arizona.edu/~chalmers/papers/espace.html

———'Soames on Two-Dimensionalism', http://www.u.arizona.edu/~chalmers/papers/soames.pdf

Forbes, G. 1985, *The Metaphysics of Modality*. Oxford: Oxford University Press.

Foster, J. 1982, 'Induction, Explanation and Natural Necessity', *Proceedings of the Aristotelian Society* 83, 88–101.

Hale, B. 1996, 'Absolute Necessities', *Philosophical Perspectives* 10, 93–117

———1997. 'Modality', in Bob Hale and Crispin Wright (eds.) *A Companion to the Philosophy of Language*, Oxford: Blackwell, 487–514.

Jackson, F. 1998, *From Metaphysics to Ethics*, Oxford: Oxford University Press.

concept of chance', although it is 'only approximately right, and that only sometimes. ... A feature of Reality deserves the name of chance to the extent that it occupies the definitive role of chance; and occupying that role means obeying the old Principle. ... Nothing perfectly occupies the role, so nothing perfectly deserves the name. But near enough is good enough. If nature is kind to us, the chances ascribed by the probabilistic laws of the best system will obey the old principle to a very good approximation in commonplace applications. They will occupy the chance-role well enough to deserve the name' (1994, 489).

12. Despite the two-way independence, this is, in an intuitive sense, more constrained. There is a huge class of epistemic possibilities which are not metaphysically possible, but (as far as I can see) one has to search hard for examples, which are rather contrived and on the whole not very important or interesting, of the metaphysically possible which is not epistemically possible.

13. This paper began life a long time ago. Its topic remains controversial, and I am aware that there is recent work which I have been unable to take into account here. I am grateful to many individuals and audiences, and in particular to Ian McFetridge for discussion in the 1980s, to David Lewis for written comments, and to Scott Sturgeon for recent comments and discussion.

Kneale, W. 1949, *Probability and Induction*, Oxford: Oxford University Press.
——1950, 'Natural Laws and Contrary to Fact Conditionals', *Analysis* 10, 121–5.
Kripke, S. 1980, *Naming and Necessity*, Oxford: Basil Blackwell.
Leeds, S. 2001, 'Possibility: Physical and Metaphysical' in Carl Gillett and Barry Loewer (ed.) *Physicalism and its Discontents*, Cambridge: Cambridge University Press, 172–93.
Lewis, D. 1973, *Counterfactuals*, Oxford: Basil Blackwell.
——1980. 'A Subjectivist's Guide to Objective Chance' in Richard C. Jeffrey (ed.) *Studies in Inductive Logic and Probability*, Volume II. Berkeley and Los Angeles: University of California Press, 263–93. Reprinted with postscripts in Lewis (1986), 83–132. Page references to this volume.
——1986, *Philosophical Papers* Vol. 2, Oxford: Oxford University Press.
——1994, 'Humean Supervenience Debugged', *Mind* 103, 473–90.
McFetridge, I. 1990, 'Logical Necessity' in his *Logical Necessity and Other Essays*. London: Aristotelian Society Series, 10, (ed.) John Haldane and Roger Scruton.
Mill, J. S. 1965, *A System of Logic*, London: Longmans. (First edition 1843, 8th edition 1872).
Peacocke, C. 1997, 'Metaphysical Necessity: Understanding, Truth and Epistemology', *Mind* 106, 521–74.
——1999, *Being Known*, Oxford: Oxford University Press.
Putnam, H. 1981, *Reason, Truth and History*, Cambridge: Cambridge University Press.
Ramsey, F. P. 1990, *Philosophical Papers*, (ed.) D. H. Mellor, Cambridge: Cambridge University Press.
Rumfitt, I. 2003, 'Contingent Existents', *Philosophy* 78, 461–81.
Van Fraassen, B. 1989, *Laws and Symmetry*, Oxford: Oxford University Press.

LEIBNIZ ON BODY, MATTER AND EXTENSION

by Daniel Garber and Jean Baptiste Rauzy

I—Daniel Garber

ABSTRACT This paper explores Leibniz's conception of body and extension in the 1680s and 1690s. It is argued that one of Leibniz's central aims is to undermine the Cartesian conception of extended substance, and replace it with a conception on which what is basic to body is force. In this way, Leibniz intends to reduce extension to something metaphysically more basic in just the way that the mechanists reduce sensible qualities to size, shape and motion. It is also argued that this move is quite distinct from the reduction of body to monads and their appetitions and perceptions, so prominent in his later writings.

I

It is well-known that extended bodies have a problematic place in Leibniz's metaphysics. What place *do* they have in his thought? In a difficult passage from the *Discours de métaphysique*, Leibniz wrote:

> *That the Notions Involved in Extension Contain Something Imaginary and Cannot Constitute the Substance of Body.* ... I believe that anyone who will meditate about the nature of substance, as I have explained it above, will find that the nature of body does not consist merely in extension, that is, in size, shape, and motion, but that we must necessarily recognize in body something related to souls, something we commonly call substantial form, even though it makes no change in the phenomena, any more than do the souls of animals, if they have any. It is even possible to demonstrate that the notions of size, shape, and motion are not as distinct as is imagined and that they contain something imaginary and relative to our perception, as do (though to a greater extent) colour, heat, and other similar qualities, qualities about which one can doubt whether they are truly found in the nature of things outside ourselves.[1]

In this striking passage, Leibniz put forward a critique of the Cartesian conception of body. According to the Cartesians, body

1. *Discours de métaphysique* § 12.

consists of extension and extension alone. Sensible qualities, such as colour and heat, don't really exist in bodies in the way we sense them. Rather, according to the Cartesian mechanical philosophers, they exist only as sensations in minds as a result of the physical interaction between the world of extended things and the human sense organs. On this view, the redness we sense in an apple, for example, is a sensation in the mind that arises as a result of the fact that light is reflected in a certain characteristic way from the surface of the apple, something that contains only extension and its modes. This light so altered, in turn, tickles the retina in a characteristic way, causing motions in the brain which result in the idea of red in the mind of the perceiver.[2] Leibniz wants to claim here that the mechanist's basic notions of extension, shape, motion and the like are not so basic as they thought, and that even these too can be analyzed further and into more basic notions, just as colour and heat are analyzed into the size, shape and motion of the constituent parts of bodies. Furthermore, Leibniz argues, the essence of body is not extension, and we must introduce into bodies 'something related to souls, something we commonly call substantial form'. In this paper I would like to explore this tangled thicket of claims and try to clarify some aspects of Leibniz's thought about extended bodies, at least as he conceived of them in this and related texts from this period of his thought.

I am quite deliberately limiting myself to talking about just *some* aspects of Leibniz's thought. There was a time when one could talk quite generally about Leibniz's view on this or that, or about *the* position that he took in his mature writings, those commencing in the late 1670s or so. The burgeoning of excellent scholarship on Leibniz in the last couple of decades, together with the wealth of new texts made available by the editors of the Akademie edition of his writings have, thankfully, made that impossible. Scholars now recognize the complexity of Leibniz's thought, and there are competing developmental stories to choose from in the literature. In particular, it can no longer be assumed without argument that Leibniz held the simple metaphysical picture of the late *Monadology* (1714) from the

2. See, e.g. Descartes, *Traité de la lumière* (1633; pub. Paris, 1664), Ch. 1 or *Principia Philosophiae* (Amsterdam, 1644) Part I, Sections 69–70 and Part IV, Sections 189–98.

1680s to the end of his life, largely without change.[3] I don't make any such assumption. Nor will I attempt to make the case for a systematic contrary reading here either. Rather, I will simply try to follow the texts where they lead us, and read them as carefully as I can, being sensitive to their nuance and their chronology, what they reveal and what they may hide.

The issues in Leibniz's thought that I intend to focus on here may be somewhat unfamiliar to the philosopher who has not kept up with the recent literature. I am not going to talk much about monads or simple substances; as terms, neither enters Leibniz's vocabulary until the mid-1690s, and it is not absolutely clear that they get the meanings that they have in Leibniz's late philosophy until even later. What I want to look at is what Leibniz has to say about *bodies* in the 1680s and 1690s. The chronological limitations are significant here. If I am right, his thought changes significantly after that, though I don't want to argue that here. I want to investigate what he has to say about bodies and their extension in this period, and the way in which extended bodies are grounded in something more basic, substance, matter, form and force. There may be a layer still deeper in which these notions are resolved into notions more basic still, and in which something like the more familiar monadology reigns. While I will touch on Leibniz's idealism or phenomenalism at the end of this paper, that will not be the primary focus of my remarks. Rather, I want to follow the texts themselves, and see where they lead us.

II

Some Historical Preliminaries. Before we can get down to business, though, there are some historical preliminaries that are important to mention.

Leibniz's discussion of body and substance occurs within the context of what might be called the mechanist revolution against scholastic Aristotelianism. The full story is, as always, complex

3. For a defense of the view that Leibniz changed his view over the course of his career, see, e.g. D. Garber, 'Leibniz and the Foundations of Physics: the Middle Years,' in K. Okruhlik and J. Brown (eds.) *The Natural Philosophy of Leibniz* (Dordrecht: Reidel, 1985), 27–130. For a defense of the position that Leibniz's view was consistently idealistic throughout his career, see, e.g., Robert Adams, *Leibniz: Determinist, Theist, Idealist* (Oxford: Oxford University Press, 1994), esp. Part III.

and ambiguous. However, the main lines go like this. For Aristotelian natural philosophy, the basic principles of explanation are primary matter and substantial form.[4] Substantial form is that which explains the particular properties that different sorts of substances have, while primary matter is the (ultimate) common element that remains constant from one substance to another. So, for example, the Aristotelian elements earth, water, air, and fire all share the same primary matter, and if one could transform a bit of earth into water, it would retain the same matter. However, by virtue of having different substantial forms, water is cold and fire hot, earth falls while air rises.[5] For the mechanical philosophy, though, there are no substantial forms (with the possible exception of the human soul). Mechanical philosophers such as Descartes or Boyle held that all body is made up of the same kind of stuff, and that the only differences among bodies were their geometrical properties, their sizes, their shapes, their motions. (Descartes went so far as to say that these geometrical properties were the only properties bodies really have: bodies are essentially extended, the objects of geometry made real.) Instead of explaining the properties of bodies in terms of their substantial forms, the mechanist explains their properties in terms of the size, shape, and motion of the tiny corpuscles that make them up. And so, the heat of fire may be explained in terms of the speed with which the parts of its constituent corpuscles move or their pointy shapes, and the wetness of water may be explained in terms of the eel-shaped particles of which it is made, whose shape allows them to slide past one another, etc.[6]

4. I omit here the third principle, privation, which plays a subsidiary role in the story.

5. For simple accounts of the view, see, e.g. St. Thomas's essay, 'Principles of Nature' in St. Thomas Aquinas, *Selected Writings*, ed. and trans. by R. P. Goodwin (Indianapolis: Bobbs-Merrill, 1965), or Eustachius a Sancto Paulo's popular textbook, *Summa philosophiae quadripartita* (Paris, 1609), *tertia pars...quae est physica, prima pars ... de corpore naturali in genere*, Sections I (*de materia*) and II (*de forma*).

6. See e.g., the explanations that Descartes gives of the manifest properties of fire and water in *Traité de la lumière*, Ch. 3 or in Disc. I of *Les météores* (Leiden, 1637). See e.g., Robert Boyle, *Origin of Forms and Qualities* (Oxford, 1666) for a clear statement of the mechanical philosophy. It was Boyle who named the programme, and included Descartes and Gassendi, among others, as its earlier adherents. However, the case could be made that, strictly speaking, the programme didn't really exist until Boyle chose certain elements of his predecessors' programmes and highlighted their similarity. However, when we are considering Leibniz, later in the seventeenth century, the prehistory of the mechanical philosophy is not at issue.

In a famous letter that he wrote Nicolas Remond in 1714, late in life, Leibniz talks about his own view of body and substance as it relates to this larger context:

> I discovered Aristotle as a lad, and even the Scholastics did not repel me; even now I do not regret this. After having finished the trivial schools, I fell upon the moderns, and I recall walking in a grove on the outskirts of Leipzig called the Rosental, at the age of fifteen, and deliberating whether to preserve substantial forms or not. Mechanism finally prevailed and led me to apply myself to mathematics ... But when I looked for the ultimate reasons for mechanism, and even for the laws of motion, I was greatly surprised to see that they could not be found in mathematics but that I should have to return to metaphysics. This led me back to entelechies, and from the material to the formal, and at last brought me to understand after many corrections and forward steps in my thinking, that monads or simple substances are the only true substances and that material things are only phenomena, though well founded and well connected.[7]

Scholars have fought over the historical accuracy of these reflections, but I think that all are agreed that, at least in gross outline, they do represent the general progression of Leibniz's thought. It is not surprising to learn that Leibniz was educated in scholastic philosophy; virtually everyone was in that time. Nor is it surprising to learn that he rejected it for some version or another of the mechanical philosophy. Many did. The details are more complicated than Leibniz lets on in this letter. He was probably a bit older than fifteen when he abandoned the scholastics, and the version of the mechanical philosophy that he adopted was thoroughly idiosyncratic, Hobbesian rather than Cartesian or Gassendist, and with large dollops of mentality

7. GP III 606 (L 654–5). As Leibniz uses the term, 'entelechy' is virtually identical with form. References to Leibniz's texts are given using the following standard abbreviations. 'GP' designates C. I. Gerhardt (ed.) *Leibniz: Die philosophischen Schriften.* 7 vols. (Berlin: Weidman, 1875–90), 'GM' designates C. I. Gerhardt (ed.) *Leibniz: mathematische Schriften.* 7 vols. (Berlin: Asher and Schmidt, 1849–63); 'L' designates L. Loemker (ed.) and trans., *Leibniz: Philosophical Papers and Letters* (Dordrecht: Reidel, 1976); 'A' designates Deutsche Akademie der Wissenschaften zu Berlin, eds., *Leibniz: Sämtliche Schriften und Briefe* (Berlin: Akademie Verlag, 1923–); 'AG' designates R. Ariew and D. Garber (eds. and trans.), *Leibniz: Philosophical Essays* (Indianapolis, IN: Hackett, 1989); 'M' designates the H. T. Mason, (ed.), *The Leibniz-Arnauld Correspondence* (Manchester: University of Manchester Press, 1967); 'Arthur' designates Richard Arthur (eds. and trans.), *Leibniz: the Labyrinth of the Continuum* (New Haven: Yale University Press, 2001). The original language text is given first, followed by a reference to the translation, when available.

thrown in for good measure. But even so, as late as March 19, 1678, Leibniz wrote to Herman Conring:

> I recognize nothing in the world but bodies and minds, and nothing in minds but intellect and will, nor anything in bodies insofar as they are separated from mind but magnitude, figure, situation, and changes in these, either partial or total. Everything else is merely said, not understood; it is sounds without meaning.[8]

But just as Leibniz reported in the later letter to Remond, this classical mechanist position was set aside when Leibniz came to the view that he must reintroduce substantial forms. A year or so after his letter to Conring, in Autumn 1679, Leibniz announces in a letter to the Duke Johann Friedrich, 'I re-establish the substantial forms with demonstrative certainty [*démonstrativement*] and I explain them intelligibly.'[9] The details of the re-establishment of substantial forms can be found in a remarkable text from the period, a plan for a book on the elements of physics, now dated from Summer 1678 to Winter 1678/9. In that text Leibniz wrote:

> Certain things take place in body which cannot be explained from the necessity of matter alone. Such are the laws of motion, which depend upon the metaphysical principle of the equality of cause and effect. Therefore, we must deal here with the soul and show that all things are animated. Without soul or form of some kind, body would have no being, because no part of it can be designated which does not in turn consist of more parts. Thus nothing could be designated in a body which could be called 'this thing,' or a unity.[10]

This is the first step in what Leibniz reported as the path that leads ultimately to monads and to the view that bodies are only well-founded phenomena. But, as Leibniz told Remond, there were 'many corrections and forward steps' between the initial revival of substantial forms and the full-blown monadology of his later years. What I would like to do right now is look more carefully at this stage in his thought, what the world looked like

8. A2.1.400 (L 189).
9. A1.2.225; cf. A2.1.490
10. A6.4.1988 (L 278–9). Cf. A6.4.2009 (L 289). Cf. A6.4.1398–9 (Arthur 245), which may be from the same period.

to Leibniz at the moment when he reintroduced substantial forms into the mechanist world.

As the passage just quoted suggests, the substantial forms that Leibniz introduced into bodies at this moment in his development were supposed to play a number of different roles. Two are particularly prominent: grounding the laws of motion, and providing genuine unity in bodies. In a purely geometrical world, such as Leibniz himself held before the reintroduction of substantial forms, there is no source of activity in bodies. As a result, bodies taken by themselves offer no resistance in impact; a body in motion, no matter how small, could put another body at rest into motion, without losing any of its own speed, no matter how large the resting body may be. This, Leibniz thought, violated certain metaphysical principles, such as the conservation of the ability to do work (the principle of the equality of cause and effect), which would allow you to build a perpetual motion machine in such a world. And so, he argued, we must reject the premise, and introduce something into bodies over and above extension.[11] Another feature of a Cartesian world of extended matter is the fact that there are no genuine individuals in such a world. Every body is divisible into smaller bodies, on to infinity, without our ever coming to anything that 'could be designated in a body which could be called "this thing", or a unity'. Souls or forms are thus introduced into bodies in order to constitute genuine individuals: a genuine individual is a body, united by virtue of having a soul or form, something that makes it *one* thing.[12]

Such genuine (and genuinely active) individuals are what Leibniz calls corporeal substances in this period. The view is sketched most completely in Leibniz's letters to Arnauld in 1686 and 1687. He wrote:

> One will never arrive at a thing of which it may be said: 'Here really is an entity', except when one finds animate machines whose soul or substantial form creates substantial unity independent of the external union of

11. For a development of this argument, see, e.g., a piece now thought to have been written between 1678 and 1681, A6.4.1976–80 (AG 245–250). A summary of the argument is given in *Discours de métaphysique* § 21.

12. This consideration is especially prominent in the Correspondence with Arnauld. See e.g., GP II 97 (M 121).

contiguity. And if there are none, it follows that apart from man there is apparently nothing substantial in the visible world.[13]

But he does think that there are such things in the world, and that they are found everywhere in nature. In another letter he wrote:

I am very far removed from the opinion which states that animate bodies are only a small part of the others. For I believe rather that everything is full of animate bodies, and to my mind, there are incomparably more souls than there are atoms for M. Cordemoy, who makes a finite number of them, whereas I maintain that the number of souls or at least forms is quite infinite, and that since matter is endlessly divisible, one cannot fix on a part so small that there are no animate bodies within, or at least bodies endowed with a basic entelechy or (if you permit one to use the word 'life' so generally) with a vital principle, that is to say corporeal substances, about which it may be said in general of them all that they are living.[14]

Such corporeal substances are organisms, organic bodies each of which is attached to a soul. Each of us constitutes such a corporeal substance. The further claim is that each organic body is, in turn, ultimately made up of corporeal substances as well. In another letter to Arnauld, Leibniz wrote:

Man ... is an entity endowed with a genuine unity conferred on him by his soul, notwithstanding the fact that the mass of his body is divided into organs, vessels, humours, spirits, and that the parts are undoubtedly full of an infinite number of other corporeal substances endowed with their own entelechies.[15]

In this way the world is composed of bugs within bugs within bugs, all the way down to infinity. (Leibniz here was influenced by the world of the microscopists such as Leeuwenhoek and Swammerdam, whose work he knew.)[16]

It should be noted here that in this context, Leibniz did not intend to give up the mechanical philosophy at all. Despite the

13. GP II 77 (M 95).
14. GP II 118 (M 151-2). It should be noted that the Hanover text quoted here (and given in GP II) has later additions that Arnauld never saw.
15. GP II 120 (M 154).
16. On Leibniz and the microscopists, see Catherine Wilson, 'Leibniz and the Animalcula,' in M. A. Stewart (ed.) *Studies in Seventeenth-Century European Philosophy* (Oxford: Oxford University Press, 1997), 153–75.

fact that the world is made up of such organisms, corporeal substances, organic bodies and souls, everything is still explicable mechanically. Leibniz wrote to Arnauld in a typical and oft-repeated passage:

> If the body is a substance and not a simple phenomenon like the rainbow, nor an entity united by accident or by aggregation like a heap of stones, it cannot consist of extension, and one must necessarily conceive of something there that one calls substantial form and which corresponds in a way to the soul. I have been convinced of it finally, as though against my will, after having been rather far removed from it in the past. Nevertheless, however much I agree with the Scholastics in this general and, so to speak, metaphysical explanation of the principles of bodies, I am as corpuscular as one can be in the explanation of particular phenomena, and it is saying nothing to allege that they have forms or qualities. One must always explain nature along mathematical and mechanical lines, provided one knows that the very principles or laws of mechanics or of force do not depend upon mathematical extension alone but upon certain metaphysical reasons.[17]

In this way forms are necessary not to explain particular phenomena in nature (why earth falls, why water is wet) but to ground the reality of the world of bodies and the laws of motion that they obey.

This doesn't look much like what most readers think of as Leibniz's metaphysics. Where are the monads in all of this? Where is Leibniz's well-known idealism? There may be a deeper level of analysis in which the bodies of the corporeal substance melt away into the perceptions of monads or the like. Perhaps. But that is not my concern at the moment. Later I will return to the question of Leibnizian idealism, but for the moment, I want to stick with what he says in these texts about bodies and the corporeal substances that make them up, and the matter and form of which they are composed.

With this historical background in place, we can now (finally!) begin to discuss some philosophical issues concerning bodies and their extension.

17. GP II 58 (M 66).

III

Matter, Form and Force. Leibniz saw himself as having revived the substantial forms of Aristotle and the schoolmen, much disdained by his contemporaries. Leibniz writes in the *Discours de métaphysique*:

> *That the Belief in Substantial Forms Has Some Basis, but That These Forms Do Not Change Anything in the Phenomena and Must Not Be Used to Explain Particular Effects.* It seems that the ancients, as well as many able men accustomed to deep meditation who have taught theology and philosophy some centuries ago (some of whom are respected for their saintliness) have had some knowledge of what we have just said; this is why they introduced and maintained the substantial forms which are so decried today. But they are not so distant from the truth nor so ridiculous as the common lot of our new philosophers imagines.[18]

Leibniz is reviving the scholastic view of corporeal substance in terms of matter and form, but he doesn't feel bound to hold everything that his predecessors did. One difference that I have already noted concerns the explanatory role of form: unlike in the scholastics, forms are not used to explain particular phenomena, but only to ground the physical world in a more general sense. But there are other important differences as well.

Leibniz talks about the notions of form and matter in a passage from a letter to Arnauld:

> Extended mass, considered without a substantial form ... is not a corporeal substance, but an entirely pure phenomenon like the rainbow; therefore philosophers have recognized that it is form which gives determinate being to matter ... Only indivisible substances and their different states are absolutely real ... But[19] if one considers as matter of corporeal substance not mass without forms but a second matter which is the multiplicity of substances of which the mass is that of the total body, it may be said that these substances are parts of this matter, just as those which enter into our body form part

18. *Discours de métaphysique* § 10.
19. The rest of this passage was not sent to Arnauld for reasons that are not clear. It is almost certainly not a later addition, unlike some passages in the Hanover ms. of the letters to Arnauld, since it appears in an earlier draft. See R. Finster (ed.) *Leibniz: Philosophischer Briefwechsel, bd. I: Der Briefwechsel mit Antoine Arnauld* (Hamburg: Meiner Verlag, 1997), 300, for an earlier draft of this passage, taken from an earlier version of the letter, only recently published.

of it, for as our body is the matter, and the soul is the form of our substance, it is the same with other corporeal substances.... But if one were to understand by the term 'matter' something always essential to the same substance, one might in the sense of certain Scholastics understand thereby the primitive passive power of a substance, and in this sense matter would not be extended or divisible, although it would be the principle of divisibility or of that which amounts to it in the substance. But I do not wish to argue over the use of terms.[20]

In this passage Leibniz gives special attention to one of the constituents of substance, the matter. He introduces a distinction between three conceptions of matter. First of all, there is matter in the Cartesian sense, 'extended mass, considered without a substantial form'. This Leibniz considers as a 'pure phenomenon like the rainbow'. He then introduces a second conception of matter, one that is more directly connected with his notion of a corporeal substance. Secondary matter, on this view, is matter attached to substantial form, presumably a collection of corporeal substances making up the organic body of one of the organisms that constitutes a corporeal substance. In this way, as Leibniz writes, 'As our body is the matter, and the soul is the form of our substance, it is the same with other corporeal substances.' But there is yet another conception of matter here. On this conception, matter is 'something always essential to the same substance'. Understood in this way, matter is just the 'primitive passive power of a substance, and in this sense matter would not be extended or divisible, although it would be the principle of divisibility or of that which amounts to it in the substance'. It is not altogether clear that Leibniz is endorsing this use of the term 'matter' here; it can be read as a nod to scholastic notions of primary matter.[21] But it should be taken seriously: it echoes themes found in some other contemporary discussions of the notion of matter in Leibniz's other writings.

A central idea here is that form and matter are to be understood in terms of force, passive force in the case of matter

20. GP II 119–20 (Mason 152–4); cf. GP III 260–1 (AG 289–90); GP IV 395 (AG 252).

21. This is also clear in the earlier version of this passage, where Leibniz characterizes this account of matter as being '...assez conforme au sens des Scholastiques...' (Finster (ed.) *Briefwechsel mit Antoine Arnauld*, p. 300).

and active force in the case of form. Leibniz writes in a passage from a note now dated between 1684 and 1686:

> Corporeal substances have parts and species. The parts are matter and form. Matter is the principle of passion, or primitive force of resisting, which is commonly called bulk or antitypy, from which flows the impenetrability of body. Substantial form is the principle of action, or primitive force of acting.[22]

This idea gets a fuller elaboration about a decade later, in the *Specimen Dynamicum*, where the primitive passive force, again identified with matter, is taken to include both impenetrability, 'that by virtue of which it happens that a body cannot be penetrated by another body', as well as resistance, 'a certain laziness, so to speak, that is, an opposition to motion, nor, further does it allow itself to be put into motion without somewhat diminishing the force of the body acting on it'.[23]

The idea that matter is really just passive force seems to be one of the important elements that lead Leibniz toward denying that extension is fundamental to body. As we have seen in the long passage quoted from the letter to Arnauld, he argues that insofar as matter is just passive force, 'In this sense matter would not be extended or divisible, although it would be the principle of divisibility or of that which amounts to it in the substance.' This also seems to be behind what Leibniz advances in a passage from the essay, 'On the Method of Distinguishing Real from Imaginary Phenomena,' now dated 1683–1686, which echoes *Discours de métaphysique* § 12. Leibniz wrote:

> Concerning bodies I can demonstrate that not merely light, heat, colour and similar qualities are apparent but also motion, figure and extension. And if anything is real, it is solely the force of acting and suffering, and hence that the substance of a body consists in this (as if in matter and form).[24]

What is real, then, in bodies is not extension, but force. As he puts it in another passage, 'Matter is the force of being acted upon or of resisting in any body whatsoever, from which follows

22. A 6.4.1508 (Arthur 285–7).
23. GM VI 236–7 (AG 120); cf. GP IV 395 (AG 252), GP II 171 (AG 173); A 6.4.1504 (L 365).
24. A6.4.1504 (L365).

a certain extension in body, unless the Author of things desires otherwise.'[25] The passage is primarily concerned with the problem of the Eucharist. In this context, the fact that God can create this force without extension is something that can only happen by miracle.[26] But even so, it is interesting the way in which extension seems to be distanced from what is real in bodies, and that Leibniz can say that even though extension and divisibility arise from passive force, there is a real sense in which bodies are not extended or divisible.

This view of matter raises a number of questions. First of all, it is not at all clear how to reconcile it with the conception of matter as the organic body of a corporeal substance. This is a question that I cannot treat here, though it is a very serious one. But it also raises very interesting questions about the status of the extension of bodies. How, then are we to think of the extension of bodies? Is to say that force is what really underlies body to say that they are really not extended? Or that they are *un*extended? To say that they are just ... monads?[27]

The issues are complex, and in the brief space that I have I cannot go into all of the issues that this raises. It is important to note that in the passage I quoted from the letter to Arnauld, Leibniz represents this conception of matter as a simple paraphrase of a scholastic conception. There is something to that. While one can find different conceptions of matter among the scholastics, a number of thinkers held that primary matter is not itself extended but is that which gives rise to extension.[28] Surely none of them could be held to be presenting a kind of Leibnizian idealism. But the analogy that Leibniz gives between the mechanist elimination of secondary qualities and what he is doing with respect to extension gives us another way of seeing what is going on here.

---

25. A6.4.2326.

26. Robert Adams, *Leibniz*, pp. 349ff discusses passages like these as part of an argument that Leibniz was an idealist in the period under discussion. However, the fact that extension can be separated from force only supernaturally makes these passages problematic for his case.

27. Cf. Adams, *Leibniz*, pp. 348–9.

28. See, e.g., D. Garber, *Descartes' Metaphysical Physics* (Chicago: University of Chicago Press, 1992), 151 for a discussion of this issue in the scholastic commentator Franciscus Toletus.

What does the mechanist mean when he says that the apple isn't really red or gold isn't really yellow? His point is simply that the colour that we sense in bodies is a causal consequence of something more basic in bodies, the size, shape and motion of the smaller parts that make up the surface of the bodies and cause the light to be reflected in a particular way. His point is that colour, understood as a particular felt quality, distinct from extension and its modes, isn't really in the physical world, and that only size, shape and motion are. In another sense, though, the mechanist should be happy to say that a ripe apple is red, if by this we understand only that it has the particular surface texture that characteristically causes the sensation of red in sentient creatures. (Actually, it is a bit more complicated than that, but this will do for our purposes here.) The mechanist would certainly not want to deny that there is a difference in colour between a ripe apple and an unripe apple, or between gold and lead. This is one of the ways in which we tell things apart, and without such cues, life would be much more difficult. But these differences in colour are just signs to us of deeper differences in corpuscular substructure.

What Leibniz wants to do is extend this picture to extension itself. What he wants to say is that like colour, extension is grounded in something metaphysically more basic: passive force, impenetrability, resistance. And just as we might want to say that there is a sense in which the apple is red, there is also a sense in which the apple is extended. It isn't *really* extended, perhaps, any more than it is *really* red. But, nevertheless, as long as we understand the basic metaphysics here, we can talk with the vulgar.

The target of the mechanists is a common-sense view of colour on which one holds that there is a real sense in which the apple is red, that redness is a quality distinct from the size, shape and motion of anything, that pertains to red apples but not to green apples. Leibniz's target here is the Cartesian orthodoxy that bodies are *really* extended, in fact, that they are nothing but extended, that they are extended substances, the objects of geometry made real. Just as a mechanist like Descartes argues that colour is just not the kind of thing that could exist in material objects, Leibniz wants to hold that extension is not the kind of thing that could possibly exist by itself in the way in which the Cartesians hold that it does, that it is simply impossible for something to be extended, *and nothing else*. As he wrote to de Volder in 1699,

> I don't think that substance consists of extension alone, since the concept of extension is incomplete. And I don't think that extension can be conceived through itself, but I think it is a notion that is resolvable and relative ... Something must always be assumed which is either continued or diffused, as whiteness is in milk, colour, ductility and weight are in gold, and resistance is in matter. For continuity taken by itself (for extension is nothing but simultaneous continuity) no more constitutes a complete substance than does multitude or number, where there must be something numbered, repeated, and continued. And so I believe that our thought is completed and terminated more in the notion of the dynamic [i.e., force] than in that of extension ...[29]

One cannot intelligibly talk about numbers made real, something that is *just* three, or twenty, *and nothing else*: one must talk about three persons, or twenty loaves of bread. Similarly, one cannot talk about something *just* being extended, *and nothing else*: the concept of extension presupposes something that is extended. And at the most basic level, what is extended is passive force, impenetrability, resistance. Or so Leibniz claims.

The view is further elaborated in an important manuscript from 1695 or 1696. In response to Leibniz's 'New System' of 1695, Simon Foucher published a brief commentary. One of the issues that he addressed was the question of the composition of the continuum. In response to Foucher's comments, Leibniz wrote one of the clearest accounts of the relation between the world of geometrical objects and the real world of bodies.[30] (Unfortunately, Leibniz chose not to publish the longer comments, making do with a short summary in the response he published.) In that text, Leibniz draws a clear distinction between the world of mathematical entities (lines, surfaces, numbers), and the world of concrete things. The problem of the composition of the continuum is concerned with the parts from which continua

---

29. GP II 169–70 (AG 171–2); cf. GP IV 393–4 (AG 251); GP VI 584 (AG 261). The earliest I could find this argument is in the 1692 comments on Descartes, GP IV 364–5 (L 390).
30. See GP IV 491–2 (AG 146–7).

can be constructed. Leibniz's point is that the mathematical continuum does not have such parts, nor does it need them: its parts come from the division of the line, and these parts are not properly elements of that line. However, in real concreta, the whole is indeed composed of parts, though those parts don't make up a genuine mathematical continuum. In the course of this discussion, Leibniz makes the following observation: 'However, number and line are not *chimerical* things, even though there is no such composition, for they are relations that contain eternal truths, by which the phenomena of nature are ruled.'[31] The view seems to be that geometrical extension is something that exists outside the world of concrete things. However, concrete things in the world *instantiate* geometrical relations, at least approximately, insofar as real extension is not genuinely continuous. In this way, geometry is applicable to the world of concreta, a world that in its nature is characterized in terms of force. That is, there are real forces in the world, which give rise to structures that instantiate geometrical relations. Bodies are extended insofar as geometry is (approximately) true of them. However, in a metaphysical sense, what is really there is force. In this way he says, again in the notes on Foucher, 'Extension or space and the surfaces, lines, and points one can conceive in it are only relations of order or orders of coexistence.'[32] To say that bodies are not extended, in the strictest sense, but contain (primitive passive) force, which gives rise to extension is meant to say something not only about body but about the metaphysical status of geometry and extension.

There is something of a gap between geometry and the real world insofar as geometrical extension is genuinely continuous, while real extension is not. But it is almost ten years later before Leibniz seems to address this question directly. This is Leibniz's theme in a letter to the Princess Sophie from 1705. He writes:

> It is our imperfection and the defects of our senses which makes us conceive of physical things as mathematical entities ... And one can demonstrate that there is no line or shape in nature that has the properties of a straight or circular line or of any other thing whose definition a finite mind can comprehend, or that retains it uniformly

31. GP IV 491–2 (AG 146–7).
32. GP IV 491 (AG 146).

for the least time or space ... However, the eternal truths grounded on limited mathematical ideas don't fail to be of use to us in practice, to the extent to which it is permissible to abstract from inequalities too small to be able to cause errors that are large in relation to the end at hand ...[33]

In this way one may say that the extensionality of bodies is, in a way, phenomenal, the result of our imperfect senses which impose geometrical concepts onto bodies which are, in their real nature, quite something different and which don't fit them exactly. In this way, the analogy between the extension of bodies and colour seems rather apt: bodies aren't really extended because the laws of geometrical extension don't really apply to bodies, in the strictest sense, even if the fit is close enough for practical purposes. Rather, bodies are extended because *we* impose geometrical concepts on them.

But even so, though there is a sense in which extended bodies are not *really* extended, this is not to say that they are unextended either, like some sort of souls. It is only to say that extension isn't the basic notion that it was for Descartes and his followers. Leibniz seems to want to say only that what is really real in bodies, at least what underlies the extension that we attribute to them, is force. In particular, it is the force by virtue of which bodies exclude one another.

IV

Conclusions and Beyond. We started with some questions about bodies and their extension: how does Leibniz understand bodies and their extension in the era of the *Discours de métaphysique* and the correspondence with Arnauld and the years following? In what way are bodies extended, and in what way are they not? We now have at least a partial answer to that question. Bodies, Leibniz argues, are not just extension, as Descartes and his followers had argued. We must also recognize in bodies substantial forms, he argues, something analogous to souls, something that grounds genuine activity and genuine individual-

33. GP VII 563–4. There is a good discussion of this passage in G. Hartz and J. Cover, 'Space and Time in the Leibnizian Metaphysic', *Noûs* 22 (1988), p. 501. This view is related to the 'no exact shape' argument Leibniz sometimes gives. See R. Sleigh, *Leibniz and Arnauld*, pp. 113ff.

ity in the physical world. Furthermore, he argues, the extension of bodies is not a primitive feature, but is something grounded in force, passive force, the force of impenetrability in particular. This force, and not extension, is what is real in bodies for Leibniz, at least during these years. Bodies are extended, in a sense, but they are extended roughly the same sense that an apple is red. Extension, like colour, is something that is simply the expression of a metaphysically more basic feature of body. For colour, it is the size, shape and motion of bodies that is more basic, and for size, shape and motion, it is force that is more basic in turn.

This is progress in understanding Leibniz's thought, I think. But we cannot end here. Earlier I mentioned the debate about Leibniz's idealism, and the question about whether in the 1680s and 1690s, he recognized the reality of extended bodies over and above souls. Does this, then, establish the reality of extended bodies for Leibniz, at least in this period? Not at all. I think that from the late 1670s on, Leibniz recognized that extension is grounded in passive force. But this, in turn, raises another question: how are we to understand the notion of passive force? Does it have a reality independent of the soul that constitutes the form of the corporeal substance? Or, alternatively, is it to be understood simply in terms of the perceptions of a mind-like simple substance? Is (passive) force itself one of the metaphysically basic constituents of Leibniz's universe at this time, or is it to be explained in terms of something more basic still? Later, in the monadological writings of Leibniz's last years, he opts clearly for the latter view, and extended bodies are clearly 'reduced' to the well-founded phenomena of perceiving substances, as he tells de Volder in a celebrated passage written in 1704 or 1705: 'I don't really eliminate body, but reduce it to what it is.'[34] At that moment he can say that 'there is nothing in things but simple substances, and in them, perception and appetite.'[35] But in the 1680s and 1690s, it isn't so clear that he is ready to go all the way, and explain away not only extension but also the force that grounds it. That is the question, but it is a question for another day.

34. GP II 275 (AG 181).
35. GP II 270 (AG 181).

SUBSTANCE

by Justin Broackes and Peter Hacker

II—PeterHacker

SUBSTANCE: THINGS AND STUFFS

ABSTRACT The categorial concepts of substance (thing) and substance (stuff) are described, and the conceptual relationships between things and their constitutive stuff delineated. The relationship between substance concepts, expressed by other count-nouns, and natural kind concepts is examined. Artefacts and their parts are argued to be substances, whereas parts of organisms are not. The confusions of seventeenth- and eighteenth-century philosophers who invoked the concept of substance are adumbrated.

I

S ubstances: Things. We conceive of the natural world as populated by relatively persistent material things standing in spatio-temporal relations to each other. They come into existence, exist for a time, and then pass away. We locate them relative to landmarks and to other material things in the landscape which they, and we, inhabit. We characterize them as things of a certain kind, and identify and re-identify them accordingly. The expressions we typically use to do so are, in the technical terminology derived from Aristotle, names of *substances.*[1]

The term 'substance' has two distinct, but importantly linked, meanings. In the Aristotelian sense, a substance (more accurately, 'a primary substance') is a concrete individual thing of a given kind, such as a particular human being (Socrates), a given tree (such as Gautama's Bo-tree) or a certain stone (the Kohinoor). The general kind (the 'secondary substance' in Aristotle's terminology) to which the individual substance belongs is

---

1. Aristotle's most accessible discussion of substance is in the *Categories*, chaps 1–5. His discussion in the *Metaphysics* is much more problematic and his hylomorphism questionable. The major contributor to modern discussion of this difficult topic is David Wiggins: see, for example, his *Sameness and Substance Renewed* (Cambridge: Cambridge University Press, 2001). I am much indebted to his writings on this theme.

specified by a substance-name ('human being', 'pipal tree', 'diamond'). Individual substances are the basic objects of reference and subjects of predication in our conceptual scheme. They *are* things of one kind or another (specified by a substance-name, as when we say that Socrates *is a man*). They are *qualified* by numerous properties, specified by non-substantial predicates (for example, *is in the agora, is snub-nosed*, or *is a philosopher*), but they are not themselves predicable of things—Socrates cannot be said *to qualify* anything or *to be true of* anything (as opposed to *being like Socrates*, which is a relational property some rare people may have) Characterizing an individual as a thing of a given kind by using such a (secondary) substance-name answers the question of *what the thing is*. Grasp of the substance name implies knowledge of what *being a such-and-such* consists in, in so far as that is logically (or, in the extended sense of the term, grammatically) determined. The substance name provides a covering concept for statements of identity concerning individual things of the relevant kind (Tully is the same *man* as Cicero, Hesperus the same *planet* as Phosphorus, Zeus the same *god* as Jupiter.) To have an adequate grasp of what a thing is, that is, that it is a thing of such-and-such a substantial kind, is to know (in more or less detail) how to distinguish one such thing from others, typically, but by no means uniformly, how to count such things, and what kinds of change or metamorphosis any individual of the kind in question can undergo compatibly with its continued existence and persistent identity. How much of such information is to be deemed constitutive of the meaning of the substance term is often indeterminate.

Substances lend themselves to hierarchical classification. Human beings are a kind of anthropoid ape, anthropoid apes a kind of mammal, mammals, in turn, being kinds of vertebrate. If a species name (such as 'human being') applies to an individual substance, and a generic name applies to the species (as 'animal' applies to human beings), the generic name also applies to the individual (primary) substance. Generic terms, no less that the subordinate names of species, signify secondary substances—that is, are names of substantial kinds. But the species name is more specific and hence informative than the generic name.

Substances are picked out by a subclass of concrete (as opposed to abstract) count nouns. For we must distinguish between 'tinker', 'tailor', 'soldier', 'sailor', which are concrete count-nouns but not substance-names, and concrete count-nouns that are substance-names, such as 'man', 'dog', 'cabbage'. One difference is that a non-substantial count-noun may cease to apply to an individual thing, without the thing ceasing to exist, whereas a substance name cannot. So, for example, NN can cease to be a tinker or tailor, yet continue to exist and be the very same human being, but he cannot cease to be a human being and continue to exist. Another is that non-substantial count-nouns that apply to substances are themselves explained in terms of the secondary substance. So, a tinker is *a man* who repairs pots and pans, a tailor is *a man* who makes clothes. Of course, a man is *an animal* of a certain kind, but knowledge of the genus of a particular thing is less specific than knowledge of the species, whereas knowledge of the professional, but accidental, activity of a being does not as such specify, although it may presuppose, the kind of being it is. Concrete count-nouns such as 'man', 'horse' or 'tree' have both singular and plural forms, take numerals as adjectives, and in their plural form take the quantifiers 'many', '(a) few', 'several', as well as phrasal quantifiers such as 'a great number of' and 'a large number of'.

Artefacts (if we admit them among substances, as I shall urge we should) are similarly classifiable. A dumb-waiter is a kind of table, a table a piece of furniture of a given sort, a piece of furniture a kind of artefact.

Scientific classification aims to be systematic, guided by clearly stateable and applicable principles of classification. These, wherever possible, aim to ensure exclusion of cross-classification, and to determine categories that are fruitful for explanatory purposes and scientific generalization. Non-scientific classification is typically less systematic, guided by a multitude of different purposes, often non-explanatory ones, characteristic of human societies. Even when the purposes are explanatory, the forms of explanation may not be those of the sciences, but pertinent to one form or another of human practice (cuisine, agriculture, manufacturing, architecture, etc.) or to societal concerns and interests (including those of morality, criminology and law). These are no less substance-invoking than the explanatory vocabulary of the sciences.

With respect to any substance, we can typically distinguish between properties that are essential for the thing to be the kind of thing it is and properties that are inessential (the *accidents*), even though we may be forced to recognize a degree of indeterminacy in the essential properties and hence borderline cases of being a such-and-such. An individual diamond must consist of carbon in appropriate crystalline structure, and must have a scratch hardness of 10 on the Mohs scale—these are essential properties. But it may be large or small; white, blue, red, green or black; be set in a crown or other setting—these are accidental properties. A tree must be a perennial plant with a woody trunk; it may be deciduous or evergreen, have smooth or rough bark. But the boundaries between what to count as a tree and what to count as a shrub or bush are not, and need not be, clearly determined. How high must a mature specimen be? Must it have branches? No decision is normally necessary. To be sure, the concept of a tree is not part of botanical taxonomy. But it would be mistaken to suppose that the substance-names of scientific taxonomies are *always* sharply defined. Given the evolution of species, it is evident that the boundary lines determining one species and differentiating it from an emerging species are not always sharp, and borderline cases are commonly to be found. We shall revert to this point again below.

Since the accidents of a substance can vary without the substance ceasing to exist, individual substances, as Aristotle noted, may admit of contrary accidents at different times. So a substance the identity of which is not colour involving, for example, may have one colour now and another colour later. A living substance may have such-and-such a size and weight now and a different size and weight later. But any given substance S remains one and the same S throughout such accidental changes.

II

Substances: Stuffs. In a different, but ordinary and familiar, sense of the term 'substance', a substance is material stuff of one kind or another.[2] It is in this sense that we speak of sticky substances and of chemical substances, and say that iron and steel, sand and

2. For more detailed treatment, see P. M. S. Hacker, 'Substance: the Constitution of Reality', *Midwest Studies in Philosophy*, IV (1979) 239–261.

water, bread and butter are substances of different kinds. Just as substances, understood as kinds of things, can be classified into genus and species, so too can substances, understood as kinds of stuffs or materials. Iron, brass and copper are species of metal; mutton, venison and beef are kinds of meat; cotton, wool and nylon are types of fabric.

Substances in the sense of stuffs are named by a subclass of concrete *non-count nouns*. For we must distinguish between concrete non-count nouns that are names of kinds of stuff, and those that are not. The latter class includes such mass nouns as 'light', 'sunshine', 'shade', 'fire', on the one hand, as well as pseudo-mass nouns such as 'furniture', 'money', 'cutlery', 'clothing', on the other.

Concrete mass nouns of the class that concern us, such as 'wine', 'metal' or 'glass', do not have a genuine plural form save when used generically to refer to general types (as in 'the wines of France' or 'the metals of the earth'). They take the quantifiers 'much' and 'a little', and phrasal quantifiers such as 'a great deal of' and 'a large (or small) quantity of'. They can be transformed into singular referring expressions by partitives that confer countability, such as 'nugget of', 'pool of', 'grain of'; when these are prefixed by an article or indexical to yield 'the nugget of', 'that pool of', 'this grain of', they form particular-designating expressions when affixed to them. An alternative transformation is by means of quantity-designating partitives, such as 'litre of' or 'pound of', which lend themselves to a different kind of particular reference, as in 'the litre of milk in the bottle', 'the pound of butter in the fridge'. Specific quantity reference here allows numerical quantification, but not countability. 'Five litres of S', unlike 'five nuggets (or puddles) of S', does not specify a number of things, but a quantity of (liquid) stuff.

What marks out the category of substance (stuff) nouns less formally than adjectives of quantity, and differentiates them from pseudo-mass nouns like 'furniture', 'money' or 'cutlery', are three further characteristics.

First, these nouns signify that of which space-occupying particulars consist. Material things, whether they be substances, partitions of stuff (such as chunks, nuggets, lumps or grains), or specific quantities of stuff (such as pints, pounds, litres), consist of stuff.

Secondly, every arbitrary division of a partition or specific quantity of a substance (stuff) yields a further partition of that stuff down to the level of *non-dissectivity*. So, for example, every arbitrary division of a chunk of gold will yield further partitions—nuggets, grains, shavings—of gold down to the atomic level (at which point dissectivity ceases, since atoms of gold do not consist of gold). Similarly, every pool, puddle or glass of water can be further divided into quantities of water, down to the molecular level. Blood, unlike water, ceases to divide into further quantities of blood at the molar level.

Thirdly, the specific quantity of stuff of which a given partition consists (the water of which the glass of water consists), as well as the specific quantity of stuff of which a given object is made (the gold of which a gold ring is made), can retain its identity *qua* specific quantity despite change of form specified by the partitive (for instance, 'glass of') or destruction of the object made of the stuff (for instance, the melting down of the gold ring). So, the puddle of water on the floor may be the very same water as was previously in the glass, and the gold of which the brooch is made may be the very same gold as that of which the ring was made. Quantities of stuff are, in respect of their identity, *form-indifferent* (the gold that was a ring is now a brooch), *fusible* (as when we pour two glasses of water into the same jug, which then contains the very same quantities of water, although no longer separable or separately identifiable), and *dispersible* (as when we scatter ashes to the wind, pour a pint of water into the sea).

Partitions and specific quantities of stuffs, like things, may undergo *qualitative* (or *accidental*) change and yet remain the same. Just as a plant may turn from green to yellow or an animal change from being fat to being thin, so too *this* quantity of cold water may be heated, and change from being cold to being hot, and *this* slice of raw meat may be cooked. Qualitative change stands in contrast to *substantial* change. Substantial change involves the ceasing to be of the substance in question—which happens both to individual substances and to partitions and quantities of stuff. When an oak is chopped down and cut into logs, it undergoes substantial change, for the oak tree no longer exists. Similarly, when wine turns into vinegar, it undergoes substantial change, for the wine no longer exists. But there is an important difference between the two kinds of cases. In the case of the destruction of things, for example the oak tree, the stuff of which it consisted (the constitutive wood) may and often does continue to exist. But in the case of the transformation of stuffs, as in the case of the wine turning into vinegar, it is the stuff itself that undergoes essential change.

III

Substance-Referring Expressions. We classify individual things in indefinitely many ways. For some purposes, adjectival classification is useful, e.g. classifying things by colour, shape, size or weight. For other purposes, nominal classification is what is needed. Not all our classificatory nominals are substance names. A human being may be a child or an adult, a parent, a doctor, an Englishman, a stamp collector, and so forth. The concept of a human being is a substance-concept, while that of a child is not—it signifies a human being *at a certain phase* (namely childhood) in the natural development of human beings. Similar phased substance-concepts are 'youth', 'adult', 'sapling', as well as metamorphic phased concepts such as 'pupa', 'tadpole', 'maggot', 'larva'—concepts that signify a thing of a given kind at a phase through which every thing of that kind must pass if it survives for long enough. A human being may cease to be a child, while continuing to exist, and whereas the adult Sir Richard Roe is not the same boy as little Dick Roe, since he is not a boy, he *was* once that very boy and *is* the very same human being as him. 'Parent' and 'doctor' are not substance-concepts, since a human being can become a parent without loss of identity, and cease to be a doctor without ceasing to exist. But, avatars and gods of mythology and religion apart, nothing that is not a human being can change into one, and, mythology and fairy tales apart, a human being cannot cease to be a human being (change into a swine or a frog) and continue to exist. 'Englishman', 'Frenchman' or 'German' are terms by which we may classify human beings, but are not substance-concepts, since they merely signify the location of birth (or country of citizenship) of a human being. Similarly, 'doctor' or 'balletomane' are not substance concepts, signifying merely professional or favoured activities that may characterize a human being. Such terms are essentially adjectival general terms, in as much as they specify a property, indeed an accidental property, of some human beings. Substance terms do, of course, occur predicatively—obviously so when we characterise a 'primary substance' such as Socrates as being a secondary substance, namely a human being. Whether that warrants conceiving of *being a human being* as a *property* depends upon how one chooses to mould the vague category of *property*. There is little to be gained, and much to be lost, from failing to segregate predicates in the category of substance from other kinds of predicates that we can readily conceive of as being used to ascribe properties to things.

There are, of course, many things and kinds of thing that are to be found in the world around us to which we refer by means of singular referring expressions, and by reference to which we may explain various phenomena that call out for explanation, which are not substances. We refer to rainbows, reflections and shadows, to sounds and smells, to holes, gaps, knots and lumps, to waves, currents, lakes and oceans, to valleys, passes, gulfs and deltas, to the atmosphere and stratosphere, and, of course, to the indefinite variety of events, states and processes. These are clearly *not* substances, although they are objects of singular reference with a rough spatio-temporal location.

Other things (or better, concepts of other things) are more difficult to classify. Is an ephemeral river (that flows once every three years) a substance? (Is *ephemeral river* a substance concept?) Perhaps not. What then of a perennial river? What of a mountain? A hill? A hillock? Or a bump? If a bump is no more than a disturbance on the surface of a solid, why is a mountain anything more than a large bump? If the Kohinoor is a substance, then so too are the stones on the garden path, and if stones, why not lumps of ice, and if lumps of ice, then why stop at pools of water?

Substance (thing) names are count nouns, but it is not uniformly the case that clear criteria for counting individuals are implicit in the meaning of any given substance name. Given the various forms of vegetative, asexual reproduction it is obvious that there can be no clear and unequivocal way of distinguishing one such plant of a given kind from another. There is surely no answer to the question of how many plants there are on one's lawn, even if one's lawn is nothing but grass; nor can there typically be any answer to the question 'How many daisies (not flowers, but plants) are there on the daisy lawn?' It is unclear how to count the number of individual trees in a copse grown from root suckers, and although it is easy to count the number of daffodils in a given clump in the spring, it is not clear how to answer the question of how many plants there are in the clump. So countability characterizes many substances—but by no means all.

The concept of substance (thing) is one of the *most* general categorial concepts, and like other such concepts it is exceedingly vague and flexible. Our general categorial concepts are not akin to variables in a formal calculus taking a sharply defined range of values as their values. On the contrary, they tend to be elastic, not rigid, frayed at the edges, not sharply circumscribed. They have their uses to be sure, but one should not expect greater precision from them than they are capable of delivering—and that is not very great.

To say that an S is a substance of a certain kind informs us of the logical character of the concept of an S rather than telling us further distinguishing material features of S's. Cabbages and cauliflowers, cats and dogs are kinds of things, just as wine and water, iron and steel are kinds of stuffs. But the concept of a substance (thing) is not the concept of yet another kind of thing, and the concept of a substance (stuff) is not the concept of yet another kind of stuff. It was a confusion of Descartes's to suggest that matter is a kind of substance, and a worse confusion to suggest that mind is another. *Matter* is simply the formal *summum genus* of stuffs. The totality of matter is not, *contra* Descartes, a kind of substance at all. 'Mind' does not signify a kind of stuff (nor indeed did Descartes think it did)—it is a count-noun, not mass-noun. In characterizing mind and matter as two kinds (the only two kinds) of substance he was cross-classifying, since count-nouns and mass nouns, if they do signify substances, do not signify substances in the same sense of the term at all and so do not signify two species of a common genus. Moreover, a mind is not a substance, a kind of entity, in any sense of the term. To be sure, what he meant was that the totality of space-matter, given the principle of conservation, and individual minds, given their absolute simplicity, causally depend on nothing other than the concurrence of God for their existence—but this too was confused and it was misconceived to appropriate the concept of substance for this purpose.

In trying to delineate the boundaries of these categorial terms, we are not endeavouring to classify everything there is (as if the philosopher were a 'meta-physicist'), but rather to differentiate between kinds of concepts or words. (We are trying to attain a synoptic view of our conceptual scheme, of the ways in which we think and speak about objects of our experience and of ourselves as subjects of experience—not to steal a march on natural science. Of course, that does not mean that we are not *also* trying to attain a synoptic view of the formal features of substances and constitutive stuff of which the world consists.) Given the multiplicity of needs in response to which our rich and refined languages have evolved, and given that languages are dynamic, it should be altogether unsurprising that the boundaries between different classes of word should be blurred, that the categories of types of expression are often not sharply circumscribed.

IV

Connections between Things and Stuffs. The two senses of the term 'substance', that is, substance as a persistent thing of a certain sort and substance as stuff of a certain kind, are systematically related. For a concrete individual thing of a given kind is a spatio-temporal continuant, and is made of, constituted of, matter of some kind, that is, a quantity of substance (stuff) or substances (stuffs) of one sort or another.

It is important not to conflate the relationship between a thing and its constitutive stuff with the relationship between the thing and its parts. The stuff of which a thing is made is neither larger nor smaller nor the same size as the thing itself, although it weighs the same. The parts of a thing are smaller than the whole of which they are parts. If a thing is wholly made of such-and-such stuff, then all the parts of the thing consist of that stuff. But if a thing is made of such-and-such parts, it does not follow that its parts are made of such-and-such parts. One may destroy the thing and its parts without destroying the stuff of which it is made, but one cannot destroy the stuff of which a thing is made without destroying the thing itself.

It is not necessary for the continued identity of a substance (thing) that it consist of the same specific quantity of stuff throughout the whole of its existence. This is most obvious in the case of living beings. Since they metabolize food from their environment, they may change all of their constitutive matter in the course of their lives while remaining the same being.

Artefacts, on the whole, do not change the totality of their constitutive stuff, and if, under the touch of a Midas, they did so instantaneously, the continued identity of the artefact would be called into question. For it is not at all obvious that the china mug, transformed into gold, is the very same mug as hitherto. However, some of the parts of an artefact can be, and often are, replaced without loss of identity. To that extent then, change of some of the constitutive matter of which an artefact is made is compatible with its continued identity. Whether gradual replacement of *all* of the parts over a prolonged period of time is compatible with continued identity or not (as in the famous example of Theseus' ship) is arguably a matter for reasoned decision sensitive to the purposes and context for which determination of identity is required. Every rotten plank of the ship that is lovingly rebuilt on shore is identical with a plank of the original vessel, but it is clear which way the marine-insurance company should decide if the question of which ship is the one insured should arise. In this case, the identity of the artefact is not impugned by the complete change of its parts, and hence its specific (as opposed to generic) constitutive stuff, over a prolonged period of time.

Among the attributes of an individual substance, there are some that are attributable to the constitutive material of the thing, for example, its plasticity, hardness, weight, solubility or insolubility in this or that solvent, commonly also its smell, taste, and texture. Thus that this bronze statuette is soluble in hydrochloric acid, is hard and weighs more than two pounds is due to the fact that the bronze of which it is made dissolves in such acid, is a hard material and that the specific quantity of bronze from which it is made weighs more than two pounds. The colour of a thing is typically the colour of the exterior surface of its constitutive stuff or of any other material forming its surface (its bark, skin, peel, and so on) which may be no more than a layer of oxides or, in the case of many artefacts, a decorative or protective coat of paint, varnish, tar (and so on).

Other attributes of things are determined by the kind of substance the thing is. If it is an artefact, for example, its size, shape and parts are typically determined by the purpose of the artefact. If it is a living being, its morphological features, characteristic organs, pattern of development and characteristic modes of behavior are determined by the nature of the organism which it is.

V

Substances and their Substantial Parts. It should be noted that the substantial parts of an individual living substance, such as a leaf or a flower, a head or a tail, are not themselves substances. Of course, the parts may be detached from the substance of which they are parts. In that sense, the constitutive parts of a substance *can* enjoy independent existence. But, in another sense, they *cannot.* For such parts are functionally defined, and they cannot fulfil their defining function once they have become detached. The amputated leg can no longer be used by an animal to walk, and the eye, removed from the sighted animal is no longer an organ of vision. (But one need not follow Aristotle in holding that it is no more an eye than a painted eye[3], since unlike a painted eye, it *was* once an organ of vision.) Furthermore, these functional parts do not long survive detachment from the organism of which they were a part. Independently of human interference, they wither or decay. Of course, human beings can graft shoots and transplant organs. But this does not significantly affect the point being made, since although these parts of an organism *are* transferable, they still only fulfil their defining function as constituent parts of a living plant or animal.

Matters are less clear with regard to parts of an artefact. Although they do fulfil a function in the whole of which they are a part, they are not *used* by the artefact of which they are a part to fulfil a function. Rather they are used by the manufacturer to construct the artefact, which may then be used *by human beings* to fulfil a function. Unlike the parts of an organism, they are created

3. Aristotle, *De Anima* 412^b 20–24.

independently of the artefact of which, on assembly, they become a functioning part. They are detachable from the whole of which they are parts without detriment to the possibility of their re-employment in the same functional role, either in the same artefact duly re-assembled or in a different one. Unlike parts of an organism that grow as the organism matures and decay when detached from the organism, they can be stored without decay or deterioration independently of the mechanism for which they are made. So it is difficult to see any overriding reason for denying that parts of an artefact can be considered as substances—*if* we resolve to consider artefacts to be non-natural substances.

Among the attributes which a substance, a concrete thing of a certain kind, has, some are actualities, such as its size, shape, colour, location, and some are potentialities or dispositional properties, such as its mobility, hardness, brittleness, solubility, inflammability. These potentialities include the wide range of active and passive powers of a substance. In the case of living things, especially animals, the active powers include their numerous different kinds of abilities (which are not dispositions) to do or refrain from doing those things they *can* do. For many of the active powers of animals, unlike those of insentient substances, are two-way powers.

VI

Substances Conceived as Natural Kinds. It would be mistaken to take the two very general categories of substances, that is, things and stuffs, to be two super-categories of *natural kinds*, where natural kinds are conceived to be discovered rather than stipulated, and subject to natural laws concerning those kinds. The salient properties of natural kinds thus conceived are sometimes held to be causally determined by a real essence constituted by their micro-structure or micro-structural proper-ties. The natural kind, it is argued, is defined by micro-structural similarity to an ostended or otherwise located paradigm. This sample, in its role as a paradigm of the (often yet to be discovered) micro-structural real essence, is conceived to be partly constitutive of the meaning of the natural kind name. Accordingly, scientific discovery holds a blank cheque from semantics, which it can fill in as science progresses.[4] This conception of the explanation of what natural kind terms mean is the contemporary heir to the venerable idea of 'real definition'. It is rooted in Locke's distinction between real and nominal essence, but unlike Locke, holds the real essence of a thing to be both discoverable and partly constitutive of the meaning of its name. It draws support from the discovery of the Periodic Table of elements, and from the discovery of DNA and its genetic role.

It is doubtful whether the categories found to be useful in the natural sciences are themselves natural kind terms *thus understood*. For this conception of natural kinds is a metaphysical rather than scientific one, rooted in a form of metaphysical essentialism, on the one hand, and misconceptions concerning meaning and explanation, on the other.[5]

It is an illusion that scientific discovery can disclose what the words we use, such as 'gold' and 'water', 'fish' and 'lily' really mean. For what a word means is determined by convention, not by discovery—although, of course, discovery may be elevated into convention by agreement on a new rule for the use of the word. What a word means is specified by the common, accepted, explanation of its meaning. Such an explanation of meaning functions as a rule or standard of correctness for applications of a term. Accordingly, our terms for kinds of things and stuffs do not draw blank cheques on future discoveries—for if they did, the explanations of what they mean could not also function as guides to and standards for correct use as they do. Science can discover what the structure of a gold atom or a water molecule really is and why gold and water behave as they do. It can explain how vertebrate sea dwellers evolved and distinguish many different kinds among them, or what lilies have in common with garlic, and it can then accept or reject the usefulness of these categories

---

4. For the view that natural kinds have an essence and are defined by reference to similarity to a paradigmatic sample, see H. Putnam, 'The meaning of meaning', repr. in his *Mind, Language, and Reality* (Cambridge: Cambridge University Press, 1975), pp. 215–71. For illuminating refutation of this conception of natural kinds from which the following discussion is derived, see J. Dupré, *The Disorder of Things* (Cambridge Mass.: Harvard University Press, 1993), Part I, and his *Humans and Other Animals* (Oxford: Clarendon Press, 2002), especially Parts I and II.

5. For examination of the semantic misconceptions see P. M. S. Hacker, *Wittgenstein's Place in Twentieth-Century Analytic Philosophy* (Oxford: Blackwell, 1996), pp. 250–3, 329f.

(*fish, Liliaceae*) for purposes of biological explanation and classification. However, in discovering that pure water consists of two parts hydrogen and one part oxygen in chemical combination, scientists did not discover what the word 'water' really means. If chemists and educated laymen now choose to define 'water' thus, that merely shows either that 'water' now has a harmlessly fluctuating meaning, or that what was inductive evidence for water has been elevated to being part of the meaning of the word in scientific parlance.

It is a mistake to suppose that natural kind terms are defined by reference to unspecified micro-structural similarity relations to a paradigm. In so far as paradigms play any role in explaining the meaning of a word, as indeed they do when a word is defined by means of an ostensive definition involving a sample, they must be usable as objects of comparison to guide the application of a word. For the role of the paradigm is as a standard for the correct application of the definiendum F: something which is *this* → [and here one points at the paradigm] or is *what this* → *is*, is rightly said to be F, or an F. So the relevant features of the paradigm must be both known and evident—otherwise the paradigm has no normative role. But if the putative 'similarity relation' concerns micro-structural properties, the paradigm can play no normative, standard-setting role. For if the micro-structure instantiated by the paradigm is unknown and still awaiting scientific discovery, the paradigm can provide no guidance in applying or withholding the term 'F'. But if the requisite micro-structure *is* known, the paradigm is redundant. For one can directly find out by appropriate chemical tests what the micro-structure of the entity under investigation is and so determine, independently of any paradigm, whether it is F or an F.

No doubt we are prone to be mesmerized by the example of the Periodic Table in chemistry and its bearing on the determination of the nature of stuffs. But it is unrepresentative; and even in this case it would be mistaken to suppose that all essential properties flow from the features determining the atomic number of what is classified. The behavior of iron atoms, for example, is very unlike that of ferric or ferrous ions, even though all have the atomic number 26 and are rightly classified as belonging to the same natural kind. Moreover, it would be absurd to suppose that the nature of scrambled eggs or Yorkshire pudding were something that is determined, independently of their nominal essences, by the atomic numbers of their constituent elements, or that we need to wait upon scientific discoveries to find out what 'beef' and 'venison', 'paper' and 'glass', really mean or really are (as opposed to discovering what their chemical analysis is). Yet names of cooked and manufactured substances are no less substance (stuff) nouns than names of the chemical elements or of compounds that are to be found in nature.

With the triumph of Darwinism, the idea that biological species are determined by a common essence, as was supposed by Aristotelian scientific conceptions, was rejected. For the theory of evolution showed the untenability of the idea of the fixity of species, and phylogenetic classification proceeded without any such assumption—often yielding equivocal and optional results. Furthermore, the latter classification is by no means uniformly the most useful in the biological sciences, and morphological classifications are often called for to satisfy explanatory needs. But evolutionary (historical) classifications, on the one hand, and morphological (structural) classifications, on the other, generate taxa of different kinds. There is no uniquely correct and omni-explanatory classificatory scheme, and Plato's distasteful metaphor of carving nature at her joints is more apt at the butcher's than on the agenda of science. Of course, not anything goes; but how we should classify things when engaged in a given science depends upon our scientific purposes, upon the peculiarities of the thing we are investigating, and upon the features we wish to explain. There is no reason to suppose a priori that there is only one scientifically fruitful way of classifying natural phenomena.

One may grant that scientific taxonomy is fruitful. It is subservient to the explanatory enterprises of science. The fruitfulness of such a taxonomy is evident in the range and explanatory powers of the ensuing generalizations. So many of the features of things and stuffs that are individuated in terms of common-or-garden concepts are explained by scientific theories that rely on more specialized and often very different classifications. But, first, not all the things that interest us and for which we have coined general names stand in need of any explanation. Secondly, not all explanation is scientific explanation. So although many phenomena that concern us do call out for explanation, the requisite explanations may involve reference to human activities and interests, to custom, law, economics and history and may employ classifications quite distinct from, but no less useful within their domains than, those of the natural sciences. Thirdly, there is no such thing as Science, but only a multitude of different natural sciences, on the one hand, and social and human sciences, on the other. The reductive ideal of unified science is an absurdity that should have died when it was abandoned by its twentieth-century progenitors, the Vienna Circle. There is no absolute final classificatory scheme for everything there is, but only a multiplicity of taxonomies that the various sciences, natural and social, find fruitful, and the multitude of more or less unsystematic substance terms, in both senses of the word, that mankind in general finds useful for the manifold purposes that inform our lives.

VII

Substances Conceived as a Common Logico-Linguistic Category.
It is evident that our ordinary classifications of material and animate things into substances of different kinds were not designed for purposes of scientific taxonomy or for scientific explanatory power, but for purposes of humdrum identification and re-identification relative to a multitude of different human concerns. Relative to our purposes and interests, it can hardly be said that we err in distinguishing between onions and garlic, or between both and lilies, even though all belong to the *Liliaceae*, or that we have made a mistake in segregating moths from butterflies, even though *Macrolepidoptera* include all butterflies and some moths. Our interests and concerns are numerous and very varied. The fact that *tree* has no place in botanical taxonomy does not mean that this term is not a substance name of a natural kind of thing (taking this term now in low key). The fact that *angiosperm*, which subsumes daisies, cacti and oak trees (since they all produce seeds in ovaries) but excludes pine trees, has no place in ordinary classifications does not show anything other than the fact that the interests of botany differ from those that underlie the classifications of ordinary language.[6]

---

6. See Dupré, *The Disorder of Things*, Ch. 1.

Similarly, it is clear that the logico-grammatical category of concrete mass nouns signifying stuffs of one kind or another is indifferent to whether the designated stuff is natural or not. Wine is no less of a substance than water, even though it is manufactured by human beings, and honey is as much a stuff as helium, even though it is made by bees. Wool or silk are natural kinds of stuff, but by the time we have finished with the natural material, the resultant wools and silks are very different from anything found on the back of a sheep or constituting the chrysalis of a silk worm. Bread and butter are no less kinds of stuffs than wheat (or indeed the flour that is produced from it) and milk. The general concepts of substances (stuffs) that we employ in our daily discourse were not introduced as a part of a taxonomy for scientific (e.g. chemical) purposes, they do not involve a systematic hierarchy of kinds of stuffs, and they invoke very different principles of classification suited to the numerous different purposes that we have. From a logico-grammatical point of view, however, there is no significant difference between natural and manufactured stuffs.

General names of artefacts are, as suggested above, no less substance-names than general names of natural things. Artefacts are enduring features of the landscapes and cityscapes we inhabit, commonly long outlasting many of their natural inhabitants. Most of the salient objects around us are, by now, artefactual. We refer to artefacts, often locate ourselves by reference to certain kinds of them, sometimes trace the provenance of other kinds, identify and re-identify them. Material artefacts (by contrast with such artefacts as works of literature or music) consist of the stuffs of which they are made. They possess active and passive powers, and they undergo various forms of change compatible with their continued identity. Artefactual names serve to identify and re-identify a persistent thing as *that* particular thing of such-and-such a sort, they provide principles for counting things of the relevant kind, and they determine, as part of their meaning, a tolerably clear array of properties the possession of which is essential for the thing in question to be said to continue to exist. St Paul's is still the same building despite having been extensively refaced, but the Winter Palace is a meticulous reconstruction of the building destroyed by the Nazis. A table can tolerate scratches and stains and the replacement of a leg or two compatible with its continued identity, but not being chopped into small pieces to feed the fire. A motor car can be repainted, have a new set of tyres, even a new engine, and yet remain the same car, but it will not remain the same car after being squashed into a cube preparatory to being melted down. Of course, there is a fair degree of indeterminacy at the borderlines, but then that is true of concepts of natural objects too.

VIII

A Historical Afterword: Misconceptions of the Category of Substance. Three strands in the classical Aristotelian account were seriously misunderstood in the seventeenth-century debate concerning substance, with long-lasting effects upon philosophical reflection. Aristotelian primary substances were rightly conceived to enjoy *independent existence* in a sense in which properties do not. They were correctly conceived to be subjects of predication, *bearers of properties*. And they were sensibly held to be subjects of changing accidents, capable of bearing contrary properties at different times, and hence *persisting through change*. Seventeenth- and eighteenth-century thinkers, whose thoughts focused to a large extent on the scientific revolution through which they were living and to which their philosophies were trying to do justice, knotted these simple strands into an unprecedented tangle.

The idea of substance as an independent existence was drastically re-interpreted by Descartes, removing it from its Aristotelian context and from its categorial status as a general form of our thought about material objects, on the one hand, and about their constitutive matter, on the other. For Descartes understood *independent existence* in causal, rather than logical terms. A substance, according to him, is 'a thing that exists in such a way as to *depend on no other thing* for its existence' (emphasis added).[7] He held that only God is completely independent of everything else, and is therefore the only substance *stricto sensu*. In a derivative sense, minds (a plurality) and matter (a totality: the plenum, the totality of space-matter)

---

7. Descartes, *Principles of Philosophy*, I. 51.

are also substances, since they depend for their existence only upon the concurrence of God (whose sustaining activity, Descartes thought, was necessary for the continued existence of all things). But God apart, the plenum is indestructible, since the total quantity of matter in the universe is, Descartes believed, conserved throughout all change. Minds are sempiternal, since, lacking parts, they are simple, and all destruction is decomposition into, and rearrangement of, constituents. But the Aristotelian sense of independent existence was non-causal. The sense in which the properties of a thing, such as its motion, shape or colour, are not independent existences is that (with qualifications for shadows, holes, gaps, shafts of light, and so on) there can be no movement that is not the movement of some thing, no shape unless there is something that has that shape, and no colour unless there is something coloured. To say that a particular substance exists is to say that there is a thing of a certain kind somewhere, somewhen. To say that a quality exists is to say that some thing somewhere, somewhen, is qualified in a certain way. So the existence of substances was not held, absurdly, to be independent *of any other substances*, let alone of *conditions* such as heat and cold, rain and snow, as well as other atmospheric circumstances and environmental accompaniments. Similarly, the Aristotelian conception of the persistence of substances through change simply meant that particular things can change their accidents and yet persist—that, contrary to what Hume later averred, change (accidental, as opposed to substantial, change) is compatible with continued identity. It did *not* mean that there is, throughout all change, something that remains unchanged. (*That* doctrine is to be found in Aristotle's hylomorphism, in his conception—a misconception—of *materia prima*.)

Matters were further exacerbated by Locke, who seized on the idea of substances as bearers of qualities—a thought fostered by the etymology of 'substance' ('substantia'—that which stands under or supports). Properties of a thing are, in Aristotle's jargon, '*in* a subject' (as we might say that they are '*had* by a subject'), a thought that was transmitted in the confusing jargon of '*inhering in* a subject'. This, in Locke's hands, yielded the misconception of *substance in general* as something that possesses properties but is distinct from them—a bare unqualified particular, a something 'I know not what' in which qualities inhere.[8] Substances, far from being conceived to be kinds of persistent spatio-temporal things, were taken to be the *substrata* of properties—something that 'supported', 'united together' the properties a thing possesses, the carcasses of the furniture of the world on which a veneer of properties is stuck. Being a mere *something* in which properties inhere, substance, as it seemed, 'in and of itself' must *lack properties*. Locke confused the bare idea of a subject of predication with the idea of a bare subject of predication.[9] The former is the perfectly coherent thought of something, as yet unspecified, which ... The latter is the incoherent idea of a thing without qualities. The idea that qualities are *collectible*[10] (other than, in a Pickwickian sense, by words) is an altogether misleading metaphor, as are the thoughts that they can, like twigs, be *bound together* or, like billboards, be *supported*.

It is small wonder that Hume washed his hands of the morass, declaring the very idea of material substance an 'unintelligible chimera' and that of a spiritual substance 'absolutely unintelligible'.[11] But nothing could have been further from Aristotle's mind than this Lockean confusion. An Aristotelian (primary) substance was anything but a bare particular—it was a persistent thing of a given kind, with an essence determined by its essential properties, a subject of accidents that may change without affecting the identity of the substance. To specify only the qualities of a thing will, Aristotle insisted, tell us *what the thing is like*. But if we want to know not what it is like, but *what it is*, we must be told, by specification of a secondary substance, what kind of thing it is.

Descartes, opposing the scholastic Aristotelian tradition, had declared that there are only two kinds of substance. Berkeley held that there is only one kind. Spinoza insisted that there is only one substance, Leibniz held that there are infinitely many. And Hume

---

8. Locke, *An Essay concerning Human Understanding*, II-xiii-17–20, II-xxiii-1–6, 15, 37, III-vi-21.

9. A point nicely made by David Wiggins in his 'Substance', in A. C. Grayling (ed.), *Philosophy 1: A Guide through the Subject* (Oxford: Oxford University Press, 1995), p. 227.

10. Op. cit., IV-vi-7.

Ibid., II-xxiii-4

11. Hume, *A Treatise of Human Nature*, I-iv-3 and I-iv-4.

denied that there are any substances at all (unless one counts each idea and impression as a substance). More than a century of philosophical reflection had reduced the subject to incoherence.

Kant sapiently attempted to rehabilitate the concept of substance. He did emphasize a point of fundamental importance, namely that the concepts of substance, agency and causation are intimately interwoven.[12] Unfortunately, however, he married the legacy of Descartes to the confusions of Locke. For, like Descartes, he associated substance in experience with what is 'abiding in its existence', and misguidedly identified it not with the relatively abiding familiar things around us, but with the supposed permanent totality of matter in space (unlike Descartes, he differentiated matter from space). 'In all change of appearances', he wrote, 'substance is permanent; its quantum in nature is neither increased nor diminished ... The substratum of all that is real, that is, of all that belongs to the existence of things is *substance*; and all that belongs to existence can be thought only as a determination of substance.' Substance, he held, 'as the substrate of all change, remains ever the same', it is 'something *abiding* and *permanent*, of which all change and co-existence are only so many ways (modes of time) in which the permanent exists.'[13] So, like Descartes, Kant thought of the various individual material substances (in the classical sense of the term 'substance') that we encounter around us as no more than passing modes of the underlying substrate of all change. Elsewhere, echoing Locke and compounding confusion, he averred that 'in all substances the true subject—namely that which remains after all the accidents (as predicates) have been removed—and hence the *substantial* itself, is unknown to us'.[14]

There is irony in all this, since what Kant needed in order to undermine the empiricism against which he warred, and to establish the conditions of the possibility of an objective spatio-temporal framework within which objects of experience can be distinguished from the experience of objects, was precisely the notion of Aristotelian substances as the *relatively* abiding, but

---

12. Kant, *Critique of Pure Reason*, B 249–50. For a helpful discussion of the flaws in Kant's treatment of substance, see P. F. Strawson, 'Kant on substance', repr. in his *Entity and Identity and other Essays* (Oxford: Clarendon Press, 1997) pp. 268–279.

13. Ibid. B 224, 225, 226.

14. Kant, *Prolegomena to any Future Metaphysics*, §46.

impermanent, independent objects of our experience. Such objects of reference and subjects of predication perfectly adequately fulfil the Kantian requirements necessary for the unity of time, on the one hand, and of a stable background against which we can apprehend change, on the other. That such objects of experience themselves come into existence and pass away does not impugn the unity of the spatio-temporal framework in which we encounter, identify and re-identify them—as long as they do not all pass away simultaneously. Nor does the demand that in every change some thing should persist require that something should persist through every change. All that is necessary is that there be Aristotelian substances among phenomena.[15]

15. I am grateful to John Dupré, Hanjo Glock and David Wiggins for their comments on an earlier draft of this paper.

THE CREATION OF THE WORLD

by Sarah Broadie and Anthony Kenny

I—Sarah Broadie

PLATO'S INTELLIGIBLE WORLD?

ABSTRACT Part 1 examines the roles of (a) *intelligent cause*, (b) *empirical materials* (fire, earth etc.), and (c) the *resulting cosmos*, in the account of world-making in the *Timaeus*. It is argued that the presence of (b) is essential for the distinctness of (a) and (c); and an explanation is proposed for why the biblical idea of creation faces no such problem. Part II shows how different suggestions implicit in Plato's doctrine of the *intelligible model* give rise to radically different kinds of Platonic metaphysics.

I

My subject is the metaphysics of the cosmology of Plato's *Timaeus*, and the relation of the cosmology to the metaphysics. These words suggest a sharp distinction between cosmology and metaphysics, which may seem anachronistic in this ancient context. But I do not think I am guilty of anachronism. Yes, it must be admitted that Plato has no term straightforwardly translatable by 'metaphysical'; but nonetheless, as everyone knows, he very clearly and self-consciously postulates non-empirical realities beyond or above the realm of changeable things. I cannot see that it distorts his purposes to label these entities 'metaphysical'.

Plato invokes his non-empirical Forms, and the discarnate soul which communes with them, in many places, including places where cosmology hardly enters in. In the *Timaeus*, however, the familiar doctrine gains additional metaphysical weight by being juxtaposed with causal reflection about empirical nature *considered in its entirety*. Here, Plato calls the empirical realm 'the all', or 'this all' (27a4; c4; 29c5; d7; 41c3; 37d2; 92c4): phrases which in the cosmological context imply that if empirical nature can be accounted for at all it must be accounted for as a whole. That it cannot be accounted for at all is an option he refuses to consider. Another possibility, that the empirical is self-explanatory and self-substantiating, is vigorously dismissed. Plato maintains that whatever can be grasped by sense, including under this heading even *the totality* of what can be grasped by sense,[1] is not ultimate; strictly, such things cannot be said to be but at most to have become; but that for him entails that they have been caused. Thus 'this all' as a whole has been caused, and (we may add) caused as the whole that it is, since Plato takes for granted that the causing is intelligent, hence intentional, agency (28a4-c5).

Before proceeding I must make clear that what Plato means when he speaks of 'this all' in the *Timaeus* is the world around us. It is not a diachronic 'all': that is, it is not the total history of everything empirical. What this world around us is, and how it came to be, are questions to be answered together. A cosmos—an ordered complex—is what this world is, and the story of how it came into being is the story of how something ordered came to be *from pre-existing unordered empirical materials*. Plato tells us to see this development as steered by an intelligent cause. Clearly, we are not to try to grasp the nature of this cause by assimilating it to any natural object already formed from matter; for the existence of any such object presupposes the causation of such a cause. By similar reasoning, this cause of the whole natural cosmos cannot be such as operates by means of a body with limbs etc., for such a body would necessarily be part of an already constituted cosmos.

Nor, for Plato, can the cause of the present order lie in some kind of ancestral thing from which this world evolved, a thing that differs from what we have today by being, for example, more hazy and indeterminate, or by consisting of something utterly massed together, or of a vast scatter of minute things in space, or of familiar materials like fire and water in a formless state. For by themselves, without the formative action of a principle of a completely different type, namely intelligence, any such materials or matter-like things could not have become or given rise to the empirical world around us. How can Plato be so sure of this?

---

1. It is not clear whether he thinks that 'sense-perceivable' applies to the whole cosmos because it applies to each part (which would not be a good inference) or that in perceiving a part we in a way perceive the whole of which it is part, just as we see London even if we visit only part of London. (That ancient Greek verbs of perception take the [partitive?] genitive facilitates the latter point.)

Because his fundamental assumption, the denial of which we are told it would be a gross impiety even to utter (29a2-4) (let alone teach as the truth), is that this world is as good, beautiful, and orderly as any empirical thing could be. Clearly, this is to be regarded as a necessary truth. It follows that we have to think of the cause of the universe as something that *reliably* targets the good and beautiful for production, hence as something that produces what is good and beautiful for its own sake. The materials of the world, or any other matter-like things, whether they are viewed as still present and constituting the world we know, or as superseded by it because of having turned into it, cannot, Plato thinks, conceivably be relied on by themselves to come up with a supremely good and beautiful universe, or on their own to behave as if they appreciated the value of such an entity by producing it. Hence although, according to him, the materials of the world were around before the world order was established, and although the world order could not, in his way of thinking, possibly have been established except out of those pre-existing materials, a cause of a kind completely different from them was needed to effect the transition from mere materials to this finished world in which we live. This cause must be intelligence, since only intelligence has the orientation towards the good, beautiful, and orderly which the explanation demands (cf. *Phaedo*, 97b8-98b6).

Summarising so far, we observe two key elements in this conception of a metaphysical cause of the empirical order around us. First, there is the assumption that the empirical order is to be accounted for as a whole, and secondly there is the assumption that this order is supremely beautiful and good. The two assumptions between them yield three results, one positive and two negative. The positive result is that this cause is an intelligence. The negative ones are that the cause is utterly unlike any formed empirical thing, and that it is utterly unlike any matter of any such thing.

Now the doctrine just presented gives us a strongly contrastive dualism between the empirical world and its cause. Let us see exactly how the contrast comes about. We have three factors distinguished functionally in relation to one another: (α) a cause, (β) materials, and (γ) a product; and the cause is related to the product as its maker, and to the materials as their user for making the product. Interestingly enough, it is precisely the presence in the scheme of *materials as used by a user* that safeguards the distinctness between maker and product. For suppose the cause were not a user of materials, but gave rise to the product by itself or immediately. In that case it would be natural and reasonable to say one of two things: either the cause-entity *has evolved into* what we were calling the product, so that in fact there is a single continuous entity of which these are successive stages; or the cause-entity *constitutes* the product. Thus in one of two ways there is a relation between cause and product which approximates to identity, in the case where the cause is such as to cause without using materials distinct from itself; whereas when the cause is such as to use materials plainly and radically distinct from itself, it is as if the presence of those materials in the product establishes the product too as plainly and radically distinct from the cause.

The plain and radical distinctness of cause and product is not adequately established by insisting that the cause is something intelligent that aims at good results, whereas the product is something material. For certainly not everyone clearly accepts that what is intelligent is, as such, immaterial. For example, Plato's older contemporary Diogenes of Apollonia found it reasonable to treat *air* as the material of the world while at the same time insisting that air is intelligent (or even that it is intelligence) and works for the good. Aristophanes makes great fun of this in the *Clouds*, but there is no reason to think that philosophers refused to take Diogenes seriously. In other words, it was possible to view the intelligent mind responsible for the universe as an extended material of which the universe is made. If this view becomes unattractive, it is not because of any flaw inherent in the sheer assumption that extended matter can be intelligent, but because of a shift to viewing matter in terms of a new paradigm (to use Thomas Kuhn's word). This is Plato's scheme, according to which intelligence figures as *that which uses a distinct matter*, and matter as *that which intelligence orders for the sake of the product*. Adopting the new scheme is of course enormously facilitated by the fact that we are extremely familiar from our own experience with the sort of intelligent activity where someone uses a distinct matter to make something. The human parallel, moreover, highlights the crucial assumption that the matter which becomes the product could not have been expected to become it on its own; since human intelligence gets to work precisely because circumstances are not going to yield up the desired result automatically. It is important too that human constructive intelligence—anyway in some of its best and most typical examples—is autonomous in aiming for and achieving the result. It is self-guided. Thus it seems absurd to think of intelligence, the intelligence that orders a distinct matter, as the kind of thing that could itself require intelligent organization by an intelligence distinct from itself. In short, Plato's scheme secures not only a dualistic contrast between *intelligent cause* and *product*, but an equally radical contrast between *intelligent cause* and *matter*. And, as I hope is obvious, the scheme relies on nothing but austerely functional interlocking notions of matter and intelligent cause. Thus without ever leaning directly on considerations to do with what is and what is not divisible or extended or bulky, Plato has established the immateriality of intelligence (or of the intelligent as such).

The points just made depend for their force on the Greek philosophical background. In that culture it was recurrently thinkable that an intelligent cause of the natural order gets to be its cause by evolving into it or by constituting it—relations close to identity, both. Hence if (for whatever reason) this culture was to generate a strong contrastive separation between the natural order and its cause, the chances are that the theory to emerge would be a triadic one in which the cause (α) causes by ordering matter (β) so that matter constitutes the product (γ). Here, the unordered matter is sharply distinct from what uses it, and this *sharp distinctness from the cause* is one of the attributes passed on to the product from the unordered matter out of which it comes to be.

With this logic in mind we should, however, wonder about our own culture's most traditional account of the origin of the world: the idea of creation *ex nihilo*, which has its roots in the book of Genesis. We should ask: what is it about that biblically inspired conception that makes *un*problematic a straightforwardly dyadic contrast between the world and its creator? For here there are just two things, the world and the creator. The creator is radically different from anything worldly, yet he creates *ex nihilo*, without mediation of matter distinct from himself.[2] One may find nothing metaphysically surprising in this combination of features, since it is traditional to regard an agent who creates *ex nihilo* as utterly unlike the world or anything worldly. Still, consideration of Plato's scheme shows too, I think, that a sense of contrastive separation of maker from product can crucially depend on seeing the maker as using a distinct material rather than as dispensing with any such aid. With biblical creation, however, there is plainly no need to include in the account a used pre-existent material in order to safeguard God's distinctness from the world that is caused to be, i.e. to keep the divine principle from merging with the world, whether as an earlier stage of it or as the matter of it. But how can this be? That is: what exactly is it about the biblical account that makes possible the framing of a genuinely complete dyadic conception involving just God and world? What is it about these two beings that ensures their perfect distinctness?

Perhaps the answer is that biblical theism assumes not only that God, the cause of the world, is holy and to be worshipped, but also that the world is *not* holy, but is a place, rather, of worshippers. To Plato, by contrast, the empirical cosmos, even though a made thing and a perceptible one, is literally itself a *god*, an appellation it shares with the god who made it from matter and with various astral deities dwelling within it (34a8; b4; 92a5-9). Compare this with a perspective which takes it for granted that whereas the cause of the world is divine and holy, the world itself, however truly seen to be 'very good' by its divine creator (Genesis i.31), is not a holy being nor a divine one. Here, the utter distinctness of cause and product is already established in terms just of the two of them and without interposition of the barrier concept of *matter used*—matter which a cause sharply different from it turns into a product likewise sharply different from itself. In the Greek context, to

2. Although 'waters' were about at the very beginning (Genesis i.2), there is no suggestion that God created everything else using them as material. However, at i. 20–2 and 24, the waters at God's command 'bring forth' the first birds and fishes, and the earth 'brings forth' land animals. At ii.7 (part of a different version) God creates man from pre-existing dust; but this is a point about the nature of man, not about the exigencies of creation in general.

remove *matter used* from the account would be fall back into a story that tends to assimilate product and cause, so that the cause either evolves into the product or constitutes it. Such possibilities are automatically excluded if, on the other hand, *holiness* is what marks off cause from product. For it is surely essential to holiness that what is holy cannot evolve into what is not holy, or freely function as stuff or matter of what is not holy. Within the world, after all, except under the constraint of some kind of emergency, it is desecration knowingly to use some holy object as material for a secular object. One may infer from this that for a holy being to turn itself into one that was not, would be self-desecration, and hence impossible.

II

Turning back to the *Timaeus*, we see at once that the few metaphysico-cosmological assumptions just assembled carry momentous suggestions concerning human nature. For if the human intellect is at all like the one that crafted the universe—and in some way it must be, if both deserve the name, and if human intellect can understand through cosmology something of the divine one's reasonings—then human intellect must, in some measure, not be part of the natural world, and in the same measure it must be immaterial. But this, which is a metaphysical consequence of Plato's cosmology, is a theme for another occasion. For the present we are still concerned with the metaphysical *underpinnings* of that cosmology.

Now, our survey of these may not have encountered any serious incoherence as yet. But I have not yet said anything about the most essentially Platonic factor in Plato's pre-cosmic metaphysical situation. This is the intelligible model, paradigm, or Form to which divine intelligence, like a craftsman, 'looks' in fashioning the cosmos (28e5ff.). Obviously, if the cosmos is formed from matter by an immaterial intelligent cause, then this cause must be assumed to be, or to possess, or to be in touch with, whatever is necessary for its intelligent-causal function to be realised. If, as Plato assumes, this requires the craftsman god to refer to an intelligible model, then that model, and his knowledge of it, are part of the show. Let us now look at this part of the show, and in particular at the model. Just here Plato's Platonism begins to run into murky waters.[3]

Let me start this ball rolling by considering the ambiguous phrase 'Plato's intelligible world'. Plato holds that this sense-perceptible universe of ours can also become intelligible to us humans because it was constructed according to a rational plan, and we are in a position to make reasonable assumptions about the content of that plan. By applying these assumptions to the empirical world, we can explain some of its important contents and features. Hence the phrase 'Plato's intelligible world' may mean: this empirical cosmos as made intelligible to us by Platonic cosmology. Alternatively, we may very well encounter Platonists using that phrase to refer to an object accessible only by the intellect, a metaphysical super-cosmos which constitutes the eternal original of which this universe is a merely temporal copy. My question is: which of these two 'intelligible worlds' is the *Timaeus* principally trying to reveal? Is Plato here offering a cosmology that explains and makes sense of our empirical world, or is he ushering us into a purely metaphysical realm by the gateway of cosmology? It is undeniable that the cosmology, if this is his topic, comes supported by metaphysics. But this is not at all to imply that metaphysical entities are really the topic: that Plato in fact is urging us up a cosmological ladder towards the pure super-cosmos and its pure ramifications, as if towards a territory he wants us to explore and contemplate for its own sake.

Whereas very many Platonists later than Plato have accepted the 'ladder to metaphysics' view of the *Timaeus*, I believe moderns agree that this dialogue gives us first and foremost a cosmology of the empirical world. This is certainly the opinion one reaches if one takes the text at face value. The main grounds for it are (1) that the relevant part of the *Timaeus* is announced in advance as a cosmology, an account of the coming to be of the universe we are in, not an account of anything else as well (27a2-6); (2) that insofar as this material points towards anything beyond itself, what it prepares for is not ascent to the domain of pure intelligibles, but downward immersion in the particularities

---

3. The worries implied by 'murky' prescind from the question whether the eternal paradigm is in the end to be identified with the Demiurge or some aspect of him; likewise from the question of the "literal" versus "non-literal" interpretation of demiurgic activity.

of human history (actually, pseudo-history);[4] (3) The *Timaeus*'s exuberantly detailed scientific explanations of a very wide range of empirical phenomena place it squarely in the genre of *peri phuseôs* writings; they go far beyond whatever might be needed for the 'ladder to metaphysics' interpretation; (4) at one place Plato indicates that although he recognises recondite metaphysical principles of reality,[5] they cannot be made clear through an account like this one (48c2-6): which may suggest that the Timaean presentation is not intended as the portal to a full-blooded examination of metaphysics for its own sake, and therefore must be intended as something else, namely a cosmology.

It is not hard to decide between these divergent approaches to the *Timaeus*, but the roots of the two approaches are not so easy to separate. For they lie in Plato's contrast of intelligible model and sensible copy or analogue, a contrast which has the potential to be developed in at least two ways.[6]

According to the first way, we are to think of the famous likeness between a Platonic Form and its this-worldly correlate (or correlates) in terms of representation: this is encouraged by Plato's frequent statements that the this-worldly object is only an image of the Form, or that it is a shadow, reflection, or dream of the Form. Our first-order interaction with representations of things, whether in words or in some other medium, is dominated by interest in the things which the representations are of (or which we take them to be of). Thus in dreaming we are typically absorbed in what the dream is about. We often look at shadows and reflections (especially of ourselves in the mirror) just in order to obtain information about the original objects whose shadows or reflections these are. No doubt it is partly because of the intensity of our interest in the originals that it sometimes seems as if the originals themselves are actually there, standing or happening in front of us or around

4. The cosmology of the *Timaeus* is, in the dialogue, offered as a prelude to a story about a heroic military achievement of pre-historic Athens (27a2-b6); this was to be told in detail in the unfinished companion dialogue *Critias*.

5. Explained, presumably, in the so called 'unwritten doctrines' of Plato, for which we have a good deal of evidence.

6. For a useful discussion covering some of the same ground as what follows, see D. Frede, 'Rationality and Concepts in the *Timaeus*', in *Rationality in Greek Thought*, M. Frede and G. Striker (eds.) (Oxford, 1996), 29–58, esp. 49–56.

us, when in fact they are in no such place and may even be non-existent, and all that is physically present to us is the representing medium. We are prone to a double mistake. Without realising it, we 'project' properties of the representing medium on to the represented original, so that the original seems to us to be, for example, 'here', when only the medium is 'here'. And we end up thinking that what is in fact an image in or borne by the representing medium is the one and only real thing; i.e. we think we are dealing with just that, not with an original *and* its representative. Now, it is plain that the *transparency* of the medium, by which I mean the fact that in our basic interaction it does *not* draw attention to itself, facilitates these mistakes.[7] Suppose we manage to correct these mistakes. Thus we no longer have the illusion that the objects represented are here with us, nor the illusion that what is in fact the image of the object is all there is. We shall now be correctly 'reading' what goes on with the objects as going on in whatever space or domain *they* are in, whether far from us or in a different world from us.

But the medium will still be transparent, if it is a good one. Thus, now that we are reading correctly we are still taking no notice of the medium as such, and we are surely giving much less attention than before to the representations in it, since we no longer confuse them with the realities we are interested in, but are instead surefootedly using them as signs of those realities. The point is that if the sensible world is essentially a representation of the intelligible original, then the right attitude towards the sensible world and things within it is not to be curious about them at all, as the cosmologist most certainly is, but simply to 'look through' them. This is so even if it is true, and we believe, that the sensible objects we are treating as signs of intelligibles are actually caused by those intelligibles, and are meant to be caused by them. For there is no reason why such a set-up should make us at all interested in the signs themselves, any more than a medical technician reading blips on a screen is interested in the blips

---

7. If the medium is a bad one, foggy, noisy, or whatever, what is supposed to be represented may hardly appear in it; in which case, if we notice anything at all we notice just some bit of the medium, and take that to be the one and only reality.

themselves just because he knows they are caused by the patient's heartbeat.

I turn now to the second of the two ways of understanding the contrast of intelligible model and sensible analogue. According to this, the Platonic Form stands to the sensible 'likeness' as a recipe or design to the product made in accordance with it. The maker who follows the design certainly does not mean to make a representation of it, even though another might be able to infer the design from the product. There is a great deal else that a product is typically intended for than to take our minds back to the recipe. For example, a shuttle is made as a tool for weaving. And if it is made according to a design, this is not so that it shall 'body forth' the design which appears through it as through a glass darkly, but so that it will be a better instrument than one haphazardly made, i.e. better at fulfilling its function in weaving. On this line of thought, the intelligent cause of the empirical world looks to an intelligible pattern in order to raise the chances of producing the best possible empirical system: that his product conforms to the pattern is not an end in itself, but ensures that the product is excellent in accordance with whatever the standard is for excellence in that type of thing. Of course, we may think it impossible to say what counts as excellence in a cosmos or empirical system, but Plato is not so timid. He clearly thinks that the best possible empirical system is a rational, intelligent, self-sufficient, animal well populated by lesser rational animals,[8] living in environments provided by it. That is the true description of this world of ours. Presumably, then, this world's *raison d'être* is: to live well and be lived in well, in a rational way.

To examine further the difficulties of the Platonic contrast between intelligible pattern and sensible copy, I now turn to a passage where he declares with tremendous emphasis that since the empirical world and its maker were as good as possible, the maker, to ensure the best, must have been guided by an *eternal* paradigm (*paradeigma*), not by one that has come to be (28c5-29b1; cf. 28a6-b2). Strangely, Plato seems to imply that the maker of this world could have chosen to use a paradigm which

---

8. According to the *Timaeus* even so called brutes are degenerate kinds of rational animal. This is bound up with the theory that the immortal reason of a depraved human being migrates on the latter's death to the body of a suitable animal (48a3-4; 90e3-92c3).

itself had come to be.[9] Was there then already something which had come to be; and who made that, and out of what, and according to what model? And why do we hear no more about this previously made article?[10] The fact is that in this passage, ostensibly about divine world-making, Plato is making a point about human construction. *We*, when setting out to make a so and so, can generally choose whether to take as our model some instance of a so and so which already exists in the spatio-temporal world, perhaps one which has been constructed by human beings before us. Plato is reminding us that human makers are at their best and most godlike (cf. 90b6-c6) if and only if they look instead to the eternal paradigm of whatever it is they propose to make.

But what does it mean for a maker to 'look to an eternal paradigm' rather than to one that has merely come to be? Here for the human case is an interpretation that stays in touch with common sense. Rather than directly try to reproduce a thing that has already come to be in the world, whether it is a shuttle someone has made or an existing political constitution,[11] the would-be shuttle- or constitution-maker should go back within himself to first principles,[12] asking what such a thing essentially is and is for. He will work out an answer, and it is common sense that he will be better guided by an intellectually sought for, intellectually worked out, answer than he would by staring at an intellectually unanalyzed pre-existing object of the kind. For if he merely tries to reproduce the latter, (a) he may labour over superficial characteristics as if they were essential ones, and (b) he may mindlessly reproduce characteristics which were appropriate

9. This is particularly suggested by the definite article *tôn* at 28c6. (For a detailed interpretation of the passage see S. Broadie, 'Theodicy and Pseudo-history in the *Timaeus*', *Oxford Studies in Ancient Philosophy* XXI (2001), 1–28, esp. 21–6.)

10. Presumably the previously made article is itself a world, if it could be the paradigm for making a world. Yet far from worrying that it is floating about somewhere beyond this world so that they might get in each other's way, Plato is entirely definite elsewhere that ours is the one and only world that has come to be (31a2-b3; 92c9).

11. Cf. *Republic* 472e1; 500e1. The *Timaeus* opens with an interchange (17c1-19a6) about 'yesterday's discourse' by Socrates, the subject of which is said to have been an ideal city state with many features of the one presented in the *Republic*.

12. This is meant in a relaxed sense, i.e. as returning to first principles of the relevant subject matter. Someone designing a gun goes back to first principles of ballistics and metallurgy, not to first principles of sub-nuclear physics.

for the context in which the original object was meant to function, but are inappropriate for the context of the new one.

So obviously it is better in crafting a an object of kind X to adopt the method we call 'looking to an eternal paradigm of X' than to adopt the one we call 'looking to a paradigm X that has already come to be'. But this way of talking is extremely misleading. No doubt there is a kind of symmetry or commensurability between the two methods, in that both are means, one better, one worse, for achieving the same end. This comparability combines with the way of talking just mentioned to create the illusion of a sort of type-symmetry or counterpart relation between *the objects involved* in the respective methods: the objects we are calling the paradigms. In fact, however, there is a profound asymmetry between the paradigm that has come to be, and that which, on the common sense interpretation, we are equating with the eternal paradigm.

The eternal paradigm, understood commonsensically, is the right answer to a 'What is X?' question. I should therefore be happy to call it a quiddity. It is plausible to think of it as eternal if it is plausible to hold that the right answer to that sort of question is necessarily always the same. So the human maker who makes the right choice of guide is guided by a quiddity (more or less perfectly grasped by him). Now it surely makes no sense to try to think of the answer to a 'What is X?' question as making any impact otherwise than as the answer to its question. Presumably there is a distinct class of such questions typified by the fact that they are asked in order to set up a guide for bringing something about, and correspondingly there is a distinct class of, let us call them, practical quiddities. The point then is that it makes no sense to think of a practical quiddity as having any role but to guide the relevant kind of maker. The asymmetry with the non-eternal case lies in the fact that the non-eternal object which is used as a paradigm, i.e. used as a *sample* or *example*, has a life of its own outside this context, contributing to weaving if it is a shuttle, constraining social activity in various ways if it is a political constitution. Here, it makes no sense to try to think of an actual shuttle's being *nothing but* a paradigm for making shuttles. Even a colour card sample of some shade can be used otherwise than as a sample: colour samples can be arranged into attractive patterns, and presumably tunes may be played using different tuning-fork sounds. And certainly of a shuttle, and of most cases, it can be said that a great many other things have to be true of them before it is true that they can be paradigms of their kinds.

Now, if we understand a paradigm to be necessarily a *sample*,[13] then a paradigm is itself an instance of the kind in question. It is an instance put to a certain use, namely that of explaining what it is for something to be of that kind.[14] Such an object is a paradigm only in the context of such a use, and it necessarily exists and operates in other contexts too. Suppose, now, that in a misguided attempt to find symmetry between looking to an eternal, and looking to a non-eternal, guide one persuaded oneself that an eternal one would be like a non-eternal one except for the difference between eternal and non-eternal, and the associated difference between intelligible and sensible. One would then note that the non-eternal guides are themselves samples of the kinds requiring to be explained, and one would infer that any eternal one is a sample too—a paradigm, according to our understanding of that word. Immediately one would be committed to the view that an eternal paradigm is an instance of the kind with respect to which it gives guidance (a 'perfect particular', as has often been said). This is a notorious implication of certain formulations of Platonism. But it has not so clearly been noticed that one would also be committed to viewing the eternal paradigm—that is, an eternal object which happens to be functioning as a paradigm—as enjoying a rich life of its own, a life not merely additional to its functioning as paradigm, but metaphysically prior. If in this fashion we imagine Plato's world-maker's intelligible guide, not as the *answer* to the question 'What would be a supremely excellent empirical system?', but as an eternal *sample illustrating the answer*,[15] then we are bound to say that the guide, like the living

---

13. But we need not, since it is not analytically true in Greek that a *paradeigma* is a sample. '*Paradeigma*' can be used of something that functions as a guide otherwise than by being a sample. For a nice unselfconscious example (!), see *Protagoras* (326c8: 'Protagoras' speaking): the laws constitute a *paradeigma* for good conduct.

14. At *Statesman* 278b4 and c3-4, things which are paradigms are said to have *become* paradigms.

15. Why should a maker need both the answer and the eternal sample? And if he doesn't, the dispensable one seems to be the latter. For perhaps he can grasp the quiddity without considering the eternal sample (he might be able to grasp it by analysing mere sensible samples); whereas he may be exercising knowledge of the quiddity (or should one say exercising the quiddity?) when he recognises the eternal object as of the kind it is. Some of Aristotle's complaints are relevant here.

world made in accordance with it, is a living being ('The Living Being'); and it then becomes irresistible to think of its life as busily and multi-directionally unfolding and being enjoyed in relation to all kinds of intelligibles rising range upon range beyond the rather humble level at which The Living Being, almost accidentally it may seem, serves as paradigm for the empirical world. I do not think Plato in the *Timaeus* really intended to pitch us into all this, but some of his language certainly pulls in this direction. It is the direction taken by Platonists for whom the cosmology of the *Timaeus* is just a portal to an exotic invisible realm which the educated intellect longs to enter, explore, and enjoy for its own sake, perhaps disconnecting itself from all this-worldly concerns including even the project of scientifically explaining this world.

But even, if, as I hope, Plato's talk of intelligible paradigms is mainly driven by the common sense intuition that in making things it is better to reflect on what is being aimed at, and to follow an answer worked out from first principles, than simply to try to copy something already in existence, he is certainly not on that account released from metaphysical commitments. He is still a Platonist, though he may be able to remain a relatively modest one by comparison with the neo-Platonic-style hyperrealist. Hyperrealism gives us an intelligible world thick with far more reality than needs to be postulated to make sense of our universe and of human intellectual endeavours. Hyperreality has its own laws of metaphysical gradation and proliferation not rooted in those humanly experienced base lines. Plato, much of the time, may be too interested in our universe as the place where human intelligence has to make the best of itself, to see it as just a sign-system or semi-transparent veil through which our intellect should permeate into some pure and far more beautiful landscape. But Plato will still maintain the objective and eternal reality, irreducible to anything empirical, of those quiddities captured in right answers to certain human questions. And he will still maintain that this world was crafted according to just such a quiddity grasped first by the divine intelligence, but more or less accessible also to ours when we engage in correctly principled cosmological investigation. It will still, therefore, be a genuinely Platonic tenet that, just as the divine cause must be something immaterial, the same must be true of the human intellect too, since its activity is similar and some of its objects are the same.

THE CREATION OF THE WORLD

By Sarah Broadie and Anthony Kenny

II—Anthony Kenny

SEVEN CONCEPTS OF CREATION

Professor Broadie identifies for us a number of features of the account of creation in the *Timaeus*:

(1) The cosmos—the ordered universe in which we live—is to be accounted for as a whole.
(2) The cosmos is supremely beautiful and good.
(3) The cause of the cosmos is non-physical, intelligent, good, and divine, i.e. God.
(4) God worked on pre-existent matter.
(5) God was copying an eternal paradigm.

It would, I think, be very widely agreed that these five theses are true of Plato's account and pick out its significant points.

Broadie makes many other points about the *Timaeus* account which may not be regarded as similarly uncontroversial. I will mention two theses which seemed to me particularly interesting: one concerns proposition (4) and the other concerns proposition (5).

Broadie's first thesis is this. It is important for Plato, she maintains, that the Demiurge should work on pre-existent matter. Otherwise there would not be a sufficient distinction in creation between the cause and the product. In the Biblical account of creation there is a sharp distinction between the creator and the created because the creator is divine and the creature is not. But for Plato 'The empirical cosmos, even though a made thing and a perceptible one, is literally itself a *god*, an appellation it shares with the god who made it from matter.' Pre-existent matter is therefore an essential part of the narrative if creation is not to collapse into some kind of pantheism, in which 'Either the cause-entity has evolved into what we were calling the product ... or the cause-entity constitutes the product.'

The second thesis is about the eternal paradigms to which the Demiurge 'looks'. Broadie offers two different interpretations of their nature. On one interpretation, the paradigms are samples. A human being, asked to produce a shuttle, might look at an existing shuttle and do his best to copy it. In such a case, the paradigm is a sample of a shuttle; and it is itself a perfectly good shuttle with a life of its own. On the other hand, the shuttle maker might start from first principles, work out what a shuttle is, and how best it can perform its function, and thus design it from scratch. Here there is no pre-existing sample, only the working out of an answer to a question. Broadie suggests that Plato wants us to think of the Demiurge's paradigms in the second of these ways. 'The eternal paradigm (on that interpretation) is the right answer to a "What is ...?" question. I should therefore be happy to call it a "quiddity".' Thinking of paradigms as quiddities rather than samples, Broadie concludes, saves us from having to take on an overpopulated neo-Platonic world of hyperreal intelligibles.

Broadie is well aware that there are a number of passages in Plato to which a neo-Platonist could appeal in order to defend the idea that the paradigms of the Timaeus are not just quiddities but actual samples. In my paper, however, I do not wish to explore that avenue of response; rather I wish to take up the invitation that Broadie's first thesis holds out, and make a comparison between the Platonic account in the Timaeus and the Biblical concept of creation. I will also explore the way in which that concept was developed and modified by Christian philosophers in the medieval and early modern period.

The book of *Genesis*, as Broadie recognizes in a footnote, contains not one but two accounts of creation. The one which comes later in our texts (beginning at verse 5 of Chapter Two) is commonly regarded as more primitive, the work of the Yahwist contributor to the Pentateuch. The account may well be earlier than the *Timaeus*. It begins thus:

> At the time when Yahweh God made earth and heaven there was as yet no wild bush on the earth nor had any wild plant yet sprung up, for Yahweh God had not sent rain on the earth, nor was there any man to till the soil. However, a flood was rising from the earth and watering all the surface of the soil. Yahweh God fashioned man of dust from the

soil. Then he breathed into his nostrils a breath of life, and thus man became a living being.

There follows the story of the making of Eden, the four rivers, the creation of animals, and the creation of woman from the rib of the sleeping Adam. Here it is not clear whether the existence of the dry dusty earth precedes the activity of God; the text can be read either way. The rising flood seems a phenomenon independent of God's activity. With regard to the creation of man, God seems to be given a Pygmalion-like role. Rather than being guided by an eternal paradigm, God seems to act in an experimental way. He tries out the various animals to see whether they are fit companions for Adam, and finds that nothing less than Eve will fit the bill.

The other account of creation, in the first chapter of *Genesis*, is usually attributed to a late, priestly, author:

> In the beginning God created the heavens and the earth. Now the earth was a formless void, there was darkness over the deep, and God's spirit hovered over the water. God said 'Let there be light' and there was light. God saw that light was good.

There follows the creation, day by day, of heaven, earth, sea, plants, sun and moon, birds, fish, land animals, and finally humans.

In this narrative God is presented as a clearly transcendent being who creates merely by uttering commands. The opening words 'In the beginning' were seized on by exegetes to show that the world had not existed for ever, but had—like the cosmos of the *Timaeus*—been brought into existence at a point in time. The order of creation differs from that in the earlier narrative: the wet precedes the dry and the other animals precede the first man. As in the *Timaeus* the beauty and order of the cosmos is emphasized. At the end of each day God sees that what he has made is good. Finally God says 'Let us make man in our own image, in the likeness of ourselves.' These mysteriously plural selves are the only paradigm to appear in the Genesis narrative.

It is the absence of paradigms, in fact, that is the most obvious difference between the Platonic and the Mosaic narratives. With regard to numbers (2), (3) and (4) of the theses we have identified, the two accounts are fairly easily reconcilable. What of the first thesis 'The cosmos is to be accounted for as a whole'? Here, I

think, there is a very important difference. Plato thinks of the
cosmos as itself alive: like any other animal it must be treated as a
whole and the nature and functions of its parts can only be
explained in terms of the nature and function of the whole. For
the Biblical tradition, by contrast, the cosmos is not itself a living
being, but is the habitat of many independent living creatures.
This is true not only of *Genesis* but of the much more poetic
accounts of creation to be found in the *Psalms* (8 and 103) and in
the book of *Job* (Chapters 38–9).

In the book of *Job*, every element and every species seems to
have its own direct relationship to God. God taunts the
complaining Job:

> Does the hawk take flight on your advice
>   When he spreads his wings to travel south?
> Does the eagle soar at your command
>   To make her eyrie in the heights?

But in *Job* no less than in the *Timaeus*, God in creating the
world seems to work on pre-existent elements:

> Where were you when I laid the earth's foundations?
>   Tell me, since you are so well informed!
> Who decided the dimensions of it, do you know?
>   Or who stretched the measuring line across it?
> What supports its pillars at their bases?
>   Who laid its cornerstone? (38,4–6)

God is the great architect, not yet the creator out of nothing.
So too in the book of *Wisdom*, where there may even be a direct
reference to the unformed matter of the *Timaeus*. Speaking of the
wickedness of the idolatrous Egyptians, the author says to God
'Your all-powerful hand did not lack means—the hand that from
formless matter created the world—to unleash a horde of bears
or savage lions upon them.' (11,18)

It is in the book of *Proverbs* that the Bible comes closest to the
Platonic idea of an intelligible world that provides archetypes for
creation. There, in the eighth chapter, a (female) personified
Wisdom sings a paeon of self-praise. 'Yahweh created me when
his purpose first unfolded, before the oldest of his works ... The
deep was not, when I was born, there were no springs to gush
with water. Before the mountains were settled, before the hills I

came to birth.' It was in accordance with this wisdom that God created: 'I was by his side, a master craftsman, delighting him day after day, ever at play in his presence.'

Only at the very end of the Old Testament do we meet with the idea of creation out of nothing. In the second book of *Maccabees* seven brothers are martyred by King Antiochus for refusing to eat pork. Their mother looks on while six of them are sadistically killed. When asked to persuade the sole surviving son to abandon his resistance, she says:

> My son have pity on me. I carried you nine months in my womb and suckled you three years, fed you and reared you to the age you are now. I implore you, my child, observe heaven and earth, consider all that is in them, and acknowledge that God made them *out of what did not exist*, and that mankind comes into being in the same way. Do not fear this executioner.' (2M, 7,27)

Henceforth creation *ex nihilo* was the fundamental Judeo-Christian orthodoxy. Theologians glossed '*ex nihilo*' as '*ex nihilo sui et subiecti*' to reject both the idea that the world is somehow spun out of God's own essence and the idea that it was made out of non-divine pre-existent matter. As Broadie has emphasized, the first idea is equally rejected by Plato; but the second point marks a definite break between the *Timaeus* and what was henceforth the mainstream Western religious tradition.

None the less, the *Timaeus* retained over centuries a great influence on philosophical concepts of creation. It is an exaggeration to say that Western philosophy consists of footnotes to Plato; but in many areas of philosophy it remains true to this day that Plato drew up the philosophical agenda. So far as concerns creation, the *Timaeus* set the following questions for centuries of investigation:

(1) What is the nature of the creator?
(2) What, if anything, was prior to the creator's activity?
(3) What, if anything, was the blueprint for creation?
(4) What entities were created?
(5) Why did the creator create?
(6) When did creation take place?

For two millennia, the answers to these questions were debated by philosophers. Many different answers we given and accordingly we find, in the history of philosophy, not one, but at least seven different concepts of creation.

The first great Christian philosopher, Augustine, did his best to reconcile Plato and the Bible. He was willing to accept that the universe was created out of formless matter, but he asked what was meant by 'formless'. If what was meant was something absolutely devoid of all forms, then it was as good as nothing. But if it was merely something comparatively formless, it must, in its turn, have been created out of nothing: 'Even if the universe was created out of some formless matter, this very matter was created from something that was wholly nothing.' (*De Vera Religione*, 18,15.)

Augustine accepted also that in creating the world God was guided by paradigms. However, he considered it impious to suggest that God, in creating, should look to anything outside himself—even to a set of ideas in a Platonic heaven. Consequently, he identified the Platonic Forms with ideas in the divine mind. From all eternity God sees in his own essence all possible limited quiddities as reflections of himself. These are the divine ideas, which are

> certain archetypal forms or stable and unchangeable reasons of things, which were not themselves formed but are contained in the divine mind eternally and are always the same. They neither arise nor pass away, but whatever arises and passes away is formed according to them. (*De Ideis*, 2)

Augustine, as is well known, was interested in the problems involved in the notion of a world created in time. What was God doing before the world began? He solved that problem by saying that when the world was not created there was no before and after. However, there were arguments in Aristotle to the effect that the world must have existed for ever. And even in the *Timaeus*, though the world as we know it had a beginning, there remained the question whether the initial unformed matter had existed for ever. And certainly the paradigm Ideas had existed for ever.

It was common ground among Christian writers that nothing other than God had existed for ever. Augustine had solved the Platonic problem by placing Ideas in the mind of God, and he had taken little interest in the Aristotelian problem. He did, indeed, separate the issue of creation from the issue of the world's duration, pointing out that something eternal could none the less be caused: an eternal footprint left in eternal sand by an eternal foot, perhaps.

Other Christian writers, such as John Philoponus, tried to prove, against Aristotle but using the Aristotelian principle that an actual infinite was impossible, that the world must have had a beginning. Philoponus was followed by much later Christian philosophers, such as Bonaventure, and more immediately by the Islamic philosophers of the Kalam. After the reception of Aristotle in the Latin West, however, it became the majority view, ably propounded by Aquinas, that philosophy could prove neither that the world had a beginning nor that it had existed for ever. Because of the *Genesis* narrative it must be accepted that the world began, but that was a matter of faith, not reason.

Another issue discussed by medieval philosophers derives from a famous passage in the *Timaeus*, but it was commonly raised in Aristotelian terms. What is the final cause of the creation? Why did God create? Many neo-Platonic and Muslim philosophers gave the answer that for God creation was not a matter of choice but of necessity. The world emanated from God in the way that light shines out from the sun.

Among Christian philosophers the pseudo-Dionysius originated the slogan '*Bonum est diffusivum sui*': goodness is self-expansive. Others spoke as if God created by necessity, but by a necessity that was not metaphysical but moral. God, said Augustine, would have been mean *(invidus)* if he had not created. He was taking his cue from *Timaeus* 29e1: '[The cause] was good, and in what is good there is never any grudging *(phthonos)* on any topic; and being devoid of anything like that he desired that everything should be, so far as possible, like himself.'

Medieval scholastics in general regarded creation as a free, unconstrained act of God. All agreed that he was free not to create, and most (but not Abelard) agreed that if he was going to create at all, he was not constrained to create any particular world (not even the best of all possible worlds). But if creation was a free act, then a further question arose: what was the motive of that action? Aquinas' answer became classic: 'Ad productionem creaturarum nihil aliud movet Deum nisi sua bonitas, quam rebus aliis communicare voluit secundum modum assimilationis ad ipsum' (*ScG* 2,46). Nothing other than his own goodness moved God to produce creatures: he wanted to share that goodness with others to the extent that they could resemble him.

A position close to Aquinas's teaching on the nature and motive of creation is beautifully expressed in Beatrice's speech in Dante's *Paradiso* 29, 13–36:

> Non per aver a sé di bene acquisto,
>   ch'esser non può, ma perché suo splendore
>   potesse, risplendendo, dir 'subsisto'
> In sua eternità, di tempo fuore,
>   fuor d'ogni altro comprender, come i piacque
>   s'asperse in nuovi amor l'eterno amore
> Né prima quasi torpente si giacque
>   ché né prima né poscia procedette
>   lo discorrer di Dio sopra quest'acque
> Forma e materia, congiunte e purette
>   usciro ad esser che non avea fallo
>   come d'arco tricorde tre saette....
> Concreato fu ordine e construtto
>   a le sustanze; e quelle furon cima
>   del mondo in che puro atto fu prodotto
> pura potenza tenne la parte ima;
>   nel mezzo strinse potenza con atto
>   tal vime che gia mai non si divima.[1]

---

1. Not that his proper good might be increas'd
     which cannot be, but that his sheen might of
     itself, in shining back, say 'I subsist'
   shrined in his own eternity, above
     all time, all limits, as it pleased him, shone
     unfolded in new loves the eternal Love.
   Nor before lay he, as with nothing done;
     for ere God moved upon these waters, know
     that of 'befores' and 'afters' there was none
   Simple and mixed did form and matter go
     forth to a being which had no defect
     like to three arrows from a three-stringed bow.
   Concrete and stablished with the substances
     was order; some were made pure act, and heaven
     as summit of the world appointed these
   pure potency the lowest place was given
     midway was potency with act clinched fast
     by such a rivet as may ne'er be riven. (tr. Bickersteth)

Here we have creation as free and unconstrained, but motivated by the desire to communicate love. The neo-Platonic comparison with the shining of the sun is maintained, but without the notion of necessitation. The 'splendour' which says 'I subsist' is, of course, the creature, not God; 'splendore', the Dante commentators tell us, is always reflected light. God has no need of a *cogito*. There is no pre-existent matter: matter, form, and being are all created simultaneously. The pure acts who exist at the summit are the angels or intelligences: Dante, like Aquinas, rejects the universal hylomorphism of Bonaventure which regarded angels as composed of form and matter (spiritual matter, whatever that may be). But Dante appears to depart from Aquinas in thinking that prime matter, formless matter, can exist on its own.

Aquinas follows Augustine in locating in the divine mind the paradigms on which creatures are modelled: they are the divine ideas. Because God is a simple undivided being, these ideas are not really distinct from his essence, and they do not depend in any way upon his will. Creation according to the ideas is free, but not the existence of the ideas in the first places.

In medieval philosophy after Aquinas, two developments occurred: the paradigms were given a degree of independence from the divine essence, and the scope of the divine will was expanded.

Henry of Ghent took up a position quite close to the *Timaeus*. He was inspired by Avicenna; I do not feel competent to decide whether he had interpreted Avicenna rightly or wrongly. The Avicennan concept, as understood by Henry, goes as follows. Prior to creation there are everlasting essences with actual being *(esse essentiae)*. When God creates he confers a new kind of being *(esse existentiae)*. Duns Scotus objected that simply adding existence to an essence that was already there was something quite different from creation. 'Creation is production from nothing. If a stone already had true real being—*esse verum reale*—then when it is produced by [God's] efficient causal power it is not produced from nothing' *(Lectura, 1,36)*.

Scotus himself, however, believed that ideas have a kind of reality that is distinct from God's essence. It was, he admitted, a pretty low level of being: an *esse diminutum*. But in compensation for giving the ideas an independent reality, however flimsy, he set much narrower limits to their content than Aquinas had done. This appears most dramatically in the field of ethics. For Aquinas the entire decalogue is part of the natural law, flowing from the divine essence and governed by the ideas; it followed that God was not free to dispense from any of the ten commandments. Scotus much restricted the scope of natural law, confining it essentially to the command to love God himself. Beyond that God's freedom to command is absolute. The divine will expressed in the later commands of the decalogue—the prohibitions on murder, adultery, theft and lying—is a free will of God, not at all constrained by his essence.

These developments—the reification of the paradigms of creation and the expansion of the scope of divine freedom—reach their climax, after the medieval period, with Descartes' doctrine of the creation of eternal truths. This doctrine is expressed in a guarded form in the fifth meditation, but is expounded much more fully in Descartes' correspondence. Let me remind you of a few key passages from his letters to Mersenne in the 1630s.

> The mathematical truths that you call eternal, have been established by God and depend on him entirely as much as all other creatures. (CSM III,23)

> You ask me by what kind of causality God established the eternal truths. I reply: by the same kind of causality as he created all things, that is to say, as their efficient and total cause. For it is certain that he is no less the author of creatures' essence than he is of their existence; and this essence is nothing other than the eternal truths. I do not conceive them as emanating from God like rays from the sun; but I know that God is the author of everything and that these truths are something and consequently that he is their author. (CSM III,25)

I have argued in several places that Descartes' account places the eternal truths in a Platonic or Meinongian heaven, quite separate from the divine essence or the human mind.[2] Recently a number of authors have contested this view. Some have attributed to Descartes a conceptualist position: the eternal truths exist only in human minds, according to which, for Descartes, God's creation

---

2. See, for instance, 'The Cartesian Circle and the Eternal Truths' in A. Kenny, *The Heritage of Wisdom* (Oxford: Blackwell, 1987), 147–164.

of numbers and figures would simply consist in his creation of minds containing the ideas of numbers and figures.[3] Such conceptualism, while it draws support from one text in the *Principles*, (I,49), seems to me impossible to reconcile with what Descartes says elsewhere—indeed with the very notion of an *eternal* truth.

More plausibly, Marleen Rozemond has argued[4] that what God does when he creates the eternal truths is to give them objective being in his own mind. In this way she brings Descartes much closer to his scholastic predecessors, even though none of them ever suggested that the truths of mathematics were free creations of God. I continue, however, to maintain that Descartes' position is much more Platonist than that. I have no doubt that the eternal truths have objective being in God's mind. So does everything, given that God is omniscient. But whatever is created is (for Descartes) really distinct from the creator. Therefore, the eternal truths cannot be located anywhere in God, for within Him there are no real distinctions. So far Descartes, as for Plato, the quiddities are eternal entities distinct from God; only for Descartes, as not for Plato, they are the object of a special, pre-cosmic, divine act of creation.

This hectic tour of the centuries has left us, as I promised, with not one but seven concepts of creation. We have the Platonic concept, the Mosaic concept, the Augustinian concept, the Avicennan concept, Thomist concept, the Scotist concept and the Cartesian concept. Each concept is differentiated from the others by giving a different set of answers to the six questions that I identified as set to candidates by Plato's *Timaeus*.

I want to end this paper with a brief discussion of a recent revisiting of one of the *Timaeus* issues. Professor Norman Kretzmann devoted the last years of his tragically shortened life to the writing of two volumes of philosophical commentary on Aquinas' *Summa contra Gentiles*. Kretzmann's commentary was probing and sympathetic; in the end, on almost all points, he either agreed with Aquinas or thought his opinions deserved serious consideration. On only one issue he disagreed, head on,

3. Cf. Vere Chappell, 'Descartes' Ontology', *Topoi* 16 (1997), 111–127.
4. In as an yet unpublished article which she kindly communicated to me.

with the teaching of the *Summa contra Gentiles*. This was the
issue of God's freedom in creating.

Both in *The Metaphysics of Theism*[5] (*TMOT*) and *The
Metaphysics of Creation*[6] (*TMOC*) Kretzmann defended the
view that God's creation of the world was not free, but necessary.
In his earlier book he set himself the following question: 'The
existence of an absolutely perfect being and nothing else at all
seems unquestionably the best of all possible worlds, so what
could motivate God to choose to create anything at all?' Aquinas'
answers to this question, he says, are unconvincing. Utility,
conceived of as widely as possible, seems entirely unavailable as
the motivation for God's volition that there be things other than
himself (*TMOT*, 221). Aquinas' conceptions of God, goodness,
creation and choice entail a necessitarian explanation and there is
an inconsistency in the notion of goodness that is unmanifested,
never shared, even though united with omnipotence.

Kretzmann is at one with pseudo-Dionysius. God is perfect
goodness itself, and goodness is essentially—from its nature and
its definition—diffusive of itself and of being. 'Doesn't it follow
that the volition to create is a consequence not of God's free
choice but of God's very nature?' God does indeed have free
choice in creation, but this is confined to the selection of which
possibilities to actualise. God's will is necessitated as regards
whether to create, but he is fully free as regards what to create
(*TMOC*, 225).

I do not wish to take issue on one side or the other of this
debate between Aquinas and Kretzmann. I merely draw attention
to it as showing something that Professor Broadie and I warmly
agree about: the lasting vitality of Plato's *Timaeus*. The most
recent philosophical monograph on creation, by one of the most
intelligent and erudite of twentieth century philosophers, still
feels the need to address the question that Augustine took from
Plato: if God had not created the world, would he have shown
himself to be a skinflint?

---

5. *The Metaphysics of Theism: Aquinas's Natural Theology in Summa contra Gentiles I*
(Oxford: Clarendon Press, 1997).
6. *The Metaphysics of Creation: Aquinas's Natural Theology in Summa contra Gentiles
II* (Oxford: Clarendon Press, 1999).

INSTRUMENTAL DESIRES, INSTRUMENTAL RATIONALITY

by Michael Smith and Edward Harcourt

I—Michael Smith

ABSTRACT   The requirements of instrumental rationality are often thought to be normative conditions on choice or intention, but this is a mistake. Instrumental rationality is best understood as a requirement of coherence on an agent's non-instrumental desires and means-end beliefs. Since only a subset of an agent's means-end beliefs concern possible actions, the connection with intention is thus more oblique. This requirement of coherence can be satisfied either locally or more globally, it may be only one among a number of such requirements on an agent's total set of desires and beliefs, and it has no special connection with reasoning. An appreciation of these facts leads to a better understanding of both the nature and the significance of instrumental rationality.

A number of theorists have recently attempted to account for the normativity of instrumental rationality.[1] Though there are significant differences, their explanations all share a common feature: each assumes that the requirements of instrumental rationality are normative conditions, of some sort, on choice or intention. If instrumental rationality were limited to situations in which we make choices or form intentions then these explanations would have some chance of being correct. But instrumental rationality is not limited in this way.

My aim in the present paper is thus to lay out an alternative explanation, one that accords instrumental rationality its proper scope. I proceed by spelling out the alternative in the form of a series of assertions which I expand upon and justify. I do not claim any originality, as the ideas on offer will be familiar from standard accounts of decision theory. My reason for putting

---

1. Christine Korsgaard, 'The Normativity of Instrumental Reason' in Garrett Cullity and Berys Gaut (eds.), *Ethics and Practical Reason* (Oxford: Oxford University Press, 1997); John Broome, 'Normative requirements', *Ratio* 12 (1999), 398–419; R. Jay Wallace, 'Normativity, Commitment, and Instrumental Reason' in *Philosophers' Imprint*, <www.philosophersimprint.org/001003> 1 (2001), 1–26.

them forward, nonetheless, is to provide the needed reminder of these ideas' significance in the context of recent discussions.[2]

I

Agents typically have both instrumental and non-instrumental desires.

Consider the following passage from Hume.[3]

> Ask a man *why he uses exercise*; he will answer *because he desires to keep his health*. If you then enquire, *why he desires to keep his health*, he will readily reply, *because sickness is painful*. If you push your enquiries farther, and desire a reason *why he hates pain*, it is impossible he can ever give any. This is an ultimate end, and is never referred to any other object.

Hume's idea here is that, much as our actions are explicable in terms of our desires and beliefs, so certain of our desires are susceptible to that same sort of explanation. We can explain why we desire some of the things we desire by citing other desires we have and beliefs about how, if the first of the things we desire comes about, this will lead to the other thing we desire coming about.

In the simplest case one thing we desire leads to another by causing it. For example, we explain why I desire to exercise by citing the fact that I desire health and believe that exercise causes health. But there are other ways in which one thing can lead to another as well. To use a familiar example, I may desire to raise

2. As will become clear to those familiar with their work, while my disagreement with Broome, and perhaps with Wallace too, turns out to be mainly a disagreement about the scope of instrumental rationality, my disagreement with Korsgaard is more complete, as she thinks that the requirements of instrumental rationality can be restated as claims about what we have reason to do. (Though note that Wallace sometimes says this sort of thing too: see, for example, his 'Practical Reason' in *The Stanford Encyclopedia of Philosophy* (Winter 2003 Edition), Edward N. Zalta (ed.), forthcoming URL = <http://plato.stanford.edu/archives/win2003/entries/practical-reason/> .) But this seems to me quite wrong, as it would require a connection between instrumental rationality and instrumental reasoning that does not exist. I will not, however, offer any explicit criticisms of these authors beyond what I have already said. My aim, to repeat, is to spell out an alternative. For more on this see my 'Is there a Nexus between Reasons and Rationality?' forthcoming in *Poznan Studies in the Philosophy of Science and Humanities: New Trends in Moral Psychology* (ed.) Sergio Tenenbaum (Amsterdam: Rodophi).

3. David Hume, *Enquiries concerning Human Understanding and concerning the Principles of Morals*, 1777 edition, (Oxford: Clarendon Press, 1975), Appendix I.

my arm because I desire to signal a turn and believe that raising my arm leads to signaling a turn, not in the sense that raising an arm causes a signaling, but rather in the sense that, given the conventions hereabouts, raising an arm constitutes giving a signal. In what follows I will call all beliefs about the ways in which one thing leads to another 'means-end beliefs'. Though the means-end beliefs discussed will typically be causal beliefs, we should bear in mind the fact that this is a simplification.

The main point Hume makes in the passage is that we cannot explain every desire we have by citing another desire and a means-end belief. Such chains of explanation must come to an end somewhere. As he sees things a chain of explanation like that described would come to an end with the desire to avoid pain. But this is, of course, an empirical claim, one which we may or may not think is typically true. People can desire anything. Moreover no particular empirical claim is crucial. What is crucial is rather the suggestion that such chains of explanation must come to an end with some desire or other which eludes explanation in this way. In some people, some of the time, the chain might come to an end with the desire to avoid pain, but in others it might come to an end with the desire for health, and in some people, some of the time, it might come to an end with the desire to exercise, or even with the desire to move their body.

Though Hume calls the desires that come at the origin of such chains of explanation 'ultimate' desires, I will call them 'non-instrumental' desires, and, accordingly, I will call the desires that are explained by such desires and means-end beliefs 'instrumental' desires. My reason for baulking at the label 'ultimate' is that this seems to suggest, misleadingly, that no rational explanation can be given of why we have the non-instrumental desires we have. But though this was Hume's own view, it seems to me quite wrong.[4] I may have a non-instrumental desire that p because I have non-instrumental desires that q, r, and s, where the desires that p, q, r, and s all fit together in a coherent way, and where I have and exercise a capacity to have non-instrumental desires that fit together in a coherent way. Or I may have a non-instrumental desire that p because I believe something that that non-instrumental desire coheres with

4. Michael Smith, *The Moral Problem* (Oxford: Blackwell, 1994), Chapter 5.

especially well—that I would non-instrumentally desire that p if I had a maximally informed and coherent and unified desire set, perhaps—where I have and exercise the capacity to have non-instrumental desires that fit together with my beliefs in a coherent way. These claims are, of course, controversial.[5] But the crucial point, for present purposes, is that we shouldn't so set things up as to preclude the truth of such claims. I will return to this at the end.

II

Instrumental desires are not distinct from the non-instrumental desires and means-end beliefs that explain them, but are rather just the complex state of having such non-instrumental desires and means-end beliefs standing in a suitable relation.

Talk of the difference between instrumental and non-instrumental desires being a matter of what explains them might suggest, again misleadingly, that when non-instrumental desires and means-end beliefs give rise to instrumental desires, these instrumental desires are new desires with their own independent existence. But this is not the right way to think about instrumental desires.

It is a striking fact that instrumental desires disappear immediately an agent loses either the relevant non-instrumental desire or means-end belief. This is, if you like, part of what it is to be an instrumental desire, as opposed to a non-instrumental desire. Yet there is no reason why this should be so if an instrumental desire were merely a desire that has a non-instrumental desire and a means-end belief somewhere in its causal history. Why should a desire disappear when (say) the desire that caused it, way back when, disappears? Instrumental desires are thus better thought of as being nothing over and above the non-instrumental desires and means-end beliefs that explain them. When we said earlier, following Hume, that instrumental desires are those that can be explained by non-

---

5. Compare Geoffrey Sayre-McCord, 'The Meta-Ethical Problem: a discussion of Michael Smith's *The Moral Problem*' in *Ethics* 108 (1997), 55–83, and Michael Smith, 'In Defence of *The Moral Problem*: A Reply to Brink, Copp and Sayre-McCord' in *Ethics* 108 (1997), 84–119.

instrumental desires and means-end beliefs, what we had in mind was this constitutive claim, not a claim about causal history.

But nor should we think of an instrumental desire as just the mereological sum of a non-instrumental desire and means-end belief. An agent may have a non-instrumental desire and a means-end belief and yet have no corresponding instrumental desire. Someone could (say) have a non-instrumental desire to be healthy and believe that he can be healthy by exercising and yet have no instrumental desire whatsoever to exercise. Non-instrumental desires and means-end beliefs must be put together, as it were, if an agent is to have an instrumental desire. We should therefore suppose that an instrumental desire is nothing over and above a *suitably related* non-instrumental desire and means-end belief.

Against this, it might be thought that the systematic employment of the criteria we use when we attribute non-instrumental desires and means-end beliefs will require us to posit appropriate instrumental desires whenever people have relevant non-instrumental desires and means-end beliefs. When someone desires to be healthy and believes that she can be healthy by exercising, it might be thought that she must be ascribed a desire to exercise: that desiring to be healthy just is desiring to exercise when you believe that exercise causes health. But this is evidently untrue.

Desires and beliefs are multi-track dispositions—there are dispositions to act, dispositions to feel pleased or disappointed, dispositions to engage in various sorts of thought processes, dispositions to say certain things in response to questions, dispositions to use certain considerations in further reasoning, and so on and so forth—and the criteria that we use in the attribution of desires and beliefs are a weighted sum of these different factors. When we attribute non-instrumental desires and means-end beliefs to people there is therefore ample room for the hypothesis that these states are present, but simply not related to each other in the way required for the people in question have the relevant instrumental desires.

III

Agents who have non-instrumental desires and means-end beliefs have a more locally coherent psychology when they have

corresponding instrumental desires, and they have a more globally
coherent psychology when the relative strengths of their instru-
mental desires covary with the strengths of their non-instrumental
desires and the levels of confidence they have in the things about
which they have means-end beliefs.

Though, as we have just seen, there is no difficulty in
attributing to someone a non-instrumental desire and a means-
end belief but no relevant instrumental desire—the desire to be
healthy and the belief that exercise causes health (say), but no
instrumental desire to exercise—it must be said that such an
attribution would be puzzling. The question is what this shows.

To desire something is to desire that some state of the world
obtains. But it is a mundane fact that states of the world obtain
as a result of the world's being some way or other: things happen
as a consequence of other things. So anyone cognisant of this fact
is in a position to see that to desire that a certain state of the
world obtains is to desire that it obtains as a result of the world's
being one of the ways it can be which will lead to the occurrence
of that state of affairs. But now consider someone who desires
that a certain state of the world obtains as a result of the world's
being one of the ways it can be which will lead to the occurrence
of that state of affairs, and who believes that the way the world
can be which will lead to the occurrence of the desired state of
affairs is the p way. For this person to fail to desire that the world
be the p way is, it seems to me, quite literally for them to be in an
incoherent state of mind. It is for them to fail to put the original
desire and belief together in the way in which they are committed
to putting them together. For, given their belief, their original
desire is already, so to speak, targeted on the world's being the p
way.

But even if this explanation of the normativity of the suitable-
relatedness of a non-instrumental desire and means-end belief in
terms of coherence is accepted, it might be thought that there is
still room for disagreement about how extensive such requirements of coherence are. For example, suppose I have a non-
instrumental desire to be healthy and that I believe there are two
ways the world could be which lead to this result. I believe that it
would result from exercise, or from my having more income, but
I do not believe that I could exercise and increase my income at
the same time. What does coherence require of me in this case?

After all, the world doesn't have to be the I-exercise way in order for it to be the I-am-healthy way, and nor does it have to be the I-earn-more way.

The answer, I think, is that coherence requires me to put my non-instrumental desire to be healthy together with each of these beliefs. For, given my beliefs, my non-instrumental desire is already targeted, so to speak, on each of these ways the world could be. I desire the realization of the possibility that I am healthy, and I believe that this possibility partitions into two sub-possibilities: the possibility that I exercise and the possibility that I increase my income. Following through the logic of the previous argument would thus seem to imply that coherence requires me to have both an instrumental desire to exercise and an instrumental desire to increase my income. Putting at least one of my means-end beliefs together with my non-instrumental desire will allow me to achieve a certain amount of local coherence, but I will achieve more if I put my non-instrumental desire together with both.

Moreover, sticking with this case, it seems that coherence also makes demands on the strengths of these instrumental desires. If, for example, I am equally confident about the two causal claims then coherence requires me to be indifferent between the two options: my instrumental desires will have to be equally strong. But if I am more confident of one than the other then it seems that, in order to satisfy the demands of coherence, my instrumental desire for the one about which I am more confident will have to be stronger. The effect of decreased confidence is, if you like, to dilute desire for that option. The upshot is thus that, even though I might meet coherence's demand that my non-instrumental desire be suitably related to my two means-end beliefs, I might still fail to meet coherence's further demand on the strengths of my two instrumental desires.

Coherence seems to make other more global demands as well. Suppose this time I have two desires, a non-instrumental desire to be healthy and a non-instrumental desire for knowledge, and that I believe all of the following: that exercise causes health, that reading causes knowledge, and that I cannot exercise and read at the same time. Finally, just to keep things simple, suppose I am equally confident about each of these things and that I have no further desires or beliefs. Does coherence require that both of my non-instrumental desires stand in suitable relations to the relevant means-end beliefs, and hence that I have both an instrumental desire to exercise and an instrumental desire to read?

The considerations adduced above would seem to apply equally to the two non-instrumental desires. Coherence demands that my two non-instrumental desires be suitably related to each of my means-end beliefs: I would have to have both an instrumental desire to exercise and an instrumental desire to read. Moreover it once again seems that, though I might satisfy that demand, I might fail to meet a further demand that coherence makes on the strengths of these instrumental desires. If my non-instrumental desires for health and knowledge are equally strong then, in order to satisfy the demands of coherence, it seems that I will have to be indifferent between the two options: my instrumental desires to exercise and to read will have to be equally strong. But if one of my non-instrumental desires is stronger than the other then it seems that, in order to satisfy the more global demands of coherence, my instrumental desire for the one which leads to the outcome that I more strongly desire will have to be stronger.

Moreover there are also mixed cases. Suppose I have a stronger non-instrumental desire to be healthy and a weaker non-instrumental desire for knowledge, and that I believe that exercise causes health, that reading causes knowledge, and that I cannot exercise and read at the same time, but that I am more confident of the connection between reading and knowledge than I am about the connection between exercise and health. In that case it seems that, once again, coherence will demand that I have instrumental desires both to exercise and to read, but it also seems that coherence will require that the strengths of these instrumental desires depend on the strengths of the two non-instrumental desires and the levels of confidence associated with my two means-end beliefs. If my confidence is greater enough, then coherence may even require that the instrumental desire to read is stronger than the instrumental desire to exercise, notwithstanding the fact that the non-instrumental desire for knowledge that partially constitutes it is weaker than the non-instrumental desire for health which partially constitutes the instrumental desire to exercise.

IV

Actions are the product of instrumental desires that are complexes of suitably related non-instrumental desires and means-end beliefs of a particular kind.

I have already alluded to the standard story of action explanation that we have inherited from David Hume.[6] According to this story, actions are caused and rationalised by a pair of mental states: a desire for some end, where ends can be thought of as ways the world could be, and a belief of the agent that something she can just do, namely move her body in a certain way, has some suitable chance of making the world the relevant way.

When we put this story together with the account we have just given of the nature of instrumental desires we get the following result. The pair of mental states that Hume says explain actions are none other than the non-instrumental desires and means-end beliefs that constitute instrumental desires when they are suitably related. Actions are therefore, according to the standard Humean story, the product of a *sub-class* of instrumental desires. They are the product of that sub-class where the means-end beliefs are about upshots of things that the agent can just do. Since this conclusion will be crucially important for what follows, let me say a little in defence of it.

Consider what must surely be the worst case for the claim that actions are the product of instrumental desires. Suppose an agent has a non-instrumental desire to do one of the things she can just do. Suppose, in other words, that she desires to perform what Danto calls a 'basic action', perhaps the basic action of moving her arm.[7] In that case it might be thought that no belief about what her moving her arm leads to could possibly be required to explain her action. No belief could be required because the agent is indifferent to the consequences. Her non-instrumental desire to perform the basic action of moving her arm must therefore suffice all by itself. Or so it might be thought.

6. David Hume, *A Treatise of Human Nature*, 1740 edition, (Oxford: Clarendon Press, 1968), especially Book II, Section III; see too Donald Davidson, 'Actions, Reasons and Causes' reprinted in his *Essays on Actions and Events* (Oxford: Oxford University Press, 1980).

7. Arthur C. Danto, 'What We Can Do', *Journal of Philosophy* 60 (1963), 434–445.

But in fact it seems that a means-end belief is still required, even in this case. For the agent still needs to believe that moving her arm will result *from something that she can just do.* In other words, she must put her non-instrumental desire together with her belief that she can perform the basic action of moving her arm and that doing so will lead to the desired result, namely, the movement of her arm. In order to see that such a means-end belief is required even in this case we must consider what happens when the non-instrumental desire to perform such a basic action is put together with the various possible combinations of belief and ability, as laid out in the following matrix.

		able to perform the basic action of moving my arm	
		yes	no
believe myself able to perform the basic action of moving my arm	yes	1	2
	no	4	3

(1) is the normal case in which I truly believe myself able to perform the basic action of moving my arm, and (2) is exactly the same, epistemically speaking, except that my belief is false: perhaps I have become paralysed without realizing it. But since, in both of these cases, if I happen to have a suitably strong non-instrumental desire to move my arm then I will presumably at least try to do so—the only difference will be that in (1) I succeed, whereas in (2) I fail[8]—neither is relevant to deciding whether a means-end belief is necessary for action. For in both cases I act, and in both cases I have the relevant means-end belief. Cases (3) and (4) are thus the real tests.

(3) is the case in which things are not as in the normal case and I am cognisant of this fact. Perhaps, being paralysed, I am unable to move my arm, and, being fully aware of my paralysis, I lack the belief that I am able to do so. This sort of case brings out the insight in the following remark of Anscombe's.[9]

8. Jennifer Hornsby, *Actions* (London: Routledge and Kegan Paul, 1980).
9. G. E. M. Anscombe, *Intention* (Oxford: Basil Blackwell, 1957), 52.

People sometimes say that one can get one's arm to move by an act of will but not a matchbox; but if they mean 'Will a matchbox to move and it won't', the answer is 'If I will my arm to move in that way, it won't', and if they mean 'I can move my arm but not the matchbox' the answer is that I can move the matchbox—nothing easier.

For even if, in case (3), I have a suitably strong non-instrumental desire to perform the basic action of moving my arm, my arm will be, for all intents and purposes, exactly like a matchbox, and my non-instrumental desire will therefore be, for all intents and purposes, just a like a non-instrumental desire I might now conceive to perform the basic act of moving a matchbox. Just as I am at a loss to know what it would mean even to try to move the matchbox in that way, I will be at a loss to know what it would mean even to try to move my arm in that way. Moreover the explanation would seem to be the same in each case, namely, that I lack the crucial means-end beliefs: that is, I lack the belief that there is something I can just do will that lead to the desired outcome. (3) is thus no counterexample to the necessity of the relevant means-end belief.

Having said that, what should we make of the case in which, being unable to (say) wiggle my ears, and believing myself unable to do so, I am none the less invited to try? 'Just do this!' I might be told by someone who demonstrates. I take it that in this sort of situation we do ordinarily succeed in at least trying to wiggle our ears. But once it is conceded that such an attempt is possible then it might be objected that, given that I don't have the belief that I can perform the basic action of wiggling my ears, that just proves that action is possible when I lack the relevant means-end belief.

But though it is true that I can try to wiggle my ears in this sort of situation I crucially do not try to do so by acting on my non-instrumental desire to perform the basic action of wiggling my ears. Rather what happens is that I see that the person who is wiggling their ears is doing something that I can just do—raising their eyebrows (say)—and what I try to do is to wiggle my ears by means of doing that. In other words, my action of trying to wiggle my ears results from my non-instrumental desire to perform the non-basic action of wiggling my ears and the belief I have as a result of the demonstration I've been given that something I can just do, namely raise my eyebrows, will lead to this result. So this case is no challenge to the necessity of the means-end belief either. It is, again, a case in which I have the relevant means-end belief.

The situation just discussed helps us understand what is going on in case (4). In (4) I have an ability to perform a certain sort of basic act, but I don't believe that I have this ability. Is it possible for me to act on the non-instrumental desire to perform the basic action alone in this sort of situation? The answer is, once again, that it is not. Lacking the belief that this is something I can just do, it seems that I would once again be at a total loss to know what it would mean even to try to just do the thing in question. In other words, since case (4) is epistemically just like case (3), case (4) presents no challenge to the necessity of the means-end belief either.

Once again, however, we should immediately acknowledge that it is possible for me to come to realise that I have the ability to perform a certain sort of basic action that I hadn't hitherto believed myself able to perform. Consider again the case in which someone asks me to wiggle my ears and then gives me a demonstration of the way in which they do it, but imagine this time that, unbeknown to me, I am one of those who is able to perform the basic action of wiggling my ears. It is certainly possible that I would succeed in trying to perform the non-basic action of wiggling my ears by copying what they do—by raising my eyebrows (say)—and it is also possible that, through subsequent experimentation, I could come to discover that I can wiggle my ears as a basic action, that is, without doing so by means of raising my eyebrows. But if this is right then this case presents no counter-example to the claim that a means-end belief is necessary for action either. It simply underscores the fact that our beliefs about which basic actions we can perform are derivable from experience.

V

Agents meet the standards of instrumental rationality to the extent that they satisfy the requirements of local and global coherence on their non-instrumental desires and means-end beliefs.

We are now in a position to say what it means for agents to meet the standards of instrumental rationality. My suggestion, perhaps unsurprisingly, is that agents meet such standards when they have non-instrumental desires and means-end beliefs that satisfy the requirements of local and global coherence as described above. In other words, their non-instrumental desires and means-end beliefs must be suitably related to each other— they must have instrumental desires corresponding to each of their non-instrumental desire/means-end belief pairs—and the relative strengths of their instrumental desires must be the right kind of product of the strengths of their non-instrumental desires and the confidence with which they hold their means-end beliefs. If this is agreed then a number of important consequences follow.

To begin, note that our defence of the normativity of instrumental rationality—the defence of the claim that having suitably related non-instrumental desires and means-end beliefs is required for psychological coherence—didn't presuppose any deep nexus between instrumental rationality and instrumental reasoning. Nor should this be surprising. For whereas reasoning is a process that takes an agent from one set of beliefs to another set of beliefs, the transitions with which we have been concerned take an agent from non-instrumental desires and a means-end beliefs to instrumental desires. There has therefore been no suggestion that an agent who has a non-instrumental desire and a means-end belief, and who goes on to form a corresponding instrumental desire, must do so by engaging in a process of reasoning. To desire something simply is not to accept a proposition that is fit for use in subsequent reasoning. Reasoning thus doesn't seem to be relevant to the task.

Of course, all sorts of reasoning processes may, as it happens, be employed when I succeed in being instrumentally rational. If (say) I have a non-instrumental desire to be healthy and I also have sufficient self-knowledge to realise this, then, if I also believe that exercise causes health, then I will be in a position to reason myself to the conclusion that exercising will cause me to get something that I non-instrumentally desire, namely health. And, having formed this belief, I will be in a position to reason myself to the further conclusion that the formation of an instrumental desire to exercise is required for local psychological coherence. Finally, equipped with this belief, I might find myself forming an instrumental desire to exercise. But it is important to emphasise the contingency of the connection between the reasoning process described and the formation of the instrumental desire. Forming the beliefs described is neither necessary nor sufficient for forming the instrumental desire to exercise.

A second important consequence concerns the scope of instrumental rationality. As we saw above, though all actions are the product of instrumental desires, these instrumental desires are a proper sub-class of the full set of such desires. Instrumental desires are simply suitably related pairs of non-instrumental desires and means-end beliefs, but actions are the product of that sub-class of instrumental desires that are constituted by suitably related pairs of non-instrumental desires and means-end beliefs to the effect that something that the agent can just do will have the desired upshot. It thus follows that an agent could be instrumentally irrational for failing to have an instrumental desire, but that the instrumental desire in question has nothing whatsoever to do with the desired result's happening as a result of anything that she can just do. Since such instrumental desires will not feed in any direct way into the agent's choices or intentions, it follows that the scope of instrumental rationality extends way beyond choice and intention.

For example, suppose I desire that my great-great-grandfather didn't suffer as a result of hearing about a crime committed by my great-grandfather, and that I have two relevant instrumental beliefs, that is, two beliefs about how this could have come about. I believe that he won't have suffered if he died before my great-grandfather's crime was committed, and I believe that he won't have suffered if, though he was alive, people tried to keep the facts from him. If the requirements of instrumental rationality are just the coherence requirements described earlier then it follows that I am instrumentally irrational if I fail to apportion my desire to these two ways in which I believe that the state of the world that I non-instrumentally desire could come about. For how could I coherently desire that my great-great-grandfather didn't suffer as a result of hearing about a crime committed by my great-grandfather, and yet be indifferent to the world's being the ways I believe it would have to be for that to be the case? Moreover, even if I do have both of these instrumental desires, the account we have given of the global coherence constraints on non-instrumental desires and means-end beliefs entails that I am instrumentally irrational if, having more confidence that my great-great-grandfather will not have suffered if he died before the crime was even committed than if people tried to keep the facts from him, my instrumental desire that the former is the case is not stronger than my instrumental desire that the latter is the case. But, and here is the crucial point, none of these instrumental desires constitutes a choice or an intention. Indeed, since the desires in question all concern the past they don't seem to have anything very obvious to do with my choices or intentions.

A third important consequence concerns the evaluation of agents. As we saw above, all actions, even those whose only purpose is to perform some basic action, are the product of a suitably related non-instrumental desire and means-end belief about the upshots of things that the agents can just do, where being suitably related is a requirement of local coherence on those non-instrumental desires and means-end beliefs. It therefore follows that anyone who acts must, thereby, meet that minimal standard of local coherence: anyone who acts is instrumentally rational.

It might be thought that this explains the appeal of the following remark of Davidson's.[10]

> In the light of a primary reason ... [where a primary reason is just a suitably related desire and means-end belief] ... an action is revealed as coherent with certain traits, long- or short-termed, characteristic or not, of the agent, and the agent is shown in his role of Rational Animal.

But the rhetoric turns out to be rather overblown. It is, after all, consistent with the local coherence required for action that an agent's non-instrumental desires and means-end beliefs fail to meet more global requirements of coherence. For example, given the strengths of their various non-instrumental desires, and the confidence with which they hold their means-end beliefs, agents might not have the instrumental desires required for global coherence. Certain instrumental desires might be missing—in other words, certain of their non-instrumental desires and means-end beliefs might not be suitably related—and, even if not missing, certain of their instrumental desires might be weaker or stronger than is required for global coherence.

10. Davidson, 'Actions, Reasons and Causes', 8.

The upshot is that it is only with a rather large pinch of salt that we can accept Davidson's suggestion that when someone acts, he is thereby shown in his role of Rational Animal. A more truly rational animal will not just meet the standard of local coherence required for action, but will have a full complement of suitably related non-instrumental desires and means-end beliefs, where the strength of the resultant instrumental desires is that required for global coherence. Such an animal will be more truly rational because it will not only be capable of action, but will be in a state of maximal preparedness to act in ways that optimally satisfy their desires, given their beliefs, under a whole range of counterfactual circumstances in which their non-instrumental desires and means-end beliefs are different.

A fourth and final consequence concerns a limitation on the ambitions of an account of instrumental rationality. The explanation of the normativity of instrumental rationality offered here makes it plain why agents could satisfy all of the requirements of instrumental rationality and yet still be vulnerable to rational criticism. For the demands of both local and global coherence described take as given the fact that agents have the non-instrumental desires that they have, they take as given the fact that these desires have the strengths they have, they take as given the fact that agents have the means-end beliefs they have, and they take as given the fact that their means-end beliefs are held with the confidence with which they are held. But in that case it is consistent with an agent's satisfying all of the demands of instrumental rationality, as these have been conceived of here, that their psychology fails to satisfy even more global requirements of coherence on the elements that are taken as given.

What might these even more global requirements of coherence be like? Certain of an agent's means-end beliefs might fail to cohere with their evidential beliefs, beliefs that provide them with ample evidence that their means-end beliefs are false. Or their non-instrumental desires might fail to cohere with each other. Or certain non-instrumental desires might fail to cohere with their beliefs about (say) which non-instrumental desires they would have if they had a maximally informed and coherent and unified desire set. In these ways, and perhaps in others too, the non-instrumental desires and means-end beliefs agents have might themselves become vulnerable to rational criticism.

The point is not, of course, that the account of instrumental rationality offered here entails that an agent's non-instrumental desires and means-end beliefs are vulnerable to such criticism. The point is rather that, at least as the requirements of instrumental rationality have been conceived of here, such rational criticism isn't ruled out. Whether or not such rational criticism is possible turns, in the end, on whether there really are the even more global requirements of coherence, like those suggested, that would underwrite the possibility of such criticism. Moreover this is, it seems to me, just as it should be. Though I do not myself believe that instrumental rationality is all there is to practical rationality, an account of the normativity of instrumental rationality should make vivid the temptation to suppose that it is.

INSTRUMENTAL DESIRES, INSTRUMENTAL RATIONALITY

by Michael Smith and Edward Harcourt

II—Edward Harcourt

ABSTRACT I argue that the incoherence Smith claims to identify in agents who desire that q, believe that p is a necessary means to q, but fail to desire that p is illusory, since it rests on the false assumption that every property I know to be possessed by an object of my desire is an object of my desire. Though the failure of Smith's account of the irrationality of this pattern of attitudes leaves it open that the pattern is indeed irrational, I argue that there are instances of it that are not irrational where the desires are desires for what the agent knows to be impossible for him. This conclusion casts doubt on the overall strategy—that of making a Humean theory of action explanation do duty as a theory of instrumental rationality—which implies that the norms of instrumental rationality apply to desires simply as such. I then try to criticise the strategy in such a way as to leave the Humean theory of action explanation unaffected.

M ichael Smith presents the theory of instrumental rationality as a generalisation of a familiar Humean theory of the explanation of action. According to the Humean theory, every action is caused and rationalised by a belief and a desire. And according to Smith if not to Hume, these are on the one hand a desire that a certain state of affairs obtains, and on the other a means-end belief to the effect that the action is apt to bring the desired state of affairs about. These two attitudes, when related in the right way, jointly constitute an *instrumental desire* to perform the action; and they are related in the right way just when they cause and rationalise an action which, in the agent's belief, is a means to bringing about the state of affairs which is the object of his desire. Explanations of this form apply, if the Humean theory is true, to every action simply as such. But thanks to the kind of content the explanatory desire and belief always have, the form of explanation in question is instrumental rationalisation. So every action is instrumentally (though not necessarily otherwise) rational in virtue of the kind of explanation it must have just because it's an action; and agents are instrumentally rational just to the extent that their desires and means-end beliefs are related (as of course they may not be) in such a way as to give rise to actions capable of this kind of explanation. What is more, one and the same form of explanation applies not only to actions but also to desires, even when, as with desires concerning the past, these are connected with action only remotely. So the norms of instrumental rationality apply not only to action but also to desire-formation. Smith's is thus an extremely economical theory of instrumental rationality: a theory—Hume's—already widely believed to play one role in the philosophy of action turns out unexpectedly, or so it is argued, to be able to play another. Moreover the fact that Smith seeks to locate the requirements of instrumental rationality within the theory of motivating reasons will give pause especially perhaps to those familiar with *The Moral Problem* in which Smith envisages, beyond these, an array of normative reasons for action foreign to the classical Humean picture.[1]

The following reply attempts no more than to identify some points of strain within the theory. Smith offers an account of why agents are instrumentally irrational if they hold attitudes which instantiate the following pattern (henceforth the 'problem combination'): desiring that q, believing that p is a necessary means to q, but failing to desire that p. In Section I below, I argue that this account is unsuccessful. The failure of the account of course leaves it open that the problem combination is indeed irrational. In Section II, however, I argue that there are instances of the pattern which are not irrational, although these instances should not be taken to establish the same conclusion for the parallel combination of attitudes in which 'intending' is substituted for 'desiring': the problem seems to arise just because Smith regards the requirements of instrumental rationality as applying to desire-formation. The suspicion is therefore that there is a flaw in the overall picture which has this implication about the scope of these requirements, that is, the picture according to which the Humean theory of action explanation can be put to work as a theory of instrumental rationality. In Section III, I try to identify what this flaw might be.

1. See e.g. Michael Smith, *The Moral Problem* (Oxford: Blackwell, 1994), pp. 94–6.

I

The norm of instrumental rationality that, according to Smith, requires us to desire that p when we desire that q and believe that p is a necessary means to q is, as Smith sees it, a requirement of coherence on our psychology.[2] Conversely to be instrumentally *ir*rational is for one's attitudes to display a certain kind of *in*coherence. The (in)coherence in question can be either local or global, but I will focus on the local case, both for simplicity's sake and because I assume that if the account is to work at all then it must work at least for that case.

Smith's account of the incoherence involved in holding the problem combination of attitudes comes in two parts. The first part argues that certain further attitudes are involved simply in desiring that q, given some supposedly platitudinous collateral attitudes. Call these further attitudes the derived attitudes. In the second part, Smith argues that to hold the derived attitudes while believing that p is a necessary means to q and failing to desire that p is patently incoherent in a way that the problem combination itself may not be. So the incoherence of the combination of attitudes arrived at by substituting the derived attitudes for the desire that q in the problem combination—call this the derived combination—is said to explain the irrationality of the problem combination. I shall argue in this section that the proffered explanation fails, chiefly on the grounds that the particular derived attitudes needed to generate the incoherence don't in fact follow from the desire that q together with the relevant platitudinous collateral attitudes.

I begin with the first part of Smith's account, which has three steps. (1) To desire something is to desire that some state of affairs obtains. (2) Every state of affairs is the effect of some other state of affairs. So (3) anyone who knows the truth of (2) will be in a position to see that to desire that a given state of affairs obtains is to desire that it obtains as the effect of the obtaining of some other state of affairs (in Smith's words, 'that to desire that a certain state of the world obtains is to desire that it obtains as a result of the world's being one of the ways it can be which will lead to the occurrence of that state of affairs').

---

2. All references are to Michael Smith, 'Instrumental Desires, Instrumental Rationality' (this volume) unless otherwise stated.

The plausibility of (1) depends on whether 'state of affairs' is taken in such a way that (for example) *my crossing my legs*, as opposed to my legs being crossed, counts as a state of affairs: if it doesn't, because it's an action of mine, (1) would be doubtful since sometimes my desires are desires to do things. But nothing in the argument of this section will depend on what to count as a state of affairs. I shall assume that (2) is unexceptionable. But what about (3)? I will raise three objections to it.

First of all, the plausibility of concluding (3) from (1) and (2) depends in part on the fact that (3) is quite a weak claim: to say that anyone who knows the truth of (2) will 'be in a position to see' that to desire that a given state of affairs obtains is to desire that it obtains as the effect of the obtaining of some other state of affairs is not to say that they will actually see it. However, if what's being claimed is that the alleged incoherence in the problem combination depends not simply on the subject's desire but on the further attitudes he forms—in particular, attitudes about what those desires consist in—it would seem to matter that subjects not only are in a position to see (etc.) but actually *do* see (etc.). For if the seeing is optional, it looks as if the proposed explanation of the irrationality applies more selectively than the fact it is intended to explain. This selectiveness problem would be remedied, perhaps, if it could be shown that one was failing in respect of (theoretical) rationality in not actually seeing (etc.), when in a position to do so. But why would this be irrational? Certainly we are not irrational for failing to believe every entailment of our current beliefs.

A similar sort of objection arises, secondly, in connection with the fact that the conclusion of this part of Smith's argument is said to depend on the truth of (1) but on knowledge only of (2). But knowledge of (1) is surely needed too. For if such knowledge is absent, someone who knows (2) could regard their desires that states of affairs obtain as a sub-class of their desires as a whole, and thus though in a position to see that to desire that a given state of affairs obtains is to desire that it obtains as the effect of the obtaining of some other state of affairs, be liable to the alleged incoherence in relation to some of their desires but not others. But however unobjectionable (1) may be, can we assume that each person will know it, just in virtue of being a subject of desires? The assumption requires all subjects of desires, implausibly, to be ready to classify the objects of their desires in the light of philosophical lines of questioning.

However, I am going to set aside these two objections in order to focus on a third, and thus make nothing further of the difference between the truth of (1) and knowledge of (1), or of that between being in a position to see (etc.) and actually seeing. For the third objection is that someone who knows the truism expressed by (2) is not even in a position to see (etc.), on the grounds that what we are alleged to be in a position to see—that a certain constitutive claim about desires and their objects holds true—is not the case. And of course if this constitutive claim *is* untrue, then all questions as to the conditions under which one might know it lapse.

Let us observe first of all that there's a scope ambiguity in Smith's formulation of his constitutive claim, that 'to desire that a certain state of the world obtains is to desire that it obtains as a result of *the world's being one of the ways it can be which will lead to the occurrence of that state of affairs.*'[3] The ambiguity depends on whether 'one of the ways' has narrow or wide scope relative to the 'desires' operator. If the phrase has narrow scope, the desire imputed is the desire that the state of affairs originally desired obtains as a result of the world's being some way or other that can lead to the occurrence of it. If it has wide scope, the desire imputed is that there is some way the world can be which can lead to the occurrence of the state of affairs originally desired, and it is desired that the state of affairs originally desired obtains as a result of the world's being that way. The significance of the distinction emerges once we are invited to consider

> someone who desires that a certain state of the world obtains as a result of the world's being one of the ways it can be which will lead to the occurrence of that state of affairs, and who believes that the way the world can be which will lead to the occurrence of the desired state of affairs is the p way.

The patent incoherence in the derived combination of attitudes resides, according to Smith, in the fact that 'given [the subject's means-end] belief, their original desire is already, so to speak,

3. My italics.

targeted on the world's being the p way.' But in what sense is it already so targeted?

On the wide-scope reading, there is a very clear sense in which this is so. I am going to assume that for any pair of states of affairs S and S', the desire that S obtains as a result of S' implies both the desire that S obtains and the desire that S' obtains. So on the wide-scope reading the desire that q implies, according to Smith, that

(A)   there is a state of affairs such as to cause q, and the subject desires that that state of affairs obtains.

Granted the subject's means-end belief that

(B)   the only state of affairs such as to cause q is p,[4]

it is now plain how the subject's desire (as reported by (A)) is 'targeted on p, given his belief'. For in (A) he is credited with the desire that a particular state of affairs with a certain property obtains, without any belief as to which state of affairs it is. (B) simply gives the missing belief: the state of affairs with that property is p. Failing in that context to desire that p is like thinking to oneself 'There's just one card which will win me the hand and I want that card; the card that will win me the hand is the ace; but I don't want the ace.' Here the subject takes contrary attitudes to one and the same object though aware of the identity, so *this* combination of attitudes is patently incoherent in a way that the problem combination is not.

There's a good reason, however, why the desire specified by (A) cannot be implied by the desire that q plus knowledge of (2). This is that there is a difference between desiring that q come about *simpliciter* and desiring that it come about from a particular cause, a difference which is reflected in the fact that the counterfactual conditions on *desiring that q* are different from the counterfactual conditions on *desiring that q as a result of p*. For example, the range of possible worlds in which I feel disappointment is greater if I have the second desire than if I have the first. So, assuming that to have a disposition is for a range of counterfactuals to hold true of one, the

4. I'm assuming here that (B) renders correctly the content of the means-end belief envisaged by Smith's 'believes that *the* way the world can be which will lead to the occurrence of the desired state of affairs is the p way' (my italics).

dispositions in which each of this pair of desires consists will overlap but not coincide. So they are different desires, notwithstanding the fact that in the actual world it may be that the only way the object of the simpler of the two desires, the desire that q, could come about is as a result of p. Examples which illustrate the difference between the two types of desire are not hard to find. Suppose a child wants to be at the funfair, but is disappointed to be there as a result of being taken by his friend's parents, because he wants to be there as a result of being taken by his own parents, even though he believes, correctly, that his own parents are busy and that being taken by his friend's parents is the only way of being there. The child may even be pleased to be at the funfair despite being disappointed at how he got to be there. But if to desire to be there were the *same* desire as the desire to be there as a result of what he believes (rightly) to be the only possible means of his being there, the child's disappointment would be inexplicable. Of course in this last case the particular cause by means of which alone the desired state of affairs could come about (i.e. the friend's parents taking the child) is known, or taken as known, by the desirer, whereas where the wide-scope reading is concerned the desirer doesn't have identifying knowledge (or anything like it) of the state of the world such that if it obtained the originally desired state of affairs would result, and such that he desires that it obtains. But the considerations that apply in the child/funfair case also apply here. Desiring that q, on the one hand and, on the other, there being a particular state of the world such that if it obtained it would cause q and desiring that q as a result of *it* have different counterfactual conditions, for the second desire is disappointed in more possible worlds than the first. So once again they are different desires.

These difficulties do not arise, however, on the narrow-scope reading of Smith's constitutive claim. If (1) is true, there will be no worlds in which the desire that q is satisfied in which q does not come about as the effect of another state of affairs, and so no world in which the desire that q is satisfied while the desire that q obtain as the result of some cause is not satisfied. So the counterfactual conditions on desiring that q and on desiring that q as the result of some cause will be the same. On the narrow-scope reading, then, the desire that q is said to imply not (A) but rather

(A*) the desire that a state of affairs obtains that is such as to cause q.

Granted the subject's means-end belief as specified by (B)—that the only state of affairs such as to cause q is p—the incoherence which results if the subject fails to form the desire that p is of the form 'I want an F; *a* is the only F; but I don't want *a*.' At least if the desire that q, along with knowledge of (2), implies the desire specified by (A*), the desire that q is 'already targeted' on the world's being the p way because the desire specified by (A*) is a desire for something of a certain kind and, in the subject's belief, p is the only thing of that kind. Let's assume that this is indeed incoherent, even if it's less impressively so than with the wide-scope reading. Moreover the problem with holding the attitudes specified by (A*) and (B) while failing to desire that p looks like a *different* problem from the (alleged) problem with the problem combination, so the one is potentially explanatory of the other. For whereas in holding the problem combination the subject's failure is failure to form a new desire on the basis of what he believes to be a causal relation, here, because the subject is now credited, additionally, with a desire for a state of affairs with a particular causal property, his failure is to form a new desire on the basis of what he believes to be a relation of unique instantiation.

However, the attitude specified even by (A*) does not—I shall argue—follow from the desire that q plus knowledge of (2). Granted knowledge of (2), one will certainly be in a position to see that to desire anything at all is to desire that a state of affairs obtains *which is*, if it does obtain, the effect of some other state of affairs. But there's an important difference between *this* knowledge and the knowledge Smith claims is made available by knowledge of (2), namely the knowledge that to desire that a given state of affairs obtains is to desire *that it obtains as the effect of* the obtaining of some other state of affairs. Call D_1 the desire that a state of affairs obtains which is, if it does obtain, the effect of some other state of affairs; and call D_2 the desire that a given state of affairs obtains as the effect of the obtaining of some other state of affairs. The difference between them is that whereas D_1 implies no more than the desire that the original state of affairs obtains, D_2 implies an extra desire over and above the desire for the obtaining of the original state of affairs, namely the desire that some other state of affairs obtains which causes the original one. The difference between D_1 and D_2 is that, on D_2, a platitudinous feature of the original state of affairs desired—the fact that it's the effect of some other state of affairs—has been moved inside the scope of the attitude of desiring. The move which gives rise to the incoherence of the derived combination on the narrow-scope reading—moving the property *being such as to cause q* inside the scope of the attitude of desiring—is just an instance of this. But the step is fallacious. It's clearly fallacious if the subject *doesn't* know that every state of affairs is the effect of some other, but it remains so even if the subject does know this, because not every known feature of a desired object is itself desired. (I can desire water and, knowing that water boils at 100°C, know that I desire something that boils at 100°C. But I need not desire that the water boil at 100°C.) So the derived combination of attitudes is not implied by the problem combination plus some platitudinous collateral attitudes, and the attempt to explain the irrationality of the problem combination by appeal to the incoherence of the derived combination fails.

Ought we to conclude, on the same grounds, that the derived combination is not itself incoherent? If we ought, we might be scared off our main conclusion which is that the derived combination is not implied by the problem combination (plus platitudes). But the additional conclusion is unwarranted, for reasons to do with the difference between causal and constitutive means-end beliefs. Whereas the causal character of the subject's belief appeared, in the problem combination, to be essential to the irrationality of that combination, it is inessential to the incoherence of the derived combination, since the relation between (A*) and (B) would be the same if the property in each were not *being such as to cause q* but (say) *being permanent*. Indeed the relation between the attitudes specified by (A*) and (B) is precisely what it would be, even without a Smith-style analysis, were the subject's belief a belief about 'constitutive means'—as in the case where I want to relax and believe that having a Turkish bath is the only available way of relaxing— rather than about causes. For the desire that q, Smith says, implies the desire that a state of affairs obtains such as to *cause* q only in conjunction with knowledge of (2). But the desire (say) to signal a turn implies the desire that a state of affairs obtains which *constitutes* signalling a turn *without* knowledge of (2), because for any state of affairs to obtain that satisfies the original desire is for a state of affairs to obtain which constitutes signalling a turn. So, because instances of the problem combination where the means-end belief is constitutive display the very same incoherence as the derived combination and are incoherent (if they are) independently of Smith's analysis, the derived combination is incoherent (if it is) independently of Smith's analysis. So the fact that the derived combination doesn't follow from the problem combination (plus platitudes) is no reason to deny that it is incoherent.

II

The fact that Smith's explanation of the irrationality of the problem combination does not succeed does not imply that another might not be found. In this section, however, I argue that there are instances of the problem combination of attitudes which are not irrational. I shall thus take issue with Smith's view of the scope of the norms of instrumental irrationality, as applying to desires *per se* rather than to choices or intentions.

One possible source of objection to Smith's view is concern over the standing of a coherence requirement on an agent's set of desires. Consider the following case. A woman desires to spend a certain amount of time bringing up her children, and believes that to do so it is necessary to reduce the time she spends on her career. However, she does not want to reduce the time she spends on her career. She thereby seems to instantiate the problem combination. Is she irrational? An objection to the idea that she is might go like this. Certainly there is a sense in which her desire set is not 'coherent', that is to say, the desires she has are not co-satisfiable. But whereas we are rationally required to rectify inconsistency in a set of beliefs, this is not the case with non-co-satisfiability in a set of desires, just because beliefs do, while desires do not, aim at truth. To be sure, persisting with a non-co-satisfiable desire set comes at a cost: if the woman lacked either the desire to spend time on her career or the desire to spend time on her children, her life would be free of the regret and frustration which, as things are, it seems bound to contain. But while absence of regret and frustration are goods, it is not obvious that in abandoning her current desire set in favour of one in which regret and frustration would not arise, and thus improving in respect of coherence in this sense, she would also be improving in respect of rationality. For the desire to spend time on her career and the desire to spend time on her children are both (let's suppose) independently well-grounded, and her life would be the poorer without either one. Coherence in this sense would be perfectly displayed, in F. H. Bradley's phrase, by the 'life of an oyster', but reason can't require us to lead such a life. So, it might be argued, the claim that the problem combination of attitudes is irrational stems from a questionable requirement of coherence on a subject's desire set.

Now Smith, at least in previous work, holds that there is a rational requirement of coherence on our desires in something like the above sense: as he says in *The Moral Problem*,

> in so far as [some] new set of desires ... exhibits more in the way of ... unity [than a previous set], we may properly think that the new ... set of desires is rationally preferable... For we may properly regard the unity of a set of desires as a virtue; a virtue that in turn makes for the rationality of the set as a whole.[5]

However, it's a mistake to defend the rationality of an instance of the problem combination by attacking this sort of coherence requirement on our desires. For though there is indeed conflict in the woman's case above, and perhaps rationally defensible conflict, the conflict arises not because she, defensibly, flouts the supposed norm which outlaws the problem combination, but rather because she conforms to that norm. It's a misdescription of the case to say that she desires to spend a certain amount of time on her career, believes that reducing the time she spends with her children is the necessary means to that, and *simply* fails to desire to reduce the time she spends with her children—thus resigning herself to the frustration of her desire to spend the time she wants on her career. The real conflict in fact occurs elsewhere. Just because she desires to spend a certain amount of time on her career and believes that reducing the time she spends with her children is the necessary means to that, she forms the desire to reduce the time she spends with her children, but this desire conflicts with her independently grounded desire to spend a given

5. Smith, *The Moral Problem*, p. 159.

amount of time with them. So whichever of these two desires she acts on, given her desire set, she is bound to experience frustration and regret.[6] But the redescription of the case makes it clear that even if the 'incoherence' of her desire set is defensible, that incoherence depends on her instantiating the pattern of desire-formation Smith describes as required by instrumental reason. One would be hard pressed, perhaps, to think of a single end such that the desire for it, together with instrumental rationality, would suffice on their own to impose coherence, in the sense of the absence of non-co-satisfiable desires, on a subject's total desire set. But more locally, in the case under consideration, instrumental rationality seems to be managing quite well.

Cases of a different kind may serve us better. Consider first the 'moral absolutist' of many an ethics course who comes to believe that the loss of millions of lives could be averted if he were to press a nuclear button. He certainly wants to avert the loss of these lives. He may form the desire that the world be otherwise than to require the pressing of the button by him in order to save the lives. But it would misrepresent the psychology of such an agent to say that he forms even a *pro tanto* desire to press the button which his principled opposition to nuclear warfare then overrules. But, arguably, he is not instrumentally irrational. Secondly, suppose that I want to pick the last fig on the tree and believe that the necessary means to this is that I climb up a branch that is (as I also believe) too thin to support my weight. The necessary means here is an action that I believe to be impossible (for me). Now if I believe that I can't climb up the relevant branch, I ought also come to believe that my picking the last fig on the tree is impossible. But there is no general problem about desiring what one believes impossible—a lifer can long for freedom, a ballerina whose career is over can long to dance again,

6. Of course there is a sense in which the woman may fail to form a desire to reduce the time she spends with her children, but this does not help the case against the irrationality of the problem combination. For 'she desires to reduce (etc.)' is ambiguous as between *pro tanto* and all things considered desires. If the woman indeed refuses to reduce the time she spends with her children, then she must have failed to form the desire, in the all things considered sense, to do so. However, this is consistent with her having formed the *pro tanto* desire to do so, under pressure from the desire to spend more time on her career, and I take it that all instrumental rationality is being said to require of her is that she form the *pro tanto* desire.

though they believe these things cannot come about—so I can go on wanting that last fig. All we can say however as to whether, guided by my means-end belief, I also form the desire to do that other impossible thing (or persist in the desire having once formed it), namely to climb up the relevant branch, is that I might but then again I might not. I can hardly be criticised for irrationality if I do form the desire to climb up the branch, but nor can I be criticised if I don't allow my desires to wander, as I might think pointlessly, down further pathways where I believe they will remain unfulfilled. Of a sample of agents equipped with the same beliefs about means which they believe lie beyond their reach, some will elaborate complex structures of instrumental desires to do things they believe they can't do, while others will be such that their desires will come to rest somewhere (as it were) higher up the structure, perhaps indeed with the non-instrumental desire in which the others' complex structures originate. And just because these are desires which none of the agents believe they can act on, neither group is superior in rationality to the other. Of course none of this shows that an agent who *intends* that q, believes that p is a necessary means to q, but does not intend that p, is not instrumentally irrational, though the explanation of why that might be so lies beyond the scope of this reply.

III

An action explanation is, in Smith's view, distinguished from a formally similar explanation of a desire that is unrelated to action only by the content of the explanatory means-end belief. Where action is in question the explanatory pair of mental states consists of

> a desire for some end ... and a belief of the agent that something she can just do, namely move her body in a certain way, has some suitable chance of [realising the agent's end].

This account of action explanations, however, presents some difficulties. One is the identification of things agents can just do with movings of their bodies: surely playing a C-major chord or changing down into third are things which, in context, I can just do, but they do not sound like specifications of ways of moving one's body. However, since it is not important for the main argument, I will not dwell on this issue. What really matters is the claim that actions are 'the product of that sub-class [of instrumental desires] where the means-end beliefs are about upshots of things that the agent can just do', whatever these things are. The problem case for this claim which Smith focuses on is the case where the agent has a non-instrumental desire to perform a basic action—to do something she can just do. The case is problematic since it might be thought that no means-end belief which relates the agent's (e.g.) moving her arm to something else as means to end 'could possibly be required to explain her action'. If that is so, then her 'non-instrumental desire to perform the basic action of moving her arm must ... suffice all by itself', and there are some actions of an agent whose explanation is not an instrumental rationalisation.

Smith replies by arguing that a means-end belief is required even in this type of case. For

> the agent still needs to believe that moving her arm will result *from something that she can just do*. In other words, she must put her non-instrumental desire [to move her arm] together with her belief that she can perform the basic action of moving her arm and that doing so will lead to the desired result, namely, the movement of her arm.

This argument, however, seems to be unsuccessful. The belief in focus is a conjunction of the agent's belief that she can (basically) move her arm and the belief that her (basically) moving her arm will lead to the movement of her arm, and only the second conjunct is properly speaking means-end. Though Smith carefully defends the claim that the first conjunct is necessary to basic action too, I confine my discussion to the second conjunct.[7] The difficulty here is that the object of desire

---

7. A brief comment on the first conjunct: with reference to Smith's case (4), where the agent can perform a certain basic action but lacks the belief that he can, Smith says that '[I]t is ... possible that, through subsequent experimentation, I could come to discover that I can wiggle my ears as a basic action, that is, without doing so by means of [e.g.] raising my eyebrows.' That is surely true. But there must be some *point at which* I become able to wiggle my ears basically rather than by raising my eyebrows. Now either I acquire my belief that I can basically wiggle them before that point or after it. If before it, certainly I don't ever basically wiggle my ears without the relevant belief, but it is a mystery how the belief is acquired. Though Smith says case (4) 'simply underscores the fact that our beliefs about which basic actions we can perform are derivable from experience', that belief acquired at *this* point can't derive from

mentioned in Smith's reply just quoted seems to be different from the one that appeared in the original problem. In the original problem, the agent's non-instrumental desire was 'to perform the basic action of moving her arm'. But in the reply the 'desired result'—that is, presumably, the object of the agent's non-instrumental desire—is said to be 'the movement of her arm'. This last phrase most naturally means 'that her arm move', and desiring that I move my arm and desiring that my arm move are different desires: the latter could be satisfied when the former was not if, for example, my arm moved because I moved it with my other arm. Now of course an agent could bring it about that her arm moves *by moving her arm*, so if the object of her desire were that her arm move, there would be a means (moving her arm) and an end (her arm moving) for the agent to have a means-end belief about. But the availability of a means-end belief in this case to complete the pattern of means-end rationalisation doesn't help to solve the original problem, where what the agent wanted was *to move her arm*.

Let's suppose, then, that 'the desired result, namely, the movement of her arm' is a way of saying that what the agent wants is to move her arm. On this interpretation, Smith is apparently committed to claiming that the agent has an instrumental desire that she move her arm which is constituted by a means-end belief (that her moving her arm is the means to her moving her arm) and her non-instrumental desire to move her arm. So, first, the instrumental desire is constituted by her means-end belief and itself; and, secondly, her moving her arm is the effect of itself. As against the second of these objections, Smith might remind us of the technicality of his term 'means-end beliefs': the belief that having a Turkish bath is a way of relaxing is a belief about what constitutes relaxing, not about what causes it, but it too counts as means-end in Smith's sense. So couldn't the agent's belief that her moving her arm is *identical* with her

experience, since the experience which would naturally give rise to the belief—i.e., that of basically wiggling my ears—*ex hypothesi* hasn't occurred yet. So it is tempting to say that this first horn of the dilemma describes an impossibility. As to the second horn, if we acquire the relevant belief *after* the point in question, the belief indeed comes from experience, but the act it's an experience of—basically wiggling my ears—must, the first time it happened, have been performed without the relevant belief. So it has not been shown that it is necessary to believe that I can perform a given basic action in order to perform it.

moving her arm be the means-end belief in question?[8] The problem with this is that no genuinely trivial belief advances one further than any other, but any other trivial belief—if the sun rises then it rises, or what have you—would not even seem to preserve the appearance that the explanatory form of instrumental rationalisation had been adhered to. And that still leaves the first objection: if A is constituted by B and itself, then A is constituted by B and B and itself, in which case it is constituted by B and B and B and itself, and so on *ad inf.*. It seems therefore that Smith has not met the challenge he himself raises to the claim that basic action requires a means-end belief on the part of the agent which relates something they can just do to their desired end. So no reason has been found to avert the conclusion that, where the agent's non-instrumental desire is to do something they can just do, it's not the case that the explanation of action takes the form of an instrumental rationalisation.

There is a question, however, as to how much this negative conclusion should matter, either to the Humean theory of action or to the theorist of instrumental rationality. Consider first the theorist of instrumental rationality. In all the cases I can think of where the agent's non-instrumental desire is to do something they can just do—a cartwheel, say—the answer to the question 'Why did you do that?' is either going to be something like 'no reason' or 'I felt like it', or else something like 'I am so happy.' In the former case it is obvious that the answer does not specify a further end such that doing the cartwheel is a means to it, and I assume that the right way to think of the latter type of answer is not as shorthand for 'I wanted to express my happiness.' (Of course one might do a cartwheel to impress somebody, but then the desire to do a cartwheel would be an instrumental desire.) But the very absence of any further desire beyond the desire to perform the action itself surely shows that the theorist of instrumental rationality should not be concerned about the case: the theorist of instrumental rationality only has something to theorise about if there is a further desire and a belief which mediates (or fails to mediate) between it and the desire to perform the action.

8. This idea appears in Smith, *The Moral Problem*, p. 97: 'The Humean will thus regard an agent's desire to ϕ, together with the trivial belief that were she to ϕ she would ϕ, as a limiting case of a motivating reason.'

Now consider the Humean theory of action. I take it that a very basic reason why Humeans think every action needs to be rationalised not only by a desire but also by a belief is the particularising function of belief: the desire to do a cartwheel is general in its object in that indefinitely many cartwheels could satisfy it, but any cartwheel the agent does is a timed particular, and belief is needed to get the agent from the one to the other.[9] Moreover if agents didn't invariably have a belief, true or false, as to the nature of the particular action they were performing, they would be helpless to judge whether or not they were thereby fulfilling their desire, so they could hardly be said to be acting intentionally. So it would be highly unsatisfactory to be left where Smith threatens to leave us if his theory of action explanation fails, namely with the conclusion that, where the agent's non-instrumental desire is to do something they can just do, the action is to be explained by their desire alone. But we aren't left there, even if we reject Smith's theory, for the particularising belief is (in the case envisaged) 'This is a cartwheel.' To say this is no more than to cite an instance of one part of Davidson's characterisation of a primary reason: 'Whenever someone does something for a reason ... he can be characterised as (a) having some sort of pro attitude towards actions of a certain kind, and (b) *believing ... that his action* [sc. the timed particular] *is of that kind.*'[10]

At this point the thought suggests itself that this particularising belief might be the means-end belief Smith is looking for, in his liberalized sense of 'means-end'. So let us suppose that it is and then think about what happens in cases where the non-instrumental desire *isn't* a desire to do something the agent can just do—for example if the agent does a cartwheel to impress. Here the explanation of the action fits Smith's instrumental rationalisation model exactly: the by-chain terminates in an instrumental desire to do something the agent can just do (a

9. This is the way Davidson justifies the presence of belief in the explanatory pair of attitudes in 'Actions, Reasons, and Causes', in his *Essays on Actions and Events* (Oxford: Oxford University Press, 1980), pp. 5–6.

10. Davidson, 'Actions, Reasons, and Causes', p. 4. Cf. also ibid., p. 5: '*R* is a primary reason why an agent performed the action *A* [sc., the timed particular] under the description *d* only if *R* consists of a pro attitude ... towards actions with a certain property [sc., being a cartwheel], *and a belief ... that* A, *under the description* d, *has that property.*' All italics mine.

cartwheel), via his non-instrumental desire to impress and his means-end belief that his doing a cartwheel will lead to his impressing. But the instrumental desire to which the means-end belief gives rise here stands as much in need of particularisation by a *further* belief, if it is to lead to action, as the non-instrumental desires in Smith's problem cases, since it too is general in its object; indeed its object is exactly the same as the object of the non-instrumental desire in the case where the agent cartwheels 'for no reason'. Thus if Smith thinks a means-end belief is necessary in his problem cases because it's needed to get from general desire to action, the need arises for *any* desire to do something the agent can just do, whether the desire is instrumental or non-instrumental. Is a belief of the form 'this is a ϕ-ing', in a context such as the present one, a means-end belief of a different sort, or isn't it? One reason to think that it isn't is the intuition that a belief is means-end only if it explains an action which I have some *further* reason to do, that is, some further end my action is a means to (causal or constitutive); but the problem cases in focus are precisely cases where I do something I can just do for no further reason. Another reason is that unless we have some prior grip on what 'means-end' as applied to beliefs is meant to rule out, there is the danger of being led to say that any belief is means-end if, in conjunction with a non-instrumental desire, it rationalises an action. But this would trivialise the idea that the theory of instrumental rationality coincides with the Humean theory of action explanation. In any case, if a belief of the form 'this is a ϕ-ing' in the present context is means-end, then though Smith's problem is more widespread than he thought in that it arises for desires to do something the agent can just do whether they are instrumental or non-instrumental, the problem also has a ready solution. If it isn't, so there is no means-end belief to hand in the case of actions explained by non-instrumental desires to do things that the agent can just do, not only is the theory of instrumental rationality safe: the Humean theory of action is safe too. A difficulty only arises if just one theory is made to perform the office of both.[11]

11. Thanks to my colleagues at the University of Kent for helpful discussion of drafts of this paper.

REFERENCES

Davidson, D., 1980, 'Actions, Reasons, and Causes', in his *Essays on Actions and Events* (Oxford: Oxford University Press).
Smith, M., 1994, *The Moral Problem* (Oxford: Blackwell).

EQUALITY, AMBITION AND INSURANCE

by Andrew Williams and Michael Otsuka

I—Andrew Williams

ABSTRACT   It is difficult for prioritarians to explain the degree to which justice requires redress for misfortune in a way that avoids imposing unreasonably high costs on more advantaged individuals whilst also economising on intuitionist appeals to judgment. An appeal to hypothetical insurance may be able to solve the problems of cost and judgment more successfully, and can also be defended from critics who claim that resource egalitarianism is best understood to favour the *ex post* elimination of envy over individual endowments.

I

One influential tendency in contemporary political philosophy claims justice requires that we share fairly in each other's good or bad luck. But what degree of redress for misfortune does justice demand?

Prioritarians argue that inequalities in fortune should be redressed so as to benefit those less fortunate.[1] Depending on how much priority it attaches to benefiting the disadvantaged, their view faces two problems. If they attach absolute priority to the disadvantaged, prioritarians face the *problem of cost*. Given the absence of decisive reasons to favour less over more advantaged individuals regardless of how small a benefit we might bestow on the former and how large the opportunity cost to the latter of our doing so, the absolute view is implausible. Instead prioritarians might endorse a more moderate view. It claims benefiting the less advantaged takes some priority over benefiting the more advantaged whilst also recognising the relevance of further factors, such as the magnitude of potential benefits, and the number of potential beneficiaries. A second difficulty arises for moderates who hope to defend principles of political morality that economise on intuitionist appeals to judgment.[2] To solve the *problem of judgment* moderates must

1. Parfit (2002: 101 and 116–21).
2. Rawls (1999: Secs. 7 and 8).

provide some principled explanation of how much priority to attach to an individual's level of advantage when deciding whom to benefit.

John Rawls makes various suggestions about how his conception of *justice as fairness* addresses these two problems. His initial suggestion rests on a restrictive view of which types of misfortune are relevant, and an additional empirical conjecture. Thus, Rawls's difference principle attaches absolute priority only to those least advantaged in terms of social primary goods, such as income and wealth. It does so, moreover, on the assumption that other principles are satisfied and that, partly in consequence, society will not face hard choices between denying the least advantaged small benefits and imposing large sacrifices on those better off.[3]

Due to its restrictive view of relevant misfortunes Rawls's initial suggestion may not be fully satisfactory. According to Amartya Sen, an exclusive focus on primary goods mistakenly denies the relevance of capabilities to interpersonal comparison and ignores variations in the ways primary goods are transformed into capabilities.[4] In his final reply to Sen, however, Rawls insists his view does attach fundamental importance to specific capabilities, namely those necessary to attain the capability threshold enjoyed by 'free and equal citizens' who are 'normal, fully cooperating members of society' (2001: 169–70). Rawls also endorses a social minimum principle that requires redress for capability shortfalls that temporarily place individuals below this threshold.[5] Thus, in the case of medical misfortune in 'the normal range of cases' he favours restoring individuals to the level of fully cooperating citizens provided the cost of doing so does not jeopardise other essential forms of expenditure. In addition, Rawls recognises the existence of more extreme cases where grave disabilities place individuals below the threshold permanently. Here he notes that it is 'obvious, and accepted by common sense, that we have a duty towards all human beings, however severely handicapped', but also expresses doubts about

---

3. Rawls (2001: 66–68).
4. Sen (1992: Ch. 5).
5. Rawls (2001: 170–76).

the weight of such duties, and admits to not knowing whether his view can be extended to such cases.[6]

Rawls's reply goes some way to responding to the problem of cost under realistic conditions. Thus, where misfortune extends beyond the economic domain, Rawls avoids the implausible implications of unrestricted absolute prioritarianism by relaxing the absolute priority he elsewhere attaches to the least fortunate. However, there are two reasons to doubt his minimum capability principle fares as well in escaping the problem of judgment. First, although the principle's requirements are to be balanced against competing requirements, Rawls provides little guidance in resolving such conflicts, and leaves unspecified our duties in extreme cases. Second, given the vagueness in the idea of a normal fully cooperating member of society, the principle's application is likely to vary greatly depending on individual judgment.[7] So, while certain incapacities may clearly generate a claim for redress under the principle, others may be more difficult to classify; compare, for example, a medical condition which precludes employment with one which causes infertility.

Despite these difficulties, Rawls's view may be more plausible than any rivals. Before drawing that conclusion, we must investigate the alternatives. In what follows, I examine the very different response to the problems of cost and judgment suggested by Ronald Dworkin's appeal to the idea of a fair insurance market.

II

According to *equality of resources*, whether a distribution of privately owned resources is just depends on the possibility of its emerging from a counterfactual market process involving individuals guided by their particular ambitions but unaware of their relative fortunes.[8] Providing illustration, Dworkin imagines castaways distributing ownership rights in a desert island. He

6. Rawls (2001: 176, n. 59).

7. Defending his difference principle against an alternative social minimum principle, Rawls voices a similar suspicion when he writes 'The difficulty here is the same as that with intuitionist doctrines generally: how is the social minimum to be selected and adjusted to changing circumstances?' (Rawls, 1999: 278).

8. Dworkin (2000: Ch. 2).

argues fairness requires nobody prefer any other individual's allocation, and that 'envy', so defined, should be eliminated via an auction amongst equally endowed bidders with lots continuously divided until the market clears and nobody wishes to repeat the process. Dworkin then asks whether some market process remains appropriate once production, investment, trade, illness, disability, and variations in talent complicate the island's economy, and prospects are shaped by differences in luck as well as ambition.

Here Dworkin distinguishes forms of inequality that arise from differing choices rather than variations in certain types of luck. For illustration, suppose castaways vary only in their preferences, and having received their fair share of resources make different economic decisions with full information about their actual consequences. If some produce more valuable crops than others, equality of resources implies the resulting inequality is just because it arose solely from differences in *choice*. Now suppose those castaways have information only about the risks associated with different decisions, and that some make more risky decisions that happen to pay off. Although the resulting inequality is not due merely to differences in choice, equality of resources implies it may nevertheless be just if it arose from differences in *option luck*. Finally, suppose that some produce more than others because of some good fortune the likelihood of which nobody could have estimated. Equality of resources then implies the resulting inequality, unless suitably redressed, will be unjust because it arose from differences in *brute luck*.

Having endorsed inequalities arising from differential choice and option luck, Dworkin then employs his crucial assumption that fairly situated individuals are entitled to expose themselves to varying degrees of risk to explain how brute luck inequalities should be redressed. Thus, he argues bad brute luck should be redressed to the extent required to mimic the operation of a counterfactual insurance market in which equally wealthy individuals, aware only of the distribution of luck rather than their personal fortunes, purchase coverage against suffering relatively bad brute luck guided by their own values and attitudes to risk.

Consider now how this proposal responds to the various problems mentioned earlier. Since equality of resources recognises the relevance of *personal resources*, such as health and talent, as well as *impersonal resources* like income and wealth, it cannot be accused of completely ignoring inequalities in capability. However, if those inequalities are so expensive to remedy that individuals would not insure against them, the theory can justify withholding benefits from the least advantaged because of the costs to more advantaged individuals of not doing so. Moreover, since the theory identifies the point at which to withhold those benefits by reference to preferences and the relative prices of different goods it is less reliant on the types of judgment involved in Rawls's appeal to an ideal of normal cooperation amongst free and equal citizens, or alternative pluralist proposals. Thus, assuming we can estimate the operation of the relevant insurance market, it is arguable that equality of resources provides a more promising way to escape prioritarian extremism whilst still economising on intuitionist appeals to judgment.

III

One familiar objection to Dworkin's proposal denies that redressing inequalities to the extent necessary to mimic the operation of a fair insurance market is sufficient to realise equality of resources. Michael Otsuka has recently provided a forceful defence for this supposedly internal critique.[9] His argument begins by granting that egalitarian justice permits certain inequalities that arise because of differences in individuals' option luck. Such acceptable inequalities include those resulting from high stakes gambles undertaken by identically and munificently endowed agents. They also include relative disadvantages borne by individuals who declined to purchase reasonably priced insurance that would have *fully* compensated them by leaving them indifferent between suffering misfortune and receiving compensation and escaping misfortune and receiving no compensation. Otsuka insists, however, that fair insurance fails to justify inequalities in outcome when reasonably priced fully compensatory insurance is unavailable.[10]

9. Otsuka (2002).
10. Otsuka (2002: 44).

Defending such insistence, Otsuka focuses on Dworkin's example of blindness. He argues individuals who become blind having declined insurance, or purchased reasonably priced partially compensatory insurance, or unreasonably expensive fully compensatory insurance, did not enjoy sufficiently valuable options to render their disadvantage unproblematic from a resource egalitarian perspective.[11] The inequality between the blind and sighted should remain problematic to resource egalitarians, Otsuka maintains, because their view requires eliminating envy over the distribution of individuals' comprehensive endowment of personal and impersonal resources. Thus, resource egalitarians cannot coherently argue justice merely requires mimicking an insurance market since the resulting distribution will not generally eliminate envy over endowments; for example, if only partially compensatory insurance is available then individuals who purchase it and become blind will still envy the endowment of those who do not become blind. Instead, Otsuka concludes, they must demand far more radical wealth transfers; in worlds like ours, populated in part by 'the severely incapacitated whom it is impossible or fantastically expensive to compensate', equality of resources implies that justice requires 'mutually shared misery' (Otsuka, 2002: 46).

Otsuka anticipates two resource egalitarian responses to the unpalatable consequences he has identified. The pluralist response renders those consequences less unpalatable by claiming that resource egalitarian principles are meant merely to provide defeasible rather than decisive reasons for political action. Though himself sympathetic to pluralist egalitarianism, Otsuka points out the first response is unavailable to Dworkin, given his well-known opposition to pluralism, and his view of equality as the sovereign political virtue. The second response involves distinguishing envy across the opportunity sets with which individuals are actually endowed from envy across individuals' prospects. Employing this distinction, Otsuka notes resource egalitarians might eschew the requirement to eliminate *ex post* envy his argument attributes to them. They might instead require only the elimination of *ex ante* envy, and claim mimicking a fair insurance market satisfies that demand.

11. Otsuka (2002: 45).

Otsuka recognises that Dworkin's remarks suggest the *ex ante* interpretation of the envy test, and also notes Dworkin's explicit rejection of the type of extremist 'rescue policy' required by the *ex post* envy test. Nevertheless, he provides at least two arguments to deny that resource egalitarians may rest content with the less redistributive envy test.

The first argument has two stages, and compares three scenarios. At the former stage, Otsuka imagines an initial scenario where on reaching adulthood each individual enjoys the same personal and impersonal resources, and is known to face the same positive risk of later developing a horrible mental illness, a misfortune that is impossible to ameliorate in any way, or insure against. Explaining why he supposes such *ex ante* equality does not by itself suffice for equality of resources, Otsuka appeals to what he implies is a necessary condition for the realisation of the resource egalitarian ideal.[12] It would not suffice, he suggests, since 'Those who come down with this illness will, through no choice of theirs, enjoy a severely diminished stock of personal resources over their lifetimes in comparison with those who are spared this ailment' (Otsuka, 2002: 50). At the latter stage of his argument, Otsuka asks us to consider a second scenario where it is possible to purchase only very expensive insurance that covers minimally effective treatment. To show that, like the first, the second scenario also fails to realise equality of resources, he compares the latter to a third scenario where some medical breakthrough makes it possible to purchase inexpensive insurance that provides a miracle cure for the horrible illness. If the elimination of *ex ante* envy via the provision of fair insurance suffices for equality of resources, then that ideal has already been realised prior to the miracle cure's discovery. According to Otsuka, however, it is clear 'With this breakthrough, we now possess the means to bring society much closer to (indeed fully to realise) the ideal of equality of resources' (Otsuka, 2002: 50). Thus, from our supposedly different responses to the second and third scenarios, Otsuka concludes we should reject the *ex ante* view, and accept his earlier claim that an equal opportunity to insure does not suffice for equality of

12. Otsuka (2002: 50).

resources in the absence of a reasonably priced fully compensatory coverage.

The second argument focuses on inequalities in impersonal resources resulting from another form of luck, differential receipt of gifts and bequests. Employing hypothetical insurance, Dworkin recommends a steeply progressive tax on such transfers, which would greatly reduce the types of inherited privilege that currently exist but still not completely eradicate *ex post* envy. According to Otsuka, however, if *ex post* envy over inherited wealth is unproblematic, then some inequalities in bidding power at the outset of Dworkin's hypothetical auction should also be unproblematic. Assuming an equal opportunity to insure against having a smaller stock of clamshells than others, these could arise if unequal stocks were randomly assigned to the castaways. Such a permissive attitude to the existence of *ex post* envy undermines hypothetical insurance since inconsistent with Dworkin's earlier, plausible claim that the 'desert island auction would not have avoided envy, and would have no appeal as a solution to the problem of dividing the resources equally, if the immigrants had struggled ashore with different amounts of money in their pockets at the outset, which they were free to use in the auction' (Otsuka, 2002: 52).

If successful, Otsuka's arguments show that hypothetical insurance fails to provide egalitarians with a plausible non-intuitionist solution to the problem of cost. I now attempt to refute those arguments, taking into account Dworkin's own responses.

IV

Though Dworkin admits having once left the issue 'in at least some doubt', he now insists that 'Equality of resources means that people should be equally situated with respect to risk rather than that they be equally situated after the uncertainties of risk had been resolved' (Dworkin, 2002: 121).[13] Rejecting the *ex post* envy test, Dworkin argues that the levelling down it demands

---

13. See also the previously unpublished remarks in Dworkin (2000: Ch. 9, Sec. VI), where Dworkin withdraws his earlier reservations, first expressed in 1981 and reprinted at p. 104, about the possibility of fair insurance delivering insufficient compensation for brute bad luck.

would not only fail to display equal concern, and so jeopardise governmental authority, but also be irrational for any individual to prefer. In addition, he criticises Otsuka's two attempts to show his view requires an *ex post* envy test.

Dworkin's first criticism flatly rejects Otsuka's response to the miracle cure. Denying Otsuka's conviction that its discovery enables equality of resources to be better realised, Dworkin writes: 'On the contrary...a new issue for equality arose when the cure was discovered. Did people have an equal opportunity to provide for that cure if needed? If, as he [i.e. Otsuka] assumes, people did have an equal opportunity, because low-cost insurance was offered on equal terms to all, then equality of resources was preserved but not improved' (Dworkin, 2002: 124, n. 33). Dworkin's denial will strike some readers as mere counter-assertion, but can be elaborated by appealing to the distinction between *deontic* and *telic* conceptions of justice.[14] Doing so provides a reply to Otsuka's ingenious example, which grants there is some sense in which the miracle cure enhances justice but denies that equality of resources is concerned with justice so understood.

On my understanding, the role played by deontic conceptions of justice is confined to guiding distributive decision-making. Thus, if some facts are unalterable, such conceptions claim they are neither just nor unjust in the deontic sense. In contrast, telic conceptions may play a broader role in practical reasoning. Since such conceptions deal with justice understood as a property possessed by a distribution in itself, they evaluate even unalterable states of affairs. Thus, if a telic conception includes normative principles that govern the production of valuable states, then like a deontic conception it too may guide distributive decision-making. In addition, however, such a conception performs further roles, like guiding aspiration and regret; for example, it may demand we hope for a particular state of affairs even when its existence is beyond our control.

Thus understood, deontic and telic judgments can be plausibly combined. For illustration, consider Rawls's remark that, like other facts beyond anyone's control, the 'natural distribution [of talents and abilities] is neither just nor unjust', and that what 'is

14. Parfit (2002: 122, n. 17, and 90).

just and unjust is the way that institutions deal with these facts' (Rawls, 1999: 87). The remark is plausible if understood as a judgment about justice in the deontic sense. However, we might also think that some of our convictions about the natural distribution resist expression by deontic judgments alone. We might, for example, criticise an individual who welcomes the infeasibility of redressing certain natural inequalities because he would otherwise be required to bear certain costs. To justify such criticism we might appeal to the telic judgment that his world is less just than one where it is feasible to redress those inequalities, and claim his attitude is objectionable because it welcomes the existence of telic injustice.

To return to Dworkin, it seems clear his project is to devise a sound theory of justice in the deontic rather than telic sense. If so, resource egalitarians have a ready response to Otsuka's three scenarios. At the outset, they can reject his assumption that equality of resources is not realised in the first scenario where the eventual victims of the illness enjoy fewer personal resources than others through no choice of their own. Such a rejection will seem odd if we take for granted that equality of resources is a telic conception that ranks states of affairs as more or less just regardless of whether they can be altered by rational agents. But, as suggested, we should scrutinise that interpretative preconception, and recognise that equality of resources, like justice as fairness, is a deontic conception. Thus, if as Otsuka stipulates 'Nothing can be done' to alleviate misfortune in his first scenario, it is not necessarily implausible to deny it exhibits any injustice in the deontic sense assumed by equality of resources. Resource egalitarians can challenge Otsuka's comparison between the second and third scenarios on similar grounds. Assuming the miracle cure's initial unavailability was beyond human control, they can echo Rawls's response to the natural distribution. Just as Rawls claims there is a sense in which a natural distribution where all are born sighted is no more just than one where only some are sighted, they might claim that equality of resources implies that the discovery of the miracle cure does not necessarily make a society more just in the deontic sense. Whether the society is more or less just depends not on the absence or availability of the cure but rather on its response to such facts, and in particular their likely effects on the operation of a fair insurance market.

Emphasising the deontic character of equality of resources is important not only because it renders more plausible Dworkin's claim that, provided that the relevant insurance schemes are mimicked, the cure's discovery does not improve equality. Doing so also enables resource egalitarians to grant the cure may enhance justice in some distinct sense. Rather than merely dismissing Otsuka's view as unsound, they can argue that his conviction that the cure enhances equality of resources is most plausibly construed as a judgment about justice in the telic sense. Thus construed, however, it does not contradict their judgment that the cure does not enhance justice in the deontic sense. I conclude then that, provided its proponents concede that equality of resources is incomplete insofar as it does not aim to account for certain telic convictions, Dworkin's first counter-argument can be elaborated in a way that effectively rebuts the miracle cure argument.

Now consider Dworkin's response to the claim that because equality of resources prohibits an unequal initial distribution of wealth in his desert island scenario it should also prohibit wealth transfers that produce unequal distributions. Dworkin alleges there are significant differences between the distribution of unowned resources in the first fictional world and previously owned resources in any actual world governed by his theory. Arguing that in the latter case the demands of equality are more complex, he claims it is not only 'inegalitarian that some people begin their lives with different levels of wealth available to them... by way of gift' but also 'inegalitarian for government to tax differentially the different choices that people make about how to spend what is rightfully theirs, and therefore inegalitarian separately to tax gifts and bequests' (Dworkin, 2002: 125). To reconcile these competing egalitarian demands, Dworkin reaffirms the insurance approach's applicability to differences in inheritance. He also insists that because it frustrates the second demand of equality to treat gifts differently from other decisions, Otsuka is mistaken to 'claim that equality unambiguously requires prohibiting gifts and bequests altogether' (Dworkin, 2002: 125).

In assessing Dworkin's response, it is worth bearing in mind that Otsuka's remarks about gifts do not simply question whether equality of resources is better realised by permitting rather than prohibiting gift-based inequalities in wealth. As I reported them, they also threatened the crucial assumption that the theory can rely exclusively on an *ex ante* version of the envy test by alleging that such reliance leads to an implausible conclusion. More specifically, they alleged that if equality of resources claims eliminating *ex ante* envy by mimicking a fair insurance suffices to render unproblematic *ex post* envy over inherited wealth then the theory should also accept *ex post* envy over initial endowments in the auction, provided that bidders enjoyed the opportunity to insure against being under-endowed. So, to rebut Otsuka's argument fully, resource egalitarians need either to show why the appeal to fair insurance does not require a permissive attitude to initial allocations that fail to eliminate *ex post* envy, or show that such an attitude may be defensible.

It is not immediately apparent how Dworkin's response, which seems designed to show only that equality of resources does not prohibit gifts, meets this particular challenge. Moreover, in claiming it is 'inegalitarian that some people begin their lives with different levels of wealth available to them . . . by way of gift' (Dworkin, 2002: 125) Dworkin even appears to lend some support to the *ex post* version of the envy test. Despite these problems, are at least two ways to respond to Otsuka's challenge.

Resource egalitarians might first deny that their appeal to insurance endorses initial allocations where 'Clamshell holdings are unequal because all the clamshells have been divided at the outset into unequal piles that will be randomly assigned to the survivors', who 'are given the opportunity to insure against failing to receive less than whatever number of clamshells they specify' (Otsuka, 2002: 53). Contrary to Otsuka, it is debatable whether he has shown that such a clamshell lottery is akin to the familiar scenario involving differential receipt of gifts, which resource egalitarians claim fair insurance can justify. Since the bidders will later enjoy ample opportunity to participate in lotteries having received their initial clamshell allocation, and purchasing insurance is costly, it is implausible to assume they would prefer to be forced into the clamshell lottery. Despite this, Otsuka's discussion provides no grounds for empowering the auctioneer to impose the lottery on them against their will. It seems more apposite to compare the lottery to a scenario in which each individual's property is stolen and then redistributed by a random and to some degree wasteful process. Given such background conditions, where some have already acted unjustly, the advocates of fair insurance could plausibly deny that their view implies the availability of theft insurance eliminates injustice. They can also, I suggest, make the same claim about the clamshell lottery. Thus, they can accept that injustice persists despite the availability of insurance, but provide an explanation of that conviction which does not concede justice generally requires the elimination of *ex post* envy but instead appeals to those unjust background conditions.

Though the second response has less appeal, resource egalitarians might also question whether, on reflection, the clamshell lottery does necessarily generate injustice. To support this suggestion, suppose an identical initial allocation takes place amongst a group of survivors, all of whom prefer their clamshells then to be redistributed through a random process, which produces certain limited though substantial inequalities in future bidding power. If those individuals instituted a post-allocation lottery, I conjecture Otsuka would not condemn the resulting inequalities as necessarily unjust. Suppose, however, that it is feasible for those same survivors to institute only a pre-allocation lottery. So, before their vessel ever encounters danger, they agree to accept the outcome of any pre-allocation lottery that produces the same inequalities in outcome. Since there seems no significant difference between the inequalities produced by the two lotteries, which vary only in their timing, I conclude that is less obvious than first appears to assume it is necessarily unjust for survivors to enter the auction with unequal bidding power.

To summarise then, this section has argued Otsuka's arguments from the miracle cure and the clamshell lottery are unsuccessful in showing that an *ex post* test is an essential element in equality of resources. Having cleared some ground, I now turn to an argument supporting the *ex ante* test.

V

As a preliminary, recall Dworkin's description of equality of resources as an attempt to satisfy two demands on a just distribution of resources, namely *ambition-sensitivity* and *endowment-insensitivity*.[15] According to the argument I shall examine, the first of these demands plays a fundamental role in justifying fair insurance. That role, however, may not be immediately apparent. The most familiar illustrations of the ambition-sensitive character of equality of resources involve individuals who differ in their preferences but are otherwise similarly situated.[16] Equality of resources satisfies ambition-sensitivity insofar as it implies, for instance, that Adrian and his less industrious fellow castaways are entitled to choose between different combinations of income and leisure, and can be held liable for the resulting differences in their circumstances. The theory is also ambition-sensitive because it favours distributing unowned resources via an auction, in which everyone's preferences help determine the structure of lots.

We might conclude from such examples that the demands of ambition-sensitivity can be satisfied merely by adopting an appropriate standard of interpersonal comparison that focuses on individuals' opportunities, and evaluates them by reference to their prices in a particular type of market. Having adopted such a standard, some further principle then determines the extent to which justice requires redress for inequality so construed.

Equality of resources rejects this familiar picture, and instead insists the twin demands just mentioned are interdependent insofar as endowment-insensitivity must be secured in an ambition-sensitive manner. To make this discrepancy more apparent compare the type of protection against relative misfortune provided by an *ex post* envy-eliminating rescue policy with that of the *ex ante* envy-eliminating insurance approach. Both types are equivalent to insurance packages combining a premium in return for some level of coverage. As already explained, granted certain assumptions about the operation of insurance markets, they differ in part because the package provided by the rescue policy provides a higher level of coverage but also demands a much higher premium. An even more fundamental difference exits, however, because the *ex post* envy-eliminating rescue policy allows individuals' preferences to count

---

15. Dworkin (2000: 89).
16. See Dworkin (2000: 83 and 67–68) for the next two examples.

only insofar as they determine whether envy exists across endowments. Like other *ex post* luck-sharing principles, the rescue policy attaches no importance in principle let alone practice to tailoring an individual's package of coverage and premium to her own estimate of its desirability compared with some other package. In contrast, the *ex ante* insurance approach assumes that, to the extent that the relevant information is available, there are reasons of justice to customise protection to individuals' actual values and the counterfactual decisions those values support.

The importance of achieving endowment-insensitivity in an ambition-sensitive manner is fully apparent in Dworkin's previously unpublished discussion of 'The Luck of the Draw' in *Sovereign Virtue* (Dworkin, 2000: 340–46). Here Dworkin defends the insurance approach with an argument proceeding in two stages. At the former stage, he describes two examples in which wealth is fairly distributed, and everyone faces the same risk of contracting a disabling disease at forty, an age none has yet reached. Regardless of whether the disease strikes randomly or on the basis of genetic endowment, Dworkin claims that the political community should ensure individuals are able to purchase insurance at market rates provided either by private firms or public programs. Appealing to the fact his proposal, unlike a rescue policy, enables individuals to decide for themselves how much protection they enjoy against misfortune, he writes that in these two cases

> It is a great strength of the insurance approach . . . that it allows people to make decisions about the relative importance of various risks for themselves, so that they can tailor their use of their own resources to their own judgments, ambitions, tastes, convictions, and commitments. That makes the insurance policy both more egalitarian and more liberal than the rescue policy (Dworkin, 2000: 344).

The latter stage of Dworkin's argument addresses a more realistic case, which differs because everyone knows which individuals will succumb to the disease; hence, an actual insurance market is absent. Dworkin argues that, nevertheless, all three cases are sufficiently similar that in the third case the community should redistribute resources to approximate what would have emerged in the first and second cases. Given the unavailability of individualised information, the community should attempt to ensure that those who succumb to the disease receive the level of coverage that would have been purchased on average, or most frequently, had risk been equally distributed.

A full treatment would question both stages of this argument, but on this occasion let us suppose if the former stage succeeds, there are weighty reasons in favour of hypothetical insurance. How might its proponents attempt to show that in the first two examples individuals are entitled to decide which risks to bear, and so justice demands they share misfortune through an insurance market?

One way to address our question appeals to prior elements within equality of resources itself. Thus, we might examine whether accepting the theory's ambition-sensitive implications in cases where individuals differ only in their preferences supports the insurance approach in cases where they also differ in their endowments. Consider first why some market process is essential to the definition of a resource egalitarian distribution. Dworkin's explanation appeals to the possibility that, depending on the form in which resources are provided, a plurality of distributions can satisfy the envy test. Assuming it would be unfair for the distributor arbitrarily to impose any one of these envy-free distributions, for example, by transforming resources into lots all of which one individual dislikes, he concludes that envy-elimination is not sufficient to eradicate all forms of fairness. To eliminate the unfairness present when lots are imposed arbitrarily Dworkin proposal an auction in which resources are divided into lots, and then sub-divided even further at any bidder's request.[17]

Elaborating this proposal in his discussion of liberty's place in equality of resources, Dworkin explains the need to specify a *baseline system* of civil and economic rights as the background against which the envy test and auction are applied.[18] Assuming that a community must treat each of its members with equal concern when distributing resources and that a market process is the best way of doing so, Dworkin defends certain principles for designing the baseline system of such a process. These include the

17. Dworkin (2000: 68).
18. Dworkin (2000: 146).

principle of abstraction, according to which 'An ideal distribution is possible only when people are legally free to act as they wish except so far as constraints on their freedom are necessary to protect security of person or property, or to correct certain imperfections in markets' (Dworkin, 2000: 148). Such a principle is plausible, Dworkin argues, because it implies a market process 'is fairer—that it provides a more genuinely equal distribution—when it offers more discriminating choices and is thus more sensitive to the discrete plans and preferences people in fact have' (Dworkin, 2000: 150-1). Thus, the principle explains why, for example, it is fairer to distribute land by an auction where individuals can bid for smaller rather than larger lots.

If the principle of abstraction is sound, resource egalitarians have a ready justification for the key assumption supporting the *ex ante* envy-eliminating insurance approach, namely that individuals themselves are entitled to decide which risks of misfortune to bear. To understand that justification, imagine a political community that is instead committed to the *ex post* equalising approach in the Dworkin's two examples, in which individuals face the same risk of succumbing to a disabling disease. Though the resulting distribution is envy-free, the principle of abstraction still condemns that community for restricting individuals' liberty to dispose of their resources as they see fit by imposing the equivalent of a particular insurance policy on each individual, regardless of her preferences. Just as a distributor who offers land only in plots large enough to build a stadium treats unfairly those individuals who want only enough land to build tennis courts, so an *ex post* equalising community treats its members comparably when it denies their entitlement to purchase a lower level of coverage.

If the community is to satisfy the principle of abstraction in such examples, it must recognise the importance of both comparative and non-comparative considerations in designing its distributive system. Thus, it should ensure not only that individuals' resource shares are equally valuable in the relevant sense, but also that the baseline system of property rights provides individuals with resources in as flexible a form as possible. When risks are equally shared, that latter consideration counts against forcing individuals to participate in any particular luck-sharing scheme, including one that secures *ex post* equality.

Instead it favours granting each individual an equally antecedently valuable entitlement to decide, on the basis of her own
attitudes to the risk of misfortune, which package of premium
and cover to purchase. Assuming such entitlements, we should
favour a corresponding understanding of the envy test. Just as we
adopt an *ex ante* test in cases involving gambling in the casino or
on the stock market, and allow that the test may be met despite
the fact some will prefer others' good fortune, we should also
favour an *ex ante* test in this case.

VI

If the appeal to abstraction succeeds, we have an immediate
argument for the insurance approach that rebuts any accusation
it compromises the resource egalitarian ideal for the sake of non-
egalitarian values. Instead the approach draws on considerations
relevant in specifying a resource egalitarian distribution in cases
where individuals differ only in their preferences, and then
extends those considerations to more complex cases involving
differential fortune. Some critics, however, will resist such an
extension, and argue it exaggerates the scope of the principle of
abstraction, and ambition-sensitivity more generally. Those
critics might accept that individuals are liable for decisions
about consumption and saving or leisure and labour, and also
agree that just inequalities may arise when fairly situated
gamblers bear risk in similar ways but enjoy differential option
luck. Nevertheless, they could still insist there are other cases
involving differential option luck where the availability of fair
insurance cannot justify unequal outcomes. Suppose, like
Otsuka, they claim these include cases where inequality is
unavoidable because fully compensatory insurance at reasonably
inexpensive rates is unavailable.

One reply to these claims questions whether the appeal to
unavoidability justifies combining a permissive attitude to
inequalities arising from conventional gambles with a restrictive
attitude to inequalities arising from certain natural lotteries. It is
quite natural to assume the difference in attitudes is defensible
because individuals, providing they are sufficiently wealthy,
voluntarily choose to expose themselves to reasonably avoidable
risks when gambling, and so have no complaint against any

resulting inequality. In contrast, when they face the chance of medical misfortune individuals have inescapable risks imposed upon them, and so may still complain if they eventually become disadvantaged.[19] This explanation appears plausible if we confine our concern to an individual's risk of *intrapersonal* disadvantage, or becoming worse off than she once was. For it may often be true that an unlucky gambler could have avoided such a risk simply by not venturing his stake. The focus of egalitarian concern, however, is *interpersonal* disadvantage, or being worse off than others. This distinction is important since it is false that if some individuals exercise their entitlement to participate in conventional lotteries others can still avoid the risk of disadvantage understood in the latter sense. Instead all they can do is either participate and risk both forms of disadvantage, or decline participation and risk only the latter. Since permitting gambling means the relevant form of disadvantage is not avoidable, the appeal to unavoidability fails to provide a stable defence of the critic's attitude to different types of option luck inequality. Given this instability, he should either abandon the criticism of unavoidable option luck inequalities, or pay the price of extending the criticism to conventional lotteries.

Even if the critic chooses the latter option, advocates of the principle of abstraction have an additional reason to doubt that the availability of reasonably inexpensive fully compensatory insurance is as important as the appeal to unavoidability supposes. As mentioned, when such insurance is available Otsuka assumes individuals are entitled to choose whether to purchase it or bear some risk of misfortune. If they decline purchase, and suffer bad option luck, then he grants that the resulting inequality is consistent with equality of resources. In the absence of such insurance, however, Otsuka insists that equality of resources requires establishing a scheme of transfers from more to less fortunate individuals that eradicates *ex post* envy, and so may under some conditions create mutually shared misery. The latter claim implies equality opposes granting individuals any entitlement to bear some risk of even greater misery by relinquishing some of the benefits of such a scheme in exchange for some corresponding relief from its burdens.

19. For a similar objection, see Macleod (1998: 99–100).

Proponents of the principle of abstraction, however, are likely to counter-assert that in both cases equality supports an entitlement to bear differing levels of risk. In doing so, they may acknowledge that in the latter case there is no reasonable alternative to accepting some risk of serious disadvantage. Nevertheless, they may also point out individuals can possess entitlements to make decisions for which there is no reasonable alternative, and that such decisions can modify their liabilities.[20] Suppose, for example, that each of us is virtually certain of an imminent painless death unless she chooses to take a drug that may restore us to good health but also carries a risk of causing a more lingering painful death. Even if we grant that there is no reasonable alternative to choosing the drug, many of us are convinced that the power to decide which risks to face rightfully belongs to each individual, and that they can be held responsible for what results. Moreover, we do not believe that in granting that entitlement we compromise equality in any sense about which we have reason to care. It is, of course, consistent to reject to such convictions, and insist that in granting the entitlement there is some respect in which equality is sacrificed. I find that response unconvincing in itself, however, and hope to have shown at least that it is not an unavoidable implication of equality of resources.[21]

REFERENCES

Dworkin, R., 2000, *Sovereign Virtue: the Theory and Practice of Equality*, (Cambridge, Massachusetts: Harvard University Press).

Dworkin, R., 2002, '*Sovereign Virtue* Revisited', *Ethics* 113, pp. 106–43.

Macleod, C., 1998: *Liberalism, Justice, and Markets* (Oxford: Clarendon Press).

Otsuka, M., 2002, 'Luck, Insurance, and Equality', *Ethics* 113, pp. 40–54.

Parfit, D., 2002, 'Equality or Priority?', in M. Clayton and A. Williams (eds.), *The Ideal of Equality* (Basingstoke: Palgrave).

Rawls, J., 1999, *A Theory of Justice*, Revised Edition (Cambridge, Massachusetts: The Belknap Press of Harvard University Press).

Rawls, J., 2001, *Justice as Fairness: A Restatement*, Erin Kelly (ed.) (Cambridge, Massachusetts: The Belknap Press of Harvard University Press).

20. Cp. Scanlon's remark that 'the fact that the only available alternative led to imminent, painful death ... would not, as Hume noted, free one from a promise to pay a surgeon.' See Scanlon (1998: 245).

21. For helpful discussion, I thank Paula Casal, Matthew Clayton, Cécile Fabre, Miriam Cohen-Chrystofidis, Mike Martin, Veronique Munoz-Dardé, Serena Olsaretti, Michael Otsuka, Thomas Pogge, Neema Sofaer, Larry Temkin, and audiences at the Cambridge Moral Sciences Club and London School of Economics.

EQUALITY, AMBITION AND INSURANCE

by Andrew Williams and Michael Otsuka

II—*Michael Otsuka*

ABSTRACT Inequality is intrinsically bad when and because it is unfair. It follows that the ideal of equality is not necessarily realised by a distribution of resources which is envy-free prior to the resolution of risks against which people have an equal opportunity to insure. Even if the upshot of such an *ex ante* envy-free distribution is just, it is not necessarily fair.

I

I nequality is intrinsically bad when and because it is unfair.[1] To say that it is intrinsically bad is to say that this badness inheres in the relational property of some being less well off than others.[2] Moreover, there is a presumption of unfairness whenever some are less well off than others through no choice of theirs.[3] These claims are not mere philosophical conceits. Rather they gain support from the attitudes and convictions of ordinary people. The phenomenon of 'survivor guilt', for example, is misdescribed as a feeling of guilt insofar as such a feeling implies a sense of culpability. Rather, survivor guilt is a feeling that it is not fair that one was spared over others who were no less worthy. 'Why me and not them?' It is worth pointing out that survivor guilt does not arise when everyone is spared. Nobody, for example, would feel survivor guilt if an asteroid whose impact

1. Here and in the next two sentences I follow Larry Temkin (2002: 129–30).

2. By contrast the badness of having less than enough to survive, while it often accompanies severe inequality, is in no way constituted by the relation of inequality. Rather it consists of the non-relational property of not having enough to live on in absolute terms.

3. In speaking of some being 'less well off' than others, I am being deliberately vague regarding the specific metric of equality. This phrase is meant to serve as a place-holder for one's preferred metric—whether it be welfare, material resources, capacities, some combination of the above, or something else. My own preference is for a welfarist metric (see Otsuka 2003: 25–9, 109–12). Therefore, whenever I condemn inequalities in material resources or mental and physical capacities as incompatible with the ideal of equality, they are, by my lights, ultimately incompatible when and because they generate inequalities in welfare.

would have obliterated all of humanity were unexpectedly to veer from a collision course with our planet. People would, however, feel survivor guilt if a meteor shower were randomly to kill their neighbours while sparing them. When some are randomly killed and others spared, this is bad not only because it is bad to be killed but also because it is unfair that some are killed and others spared. It would have been better in one respect because fairer, even though of course not all things considered better, if everyone had been killed.[4]

Not all inequalities are intrinsically bad because not all inequalities are unfair. The clearest case of inequalities which are not unfair are those which are the result of the differing free choices of different individuals where everyone had the opportunity to end up as well off as anyone else by making the same choices as that other person and the consequences of all choices could be predicted with certainty. Here luck plays no role. Imagine two people who are equal in all respects, including their personal resources and their rate of conversion of impersonal resources into welfare, except for the fact that their preferences regarding work and leisure differ.[5] They each begin their adult lives with equal allocations of impersonal resources, but the one person freely chooses to spend his days surfing and living off whatever food he can gather at his leisure from the plot of trees he owns, whereas the other freely chooses to spend his days cutting down his trees in order to construct a magnificent house and garden.[6] Although the net worth of their holdings will differ considerably over time, it is in no way unfair that the one ends up wealthier than the other, given the dependence of the difference in their resources upon nothing other than their free choices.

Even when we introduce inequalities which are due to luck, not all such differences are unfair. When we introduce the possibility of the 'option luck' of gambles, it will not always be possible to

4. See Temkin (2002: 154–5) for a defence of the claim that 'levelling down' in cases such as the above is better in one respect because fairer even though not all things considered better.

5. Following Ronald Dworkin, I define a person's 'impersonal resources' as 'his wealth and the other property he commands' and his 'personal resources' as 'his physical and mental health and ability—his general fitness and capacities' (Dworkin 2000: 322–3).

6. This example is modelled on Dworkin's example (2000: 83–5) of Adrian and Bruce.

end up as well off as another.[7] Hence, disadvantage relative to others will not always be avoidable.[8] You might choose to purchase a lottery ticket which turns out to be the sole winner. This jackpot might be sufficiently large that, whatever my choices, I will not end up as wealthy as you. Nevertheless, our inequality might be traceable to our free choices in a way that answers any charge of unfairness. In the remainder of this section I shall defend the following claim: *inequalities traceable to luck are not unfair if and only if they are the result of option luck arising from gambles when there is a reasonable alternative to gambling whose outcome is certain (or at least nearly so).*[9]

To provide an illustration, consider a case in which each of two individuals in a state of nature has a choice between a high-risk option and an option whose outcome is certain. Suppose that they each possess an equally large supply of seeds. Each person is faced with a choice between (i) planting crops on a plateau, which is sure to yield a harvest of food which will allow him to live at a modest level comfortably above subsistence, or (ii) planting crops in the hills, which is 50 per cent likely to yield just enough for bare, Spartan subsistence and 50 per cent likely to yield a rich abundance of food which will allow him to feast in splendid luxury. Whether one chooses to plant one's crops on the no-risk plateau or on the high-risk hills will depend on one's level of risk aversion, and reasonable people will differ with respect to this choice.[10] Here there don't seem to be any grounds for a complaint of unfairness if

7. 'Option luck', as Dworkin defines it, is 'a matter of how deliberate and calculated gambles turn out—whether someone gains or loses through accepting an isolated risk he or she should have anticipated and might have declined'. 'Brute luck', by contrast, is 'a matter of how risks fall out that are not in that sense deliberate gambles' (2000: 73).

8. Andrew Williams makes this point. References to Williams are to his article in this volume unless I indicate otherwise.

9. Here I assume that the individuals in question are equal in the following respects: they are initially equal in their personal and impersonal resources and their probability of becoming the victims of bad luck or the beneficiaries of good luck in the future. There is also at least rough overall parity even if not exact similarity in their rate of conversion of impersonal resources into welfare. These assumptions will hold throughout the rest of this article unless I indicate otherwise.

10. It might be an implication of differing levels of risk aversion that people have different rates of conversion of impersonal resources into welfare, with a more steeply diminishing marginal utility of resources in the case of the more risk-averse. Hence we may need to assume rough overall parity rather than exact similarity in their rate of conversion of resources into welfare.

resources differ because the one person chooses to plant on the plateau and the other in the hills. If planting in the hills yields abundance, the person who chose the plateau has no grounds for complaint that he's poorer than the person who chose the hills, since he chose not to pay the cost (of exposure to risk in this case) which was a necessary condition of abundance. In this respect, he is in no different a position from the surfer who is poorer than the property developer because he chose not to pay the cost (of toil and sweat in this case) which was a necessary condition of great wealth. If the hills yield nothing more than bare subsistence, the person who chose them has no grounds for complaint that he is poorer than the person who chose the plateau, since he had a reasonable alternative whose outcome was certain; nevertheless, he found it worth his while to expose himself to this risk for the prospect of great gain. Similar things can be said about a case in which both individuals choose to gamble by planting in the hills and the one person's crops yield an abundant harvest and the other's bare subsistence: they each had a reasonable alternative whose outcome was certain; nevertheless, they chose an option which carried with it the known risk of loss. It was in the nature of this gamble to which they had a reasonable alternative that they might end up less well off than others who made the same gamble, and they nevertheless proceeded with their eyes open.[11]

When, however, the only available options are gambles involving significant exposure to luck, we cannot rebut the charge that the inequalities which result from such gambles are unfair. To illustrate, assume first that each person's worldly possessions consist of a single seeded hill which he has inherited at birth. Assume further that each person's hill bears a 50–50 per cent chance of yielding subsistence or abundance and no pooling of risk is possible. Now this is a case in which people literally have no choice but to be exposed to a given 50–50 per cent chance of subsistence versus abundance. So this is a case in which any differences in resource holdings are unfair because purely a matter of brute luck. It doesn't make things any better if one

11. My explanation of the fairness of such gambles differs from Dworkin's (2000: 74–5), which appeals to the cost to others of one's purchases in an auction. My own scenario doesn't involve an auction and costs to others, which suggests that appeal to such costs is inessential to the case for the fairness of differences in resources which arise from gambles.

transforms this case into one which differs only insofar as everyone is now free to trade his hill in for another which also bears a 50–50 per cent chance of subsistence or abundance. Such a choice among equally risky alternatives does not transform brute luck into option luck in a manner which eliminates the unfairness of differential outcomes. The unfairness of outcomes dependent on luck might be mitigated somewhat, but it would not be eliminated, if the variety of luck-involving alternatives were increased, with some variation in the odds of and degree of good and bad luck, but in the continued absence of any reasonable option with an at least nearly certain outcome.

What is necessary and sufficient to eliminate the complaint of unfairness is, as I have proposed above, a reasonable alternative to gambling whose outcome is at least nearly certain. A necessary condition of such a reasonable alternative is that it be sufficiently good in absolute terms—one which guarantees those goods which one needs in order to lead a decent life. This is a necessary but not a sufficient condition of a reasonable alternative. For assume that we all have an option whose outcome is both known for certain and sufficiently good in absolute terms. This option might nevertheless be so clearly inferior to a luck-involving alternative to it that one could not reasonably opt for it. One such case would involve a certain outcome which, though sufficiently good in absolute terms, is trumped by an alternative which, though luck-involving, guarantees an outcome at least as good as the certain outcome. For example, we might all have two options, one which involves the certainty of precisely x units of impersonal resources which is sufficiently good in absolute terms and another which involves a gamble any outcome of which would yield *at least* x units of resources.[12] Even in other cases in which the luck-involving alternative to a certainty of x involves the possibility of something less than x, it might be unreasonable to decline such a gamble. For in such cases the downside of the gamble might be sufficiently bearable or improbable, and the

12. Kasper Lippert-Rasmussen (2001: 572–3) presents one such example which involves either (i) a certainty of 100 or (ii) a 95 per cent chance of 100 units and a 5 per cent chance of 200 units. He maintains that it would be unreasonable to decline this gamble even though the certain alternative to it is sufficiently good in absolute terms. He says of this case and more generally: 'There is something bad, from an egalitarian standpoint, about inequality resulting from gambles that it would be unreasonable to decline' (2001: 575).

expected gain sufficiently great, that all reasonable people would prefer this gamble to a certain outcome which guarantees a sufficient amount.[13]

I have maintained above that inequalities arising from gambles are unfair even though those gambles are chosen when there is literally no option apart from gambles. Here I would add that cases involving options whose outcomes are certain but which it would nevertheless be reasonable to reject in favour of gambling do not differ in moral significance from otherwise similar cases where the only options are gambles. The addition of unreasonable options does not make things any better from a moral point of view. In particular, options to gamble aren't rendered any fairer simply by virtue of the addition of options which guarantee certain outcomes which it would be reasonable for all to reject.

II

In *Sovereign Virtue*, Ronald Dworkin defends 'a conception of equality according to which ideal equality consists in circumstances in which people are equal ... in the resources at their command' (2000: 120). A distribution of such resources is equal only if it passes an 'envy test' which stipulates that nobody prefer anyone else's set of resources to his own (2000: 67, 139–41; see also 1996: 46–7). This test is to be applied to 'resources over an entire life' and not merely at a certain point in time. On this 'diachronic' approach, 'Our final aim is that an equal share of resources be devoted to the lives of each person' (2000: 83–5). Dworkin acknowledges that, given its diachronic reach, a government 'cannot wholly satisfy the envy test when people differ ... in productive ability' or otherwise 'have different good and bad luck'. In particular, he notes that compensation based on hypothetical insurance 'cannot wholly cure the disadvantage, so the envy test will continue to fail' (2000: 484, n. 28).[14]

13. Lippert-Rasmussen (2001: 574) presents such an example which involves either (i) a certainty of 100 units or (ii) a 5 per cent risk of 98 units and a 95 per cent chance of 200 units.

14. Similarly, Dworkin also writes that full satisfaction of 'the "envy" test' entails the equalisation of the 'resources that equally industrious people command over their lives ... no matter what native talents they are born with' and notes that hypothetical insurance payouts would not so equalise resources (2000: 340–1).

If, by contrast, one were to abandon the diachronic approach in favour of a narrower, synchronic application of the envy test *ex ante* the resolution of risks against which people purchase insurance, it would be possible to satisfy this test even when insurance payouts do not fully compensate for bad luck. For the sake of illustration, assume that people possess equal personal and impersonal resources at the beginning of their adult lives. Each, moreover, has the same known risk of suffering future harm and is given an opportunity to purchase whatever insurance against such harm the market provides.[15] In these circumstances, the resources of individuals—including any insurance policies they have purchased—will be envy-free at that point in time: nobody will prefer anybody else's overall set of resources to his own, since he could have purchased a set of resources identical to anybody else's but chose not to. Equality of resources would, on this account, be satisfied by virtue of this *ex ante* envy-free distribution of resources even if inequalities subsequently arise as a result of future harms which insurance does not fully compensate, thereby frustrating a wider diachronic test.[16]

In a departure from the diachronic version which features in *Sovereign Virtue*, Dworkin now endorses just such an *ex ante*, synchronic version of the envy test.[17] Is the best account of equality, as Dworkin now affirms, one which calls for nothing more than an envy-free distribution of resources prior to the resolution of risks against which people have an equal opportunity to insure? Building on the claims I have advanced in Section I, I shall argue that it is not. Such *ex ante* envy-

15. Dworkin refers to the circumstances described in this sentence as an 'equal opportunity to insure' (2000: 77).

16. In Otsuka (2002: 49–51), I propose but also criticise such an *ex ante* application of the envy test.

17. See Dworkin's reply to Otsuka (forthcoming) in Dworkin (forthcoming). Dworkin (ibid.) also advances the exegetical claim that he stressed such an *ex ante* application of the envy test throughout both his book (2000) and a more recent article (2002). The passages I have quoted in the first paragraph of this section show that this exegetical claim misrepresents his book. This claim also misrepresents his article, since there he states as 'fact' that 'the envy test would fail even after insurance indemnities had been paid' (2002: 121). I acknowledge that, in both 2000 (Ch. 9) and 2002, Dworkin endorses an *ex ante* approach to equality of resources. Yet in those two works he draws a contrast between such an *ex ante* approach to equality and the envy test, and hence this *ex ante* approach cannot be read in those works as an application of that test.

freedom might be sufficient to ensure that the ensuing pattern of distribution is fully just, but it is not sufficient to ensure the realisation of the ideal of equality.[18]

III

I shall begin with an example involving Dworkin's desert island auction in which shipwreck survivors employ clamshells as money with which to bid on the island's natural resources.[19] Suppose that some prefer to enter the auction with a guaranteed 1,000 clamshells, which is the average number. Others prefer the prospects of bidding with a higher-than-average number of clamshells at the risk of ending up with a lower-than-average number. Perhaps they would like to run a 50–50 per cent gamble of starting off with either 1,500 or 500 clamshells. Now suppose that the auctioneer can either (i) give everyone 1,000 clamshells or (ii) provide everyone with a 50–50 per cent chance of 500 or 1,500 clamshells. Suppose further that it is impossible, either through insurance or gambles, to transform one's initial allocation of clamshells once the auctioneer has distributed them. Even if the auctioneer chooses (ii), envy freedom will be realised *ex ante* the resolution of risks, since everyone will face the same odds of the same gains and losses. Nevertheless it would be inegalitarian of the auctioneer irrevocably to impose (ii) even if some would prefer the uncertain prospect of a greater-than-equal share to the certainty of an equal share. For this would be to impose on everyone a distribution in which, through no choice of anyone's, some are three times wealthier than others. Such inequalities would be a matter of brute luck. In these circumstances any plausible conception of equality would call for an equal distribution of clamshells.[20]

---

18. I have defended these points once before in Otsuka (2002). In response to Williams's insightful objections to that article, I have been prompted to revisit, elaborate, and offer new arguments on behalf of these points here.

19. See Dworkin (2000: 65–71) for a description of the auction. My example builds on an example which I first presented in Otsuka (2002: 51) and which Williams criticises.

20. Perhaps if, as Williams supposes, everyone prefers an unequal distribution to an equal distribution, then the auctioneer ought to divide clamshells unequally. I would describe this as a justifiable Pareto-departure from equality rather than consistent with equality.

If, to consider a second scenario, any individual could costlessly transform the certainty of 1,000 clamshells into a 50–50 per cent chance of 500 or 1,500 clamshells, and costlessly transform a 50–50 per cent chance of 500 or 1,500 clamshells into the certainty of 1,000 clamshells, then it would, by contrast, be a matter of indifference whether or not the auctioneer opts for (i) or (ii). Whichever the auctioneer chooses, it would be open to everyone to take a 50–50 per cent gamble of ending up with either 500 or 1,500 clamshells or to opt for the reasonable, risk-free alternative of the certainty of 1,000 clamshells. This would be akin to the case discussed in Section I, which is unobjectionable from an egalitarian point of view, in which each has the option either to plant crops on the risk-free plateau or to take the gamble of planting crops in the hills.

But now suppose that it would be possible, but only at some cost, for any individual either to transform the certainty of 1,000 clamshells to a 50–50 per cent chance of 500 or 1,500 clamshells, or vice versa. Casinos are available to transform the former to the latter and insurance policies to transform the latter to the former. But in each case one would need to pay a transaction cost in order to effect this transformation.[21] If the transaction cost were negligible, then this case would differ insignificantly from the second scenario. But the more substantial this cost becomes, the more like the first scenario this becomes. And in the first scenario, equality calls for an equal division of clamshells. Hence there is an egalitarian presumption in favour of an equal division of clamshells except in those cases in which an unequal distribution can be transformed into an equal distribution at little or no cost. The moral of this story is that *ex ante* envy-freedom conjoined with an equal opportunity to insure against unequal holdings will not always be sufficient to realise the ideal of equality.

---

21. In arguing against the auctioneer's imposing an unequal distribution, Williams assumes that it would be costly to transform an unequal distribution into an equal distribution via insurance but non-costly to transform an equal distribution into an unequal one via gambling. I don't see any grounds for assuming such asymmetry. Presumably, insurance schemes are costly to administer and nobody will sell insurance policies if they can't cover these costs and earn a bit of profit. Likewise, lotteries are costly to administer, and nobody will sell lottery tickets if they can't cover these costs and earn a bit of profit.

IV

To cast further doubt on Dworkin's *ex ante* account of equality, I shall now consider an example in which people who are initially identical in their personal and impersonal resources also have the same greater than zero but less than one hundred per cent chance of developing a horrible mental illness later on. They are provided with an equal opportunity to insure against such illness but the only available insurance is very expensive and would cover nothing more than a costly but minimally effective treatment which succeeds in making the effects of this illness only very slightly less horrible.[22] Here people possess an equal opportunity to insure against brute bad luck but neither that insurance nor anything else provides them with a reasonable option whose outcome is at least nearly certain. It follows from what I have claimed in Section I that such an equal opportunity to insure is insufficient to eliminate the unfairness of inequality in these circumstances. Only a brutally levelling policy which renders everyone else as badly off as those who develop the illness would eliminate such unfairness since only such a policy would ensure that nobody ends up, as luck would have it, with resources over a lifetime which are radically inferior to those of others.

Williams follows Dworkin (2000: 149–52) in maintaining that a distribution of resources is fairer insofar as it is more sensitive to the ambitions of individuals as captured by their actual plans and preferences. He also notes that allowing people to decide whether or not to purchase insurance against the illness described above would be more ambition-sensitive than a levelling policy. I grant that the levelling policy would be less ambition-sensitive than the provision of an option to insure, but I deny that the decrease in ambition-sensitivity corresponds to any decrease in fairness in this case. This is because the levelling policy does not discriminate against the preferences of some and in favour of the preferences of others. Everyone would *ex ante* prefer, and to a roughly equal degree, an option to insure to the levelling policy. Hence this case differs from Dworkin's case (2000: 67) to which Williams refers in which the auctioneer unfairly transforms a diverse variety of

22. Here I describe a case which I originally presented in Otsuka (2002: 50).

resources into nothing but plover's eggs and claret which one islander hates and the others love.

Note, moreover, that Dworkin is willing, in other cases, to sacrifice ambition-sensitivity for the sake of realising a fairer because more endowment-insensitive distribution of resources, by which I roughly mean a distribution in which differences in people's resources are not traceable to unchosen differences in their personal resources. Consider a case in which people have initially equal holdings of impersonal resources yet differ in their initial personal resources and their risk of becoming incapacitated or ill in the future. Suppose that each person's initial endowment of personal resources and risk of future harm is publicly known and that everyone is granted complete freedom to purchase, insofar as his budget will allow, whatever insurance policies the market offers. Such purchases would be guided by each person's actual plans and preferences and made in the light of knowledge shared by all of his initial endowment of personal resources and risk of suffering future harm. Why isn't each person's initially equal sum of impersonal resources with which to purchase insurance sufficient to realise the ideal of equality in this scenario? Presumably Dworkin would condemn such a scenario as inconsistent with the ideal of equality because it would give rise to too endowment-sensitive a distribution. Given their unequal vulnerability to risk and unequal initial endowment of personal resources, individuals would have manifestly unequal opportunities to insure in these circumstances and a highly unequal and endowment-sensitive distribution would be likely to arise. Dworkin would endorse a different and more equal distribution which would follow from the universal imposition of whichever insurance policy would be chosen by a hypothetical individual who is average in all respects, including his preferences, initial endowment of personal resources, and vulnerability to risks.[23] Since this latter distribution would be less ambition-sensitive than one which arises as the result of the exercise by actual people of their

23. The averaging assumption isn't necessarily merely an administrative convenience. The average person can't always even in principle be replaced, without generating theoretical difficulties, by actual individuals who choose insurance policies for themselves in light of their actual preferences when placed behind a veil which deprives them of knowledge of their actual endowment of personal resources and

unequal opportunities to purchase insurance, Dworkin man-
ifests a willingness to sacrifice ambition-sensitivity for the sake
of the greater endowment-insensitivity of a distribution
modelled on the insurance preferences of the hypothetical
average person.[24]

But why stop at hypothetical insurance? Why not go further to
secure greater endowment-insensitivity when the only insurance it
would be sensible for the hypothetical average person to purchase
would provide almost nothing by way of compensation for illness
or disability?[25] Why not go on, in this case, to impose a more
radically levelling distribution than that which the hypothetical
average person would have chosen? One who endorses the
imposition of hypothetical insurance is already willing to sacrifice
ambition-sensitivity for the sake of endowment-insensitivity.
How can such a person be so confident that hypothetical
insurance always achieves enough endowment-insensitivity, even
in the case in which it would be sensible to purchase nothing
more than minimally effective insurance which hardly mitigates
the rise of great inequality in personal resources? Perhaps in this
case a greater sacrifice of ambition-sensitivity for the sake of
endowment-insensitivity would be necessary in order to realise
the ideal of equality.

A defender of Dworkin might respond that we ought to stop
at hypothetical insurance because it picks out that distribution
which we ought all things considered to realise as a matter of
justice—nothing more and nothing less. In the next section, I
shall offer the following rebuttal to this claim: I might agree
that even in these circumstances the distribution which is
modelled on the hypothetical average person's choice of
minimally compensating insurance is a uniquely just distribu-

probability of future harm. Such difficulties arise because a person's actual
preferences might have been adaptively shaped by his personal resources in such a
manner as to render problematic those choices from behind the veil which are
informed by these preferences. (For discussions of these difficulties, see Dworkin
2000: 78 and Williams 2002.)

24. W. Thomas Porter (2003) nicely exposes the depth of the theoretical conflict
between Dworkin's endorsement of sensitivity to plans and preferences and his
imposition of a distribution dictated by the insurance policy which the average person
would purchase.

25. Recall the ineffective nature of insurance against mental illness in the case I
discuss at the outset of this section.

tion.[26] But this would be to say that justice condemns the full realisation of the ideal of equality—i.e., that justice calls for the sacrifice of a form of fairness which is genuinely valuable. We cannot assume that what we ought, from the standpoint of justice, to do will fully realise all values.

V

Returning to the case I presented at the outset of the previous section, I have argued elsewhere that an *ex ante* equal opportunity to purchase expensive and ineffectual insurance against a horrible, untreatable illness would not be sufficient for the following reason fully to realise the ideal of equality: if it were sufficient, then we would not be entitled to say that a subsequent medical breakthrough which provides an inexpensive miracle cure would allow for a fuller realisation of equality; but surely we are entitled to say this.[27] Williams offers the following response on Dworkin's behalf:

> Assuming that the miracle cure's initial unavailability was beyond human control, [resource egalitarians such as Dworkin] can echo Rawls's response to the natural distribution. Just as Rawls claims there is a sense in which a natural distribution where all are born sighted is no more just than one where only some are sighted, they might claim that equality of resources implies that the discovery of the miracle cure does not necessarily make a society more just in the deontic sense [according to which unalterable facts are neither just nor unjust]. Whether the society is more or less just depends not on the absence or availability of the cure but rather on its response to such facts, and in particular their likely effects on the operation of a fair insurance market.

Williams's reply is undermined by his neglect of the distinction between justice and equality which I draw during the course of my discussion of this example.[28] When we attend to this

---

26. I am sympathetic to Peter Vallentyne's argument (2002: 543–9) that *ex ante* equality involving a rationally selective purchase of insurance against brute bad luck might be superior, from the standpoint of justice, to the elimination of all brute luck over people's lifetimes because the latter might involve too great a sacrifice of everyone's expected welfare.

27. Here I summarise an argument which I made in Otsuka (2002: 50–1). Williams refers to this argument as my 'first argument'.

28. I confess that I am guilty of blurring this distinction when I speak of 'egalitarian justice' in Otsuka (2002: 41–2).

distinction, it will become clear that, whether or not Williams's claim about the attainability of justice is true, no analogous claim holds true in the case of equality.

What is the difference between justice and equality? I understand a just state of affairs to be a feasible state of affairs in which a plurality of distinct and potentially conflicting values are in best balance relative to other feasible combinations, provided that this balance is good enough, where these values encompass such things as equality, utility, liberty, the satisfaction of needs, and respect for individuals as ends in themselves rather than mere means.[29] Justice is therefore a second-order property of best and good enough balance among first-order values. This balancing is necessitated by the fact that it is impossible fully to realise all first-order values simultaneously given the circumstances in which human beings find themselves. Trade-offs must be made and a judicious balance struck. Within the feasible set of available combinations of these values, a combination might strike a balance which is no less good than any other combination. That combination is just, provided that it is good enough. I say that a just state of affairs must involve a combination which is 'good enough' because I do not want to rule out the possibility that even the best available combination of first-order values involves too great a sacrifice, or otherwise contains too little, of one or more first-order values to qualify as just. Human circumstances might be so horrible that even the best available combination of values is not good enough to be dignified by the name 'justice'.

I did not, however, claim in (2002) that the horrible mental illness against which there is no adequate insurance was a case in which justice is impossible to realise. Rather, I wrote:

> Even when ... insurance provides hardly any protection against severe brute bad luck, justice might nevertheless call for that distribution which arises when each is given an equal opportunity to insure rather than a leveling-down distribution which would realize equality of resources. ...[But] this would be because justice encompasses a plurality of potentially conflicting values and principles, of which distributive equality is only one among others, none of which is

29. Here I develop an account of justice which I first sketched in Otsuka (2002: 47–8, 51).

lexically prior. An equal opportunity to insure might plausibly be regarded as that policy which strikes the proper balance between the competing considerations, among others, of distributive equality and utility. But it cannot always plausibly be regarded as that policy which realizes distributive equality considered on its own rather than in combination with the full range of values and principles which jointly and disharmoniously constitute the more encompassing virtue of justice. (2002: 51)

When it comes to a given first-order value whose proper balance with conflicting first-order values determines a just state of affairs, an ideally best state of affairs with respect to that first-order value might be impossible to realise. This holds true irrespective of what we might be inclined to say about the attainability of justice itself.

One can provide concrete examples of first-order values whose full realisation is impossible. First consider, by way of illustration, the satisfaction of needs, which is among the first-order values which figure in a determination of what is just. Nourishment is one such need. Yet the elimination of malnutrition is a value irrespective of whether this is possible. The value did not emerge only after we discovered the means to eliminate malnutrition. Such elimination was a good thing even before we learned how to meet our nutritional needs fully. It was, in fact, the badness of malnutrition which prompted us to try to eliminate it. Moreover, it would have been bad even if we had not discovered and knew that we would never discover a means of eliminating it. Equality is another first-order value which figures in a determination of what is just. As in the case of needs, it might be impossible fully to realise the value of equality. Inequalities might be intrinsically bad because unfair even if this unfairness is ineliminable. Return to the case of the meteor shower which randomly kills some and spares others. Such inequality is bad because unfair even if unavoidable and equality therefore a value in this case even if impossible to realise. The unfairness of some being killed and others spared is not contingent on the possibility that the survivors be killed too, thus eliminating the inequality. It would be unfair if some were killed and others spared even if—perhaps especially if—the survivors were rendered immune from premature death by mysterious rays which these meteors emit.

Justice might be realised in a world in which it is impossible to eliminate malnutrition. But it does not follow that unavoidable malnutrition in such a world is not bad and that the ideal of needs-satisfaction has been realised in that world too. Likewise, justice might be realised in a world in which it is impossible to eliminate inequality. But it does not follow that unavoidable inequality in such a world is fair and that the ideal of equality has been realised too.[30]

REFERENCES

Dworkin, R., 1996, 'Do Liberty and Equality Conflict?', in P. Barker (ed.), *Living As Equals* (Oxford: Oxford University Press) pp. 39–57.

Dworkin, R., 2000, *Sovereign Virtue: the Theory and Practice of Equality* (Cambridge, Massachusetts: Harvard University Press).

Dworkin, R., 2002, 'Sovereign Virtue Revisited', *Ethics* 113, pp. 106–43.

Dworkin, R. (forthcoming): 'Reply to Critics', in J. Burley (ed.), *Dworkin and His Critics* (Oxford: Blackwell).

Lippert-Rasmussen, K., 2001, 'Egalitarianism, Option Luck, and Responsibility', *Ethics* 111, pp. 548–79.

Otsuka, M., 2002, 'Luck, Insurance, and Equality', *Ethics* 113, pp. 40–54.

Otsuka, M., 2003, *Libertarianism without Inequality* (Oxford: Oxford University Press).

Otsuka, M. (forthcoming): 'Liberty, Equality, Envy, and Abstraction', in J. Burley (ed.), *Dworkin and His Critics* (Oxford: Blackwell).

Porter, W. T., 2003, 'Sensitivity, Choice, Luck and Insurance: a Reading of Ronald Dworkin's Egalitarianism', M.Phil. thesis, University of London.

Temkin, L., 2002, 'Equality, Priority, and the Levelling Down Objection', in M. Clayton and A. Williams (eds.), *The Ideal of Equality* (Basingstoke: Palgrave), pp. 126–61.

Vallentyne, P., 2002, 'Brute Luck, Option Luck, and Equality of Initial Opportunities', *Ethics* 112, pp. 529–57.

Williams, A., 2002, 'Dworkin on Capability', *Ethics* 113, pp. 23–39.

30. I would like to thank G. A. Cohen, Alon Harel, Kasper Lippert-Rasmussen, Véronique Munoz-Dardé, Peter Vallentyne, Andrew Williams, and Jonathan Wolff for their comments.

ON EPISTEMIC ENTITLEMENT

By Crispin Wright and Martin Davies

I—*Crispin Wright*

WARRANT FOR NOTHING
(AND FOUNDATIONS FOR FREE)?

My *life* consists in my being content to accept many things
(Wittgenstein *On Certainty* §344)

ABSTRACT   Two kinds of epistemological sceptical paradox are reviewed and a shared assumption, that warrant to accept a proposition has to be the same thing as having evidence for its truth, is noted. 'Entitlement', as used here, denotes a kind of rational warrant that counter-exemplifies that identification.[1] The paper pursues the thought that there are various kinds of entitlement and explores the possibility that the sceptical paradoxes might receive a uniform solution if entitlement can be made to reach sufficiently far. Three kinds of entitlement are characterised and given *prima facie* support, and a fourth is canvassed. Certain foreseeable limitations of the suggested anti-sceptical strategy are noted. The discussion is grounded, overall, in a conception of the sceptical paradoxes not as directly challenging our having any warrant for large classes of our beliefs but as crises of intellectual conscience for one who wants to claim that we do.[2]

I

Two Kinds of Sceptical Paradox. Call a proposition a *cornerstone* for a given region of thought just in case it

---

1. The term is already in use in contemporary epistemology in a number of contrastive senses. My use of it contrasts in particular—though it also has points of contact—with that of Tyler Burge in a number of important recent articles (see e.g. Burge [1993]). Such overlap in terminology is unfortunate but, given that English has only so many expressions for norms of doxastic acceptance, all of which are already in use with multiple connotations, it is too late to hope to avoid it.

2. The paper originates in ideas that go back to my Henriette Hertz British Academy lecture (Wright [1985]) which shared the root idea that an attractive response to scepticism might draw on the possibility of non-evidential warrant. The major strategic contrast with the present proposals is in how such warrant is conceived as possible. In the lecture, I proposed that at least some 'cornerstones' might be regarded as defective in factual content and that acceptance of them might accordingly be freed from the requirements of evidence that I took to be characteristic of the factual. In the present discussion, non-factuality is no longer assigned a role in making a case that rational acceptance need not be evidence-based.

would follow from a lack of warrant for it that one could not rationally claim warrant for *any* belief in the region. The best— most challenging, most interesting—sceptical paradoxes work in two steps: by (i) making a case that a certain proposition (or restricted type of proposition) that we characteristically accept is indeed such a cornerstone for a much wider class of beliefs, and then (ii) arguing that we have no warrant for it.

The 'best' such paradoxes are, I think, of essentially two kinds, though they each allow of minor variations of detail. The first— what we may call *Cartesian*—makes a case that it is a cornerstone for a large class of our beliefs that we are not cognitively disabled or detached from reality in a certain way—the scenarios of a persistent coherent dream or hallucination, persistent deception by a *malin génie*, the envatment of one's disembodied brain, and 'The Matrix' are examples of such detachment—and then argues that we have no warrant to discount the scenario in question. So the upshot is a challenge to our possession of warrant for any of the large class of dependent beliefs in question.

There are various ways a Cartesian sceptical argument may support its two ingredient lemmas. The details cannot concern us now—otherwise we won't get to the issues I want to get to. But we do need to register a point about how the second lemma—that we have no warrant to discount the relevant scenario— is usually supported. Suppose I do have warrant to discount the suggestion that I am right now in the midst of a sustained and coherent dream? Well, if I have such a warrant, how did I get it? The proposition that I am not right now suffering such a dream is, broadly speaking, an empirical one, so any warrant I have for it must presumably consist in empirical evidence, acquired by executing some appropriate empirical procedure. However—the sceptical argument says—evidence acquired as the result of an empirical procedure cannot rationally be regarded as any stronger than one's independent grounds for supposing that the procedure in question has been executed properly. For instance, measurement-based evidence to regard the edge of my desk as near enough 1.75 metres long cannot rationally be regarded as any stronger than my independent warrant to suppose that the measuring procedure was carried out to appropriate tolerances, using a properly calibrated tape measure, and the results carefully observed, etc.

A fortiori, then, evidence for the proposition that I am not now dreaming, acquired as a result of executing some appropriate empirical procedure, cannot rationally be regarded as any stronger than my independent warrant for thinking that the relevant procedure was properly executed, and hence for thinking that it was executed *at all*—ergo: that I did not merely dream its execution! So it appears that my acquiring a warrant by empirical means for the proposition that I am not now dreaming requires that I *already have* a warrant for that same proposition. So I cannot ever acquire such a warrant (for the first time.)

No doubt that reasoning is very discussible. The only point I want to call to your attention at this stage is that—strictly—its conclusion falls short of the needed sceptical lemma. The conclusion is that I can't get evidence to discount the supposition that I'm right now in the midst of a sustained and coherent dream. The needed lemma is that I *don't have* any warrant to discount that supposition. The lacuna will matter if it's possible to have warrant (for an empirical proposition) which does not consist in the acquisition of empirical evidence. I conjecture that this lacuna will be left unfilled by all likely ways of arguing that a Cartesian sceptical scenario cannot warrantedly be discounted.

The second principal genre of (interesting) sceptical paradox is typified by Hume's inductive scepticism. Here there is no play with a scenario of cognitive disablement or dislocation. Rather, the sceptical argument makes a case that our epistemic procedures involve a vicious circle. The challenge posed by inductive scepticism, in the simplest case, is to show that and why a certain kind of ampliative inference is rational—one which passes from finitely many observed examples of (and no observed counterexamples to) a natural pattern to the projection that the pattern extends indefinitely to unobserved cases. The problem is sometimes presented (though not actually by Hume[3]) as that of finding supplementary premises to render the type of inference in question *deductively* valid, and then to explain how such premises

---

3. Hume merely challenges his reader:
    'But if you insist that the inference is made by a chain of reasoning, I desire you to produce that reasoning' (*An Enquiry Concerning Human Understanding*, Section 4, Part 2, 29).

might be justified. This, though, misrepresents matters. There is nothing general which we actually believe that will serve to transform an ampliative inductive inference into a deductively valid one. Consider—forgive the usual simple-minded schema— the inference from 'All observed Fs are G' to 'All Fs are G'. The belief that this is—in the right kind of context, and subject to the appropriate controls—a reasonable inference is based on the thesis (what used to be called the Uniformity of Nature) that the world abounds in natural regularities. But that thesis does not provide a premise which, conjoined with the datum that all observed Fs are G, will entail the conclusion that all Fs are G. That argument is *still* deductively invalid. The role of the Uniformity Thesis is rather to provide an *informational setting* in which the observed pattern of co-occurrence between Fs and Gs defeasibly warrants generalisation. The contention of the inductive sceptic is then that there is an implicit circularity in our procedures. Without the collateral information of the Uniformity Thesis, no inductive inference, even the very simplest, is reasonable. But the only way in which the Uniformity Thesis might itself be justified is by inductive inference. Or so the sceptical thought runs.

It's not often observed that this pattern of scepticism generalises—that essentially this form of argument may be put to the service of scepticism about each of, for example, the material world, other minds and the past. Let P be any proposition purporting to express a routine observation about my local perceptible environment—say: that I have two hands— and consider the following trinity:

I   My current experience is in all respects as if P
II   P
III   There is a material world

Here, the sceptical thought is, proposition I typifies the best possible evidence anyone can have for P—evidence, plausibly, such that if it and its ilk are not sufficient evidence for claims about the material world, then nothing is—and yet, as in the case of induction, movement from I to II is ampliative: the inference is a defeasible one. Moreover, so the sceptical thought contends, the evidential bearing of I on II is not unconditional: the warrant provided by I for II is, as I've expressed the matter elsewhere, *information-dependent.*[4] And paramount among the pieces of information that have to be in place in order for the move from I to II to be warranted is III: that there is a material world in the first place (whose characteristics, at least at the level of description typified by P, are representable, and normally successfully represented, in sense experience.) But the only foreseeable way of acquiring a warrant for III, so the argument goes, would be to infer it from a warranted belief of the kind typified by P. So, again, there is a vicious circle: it is if only I can get a warrant for a specific proposition about it that I can acquire a warranted belief that there is a material world, yet it is only if the latter is already warranted and part of my collateral information that I can draw on my experience to provide warrant for specific beliefs about it.

It's obvious enough that the same pattern of sceptical argument—I'll call it the I-II-III argument—can be enveloped around each of

I	(Where X is distinct from oneself) X's behaviour and physical condition are in all respects as if she was in mental state M	I	It seems to me that I remember it being the case that P yesterday
II	X in mental state M	II	It was the case that P yesterday
III	There are minds besides my own	III	The world did not come into being today replete with apparent traces of a more extended history

And, although the case does not schematise quite so succinctly, the paradox also afflicts so-called *abductive* inference, or inference to the best explanation (when realistically conceived). Roughly, inferring from a body of attested empirical generalisations to a theory which purportedly depicts the underlying causes of their holding is justified, it will be contended, only in the context of the collateral information that there is an appropriate underlying realm of causes in the first place—yet that is something which in turn could only be known by inference from prior knowledge of the truth of particular such theories.

4. Wright [2002].

To generalise. A version of this paradox will be available whenever we are persuadable (at least temporarily) that the ultimate justification for one kind of claim—a type-II proposition—rests upon ampliative inference from information of another sort—type-I propositions. In any such case the warrantability of the inference will arguably depend upon the presupposition that there is indeed a tract of reality suitable to confer truth on type-II propositions in the first place, a domain whose details are, in the best case, broadly reflected in type-I information. *A fortiori*, it will depend on the first component of that: that a domain of fact which type-II propositions are distinctively apt to describe so much as exists. That is the relevant type-III proposition—a proposition of sufficient generality to be entailed by any type-II proposition. The schematic form of the resulting sceptical argument is then given by these five claims:

(i)   Type-II propositions can only be justified on the evidence of (by ampliative inference from) type-I propositions.

(ii) The evidence provided by type-I propositions for type-II propositions is information-dependent, requiring (among other things) collateral warrant for a type-III proposition.

(iii) So: type-III propositions cannot be warranted by transmission of evidence provided by type-I propositions for type-II propositions across a type-II to type-III entailment—rather it's only if one already has warrant for the type-III proposition that any type-II propositions can be justified in the first place.

(iv) Type-III propositions cannot be warranted any other way.

If all four propositions are accepted, then type-III propositions are cornerstones for type-II propositions (thesis ii) which cannot themselves be warranted (theses iii and iv). So

(v)   There is no warrant for any type-II proposition.

No doubt the justificational architecture postulated by the I-II-III argument is contestable in some of its local applications but there seems to be no hope whatever for the thought that it might successfully be contested *everywhere*. The relevant structure seems to be implicit in the very idea of *cognitive locality*.

Cognitive locality is the circumstance that only a proper subset of the kinds of states of affairs which we are capable of conceptualising is directly available, at any given stage in our lives, to our awareness. So knowledge of, or warranted opinion concerning the remainder must ultimately be based on defeasible inference from materials of which we are so aware. As we observed, type-III propositions are implicitly in play whenever our best justification for the truth of propositions of one kind— propositions of one distinctive type of subject matter—consists in the assembly of information about something else. That's the architecture which I-II-III scepticism attempts to impose, with varying degrees of plausibility, on the justification of propositions about the material world, about the past, about other minds and on inductive justification. And wherever such is indeed the justificational architecture, it will be plausible that a type-III proposition will form part of the informational setting presupposed in order for the relevant transitions to rank as warranted. Putting the matter in the most abstract form: suppose it granted that the best justification we can have for a certain kind of proposition—P-propositions—consists in information of another kind—Q-propositions—such that no finite (consistent) set of Q-propositions entails any P-proposition.[5] The use of P-propositions in accordance with this conception will then carry a double commitment: a commitment to there being true P-propositions—and hence truth-conferring states of affairs for them—at all, and a commitment to a reliable connection between the obtaining of such truth-conferrers and the truth of finite batches of appropriate Q-propositions. That is the broad shape of the commitment which surfaces in the specific instances:

> that there is a material world, broadly in keeping with the way in which sense experience represents it;
>
> that other people have minds, whose states are broadly in keeping with the way they behave;
>
> that the world has an ancient history, broadly in keeping with presently available traces and apparent memories;
>
> that there are laws of nature, broadly manifest in finitely observable regularities,

5. This way of putting the point requires, if it is to be fully general, that infinite conjunctions of Q-propositions do not count as Q-propositions.

where each first conjunct presents a type-III proposition, while the second conjunct effects the connection necessary for the favoured kind of evidence to have the force which we customarily attach to it.

Philosophers may argue about, and be more or less generous concerning, what should be regarded as cognitively local. Descartes, at least for the purposes of the project of the *Meditations*, was relatively miserly, restricting the cognitively local to what was available to his reason and to certain forms of psychological self-knowledge. Twentieth century direct realism, by contrast, in the spirit that informs John McDowell's *Mind and World* and Hilary Putnam's Dewey Lectures,[6] has been much more generous. But however generous one wants to be, a bound will surely have to be placed on cognitive locality at some point. Concerning what lies beyond it, our options will then be to regard it either as lying beyond our ken altogether, or as accessible to us only via the kind of inferential routine which the I-II-III argument purports to show is viciously circular.

Notice once again, however, that the thrust of this second genre of sceptical argument is that an evidential justification for the cornerstone—the type-III proposition—cannot be *acquired*: the claim is that in order to arrive at such a justification, one would have first to accomplish a process of justification (for a type-II proposition) which would presuppose it. So again there is a lacuna between the most that is strictly accomplished by the sceptical argument—that evidence for a cornerstone cannot be acquired by any foreseeable justificatory process—and the claim, that we have no warrant for it, which is actually what is needed to elicit the catastrophic conclusion (that there is no warrant for any belief of the type-II in question).

If I am right that the two distinguished—Cartesian and Humean—forms of sceptical argument between them capture, in essentials, all that we have to worry about, then their common lacuna suggests a common strategy of response—what I will call the *unified strategy*. Suppose there is a type of rational warrant which one does not have to *do any specific evidential work* to earn: better, a type of rational warrant whose possession does not require the existence of evidence—in the broadest sense,

6. Putnam [1994].

encompassing both *a priori* and empirical considerations—for the truth of the warranted proposition. Call it *entitlement*. If I am entitled to accept P, then my doing so is beyond rational reproach even though I can point to no cognitive accomplishment in my life, whether empirical or *a priori*, inferential or non-inferential, whose upshot could reasonably be contended to be that I had come to know that P, or had succeeded in getting evidence justifying P. The sceptical arguments purport to show that the rejection of Cartesian scenarios, and the acceptance of type-III propositions, are both beyond warrant by such investigative accomplishment. If they were nevertheless entitlements, warranted without evidence—whether by my own work, or that of experts in my community, or that of my precursors— no sceptical conclusions need automatically follow. I would be entitled to discount the idea that my experience might be no more than a sustained lucid dream, and entitled to accept that there is a material world just as we ordinarily suppose. The cornerstones could warrantedly remain in place, even though it was conceded that our right to leave them there was unsupported by evidence for their truth. And, that being so, it wouldn't matter if, just as the sceptical arguments contend, they are indeed cornerstones whose removal would be catastrophic.

The suggestion merely that there are such things as entitlements in this general sense—much less that they extend far enough to service the serious anti-sceptical mission called for by the unified strategy—may seem like wishful thinking. Still, my purpose here is to take it seriously, though a discussion on the present scale is bound to leave many loose ends. In what follows I'll try merely to outline a *prima facie* case for a number of different possible species of entitlement and review some of the salient obstacles and further issues. The overall upshot will be, I believe, a prospect of at least some partial successes, and a clearer sense of what it might take to execute the unified strategy right across the board and of its foreseeable limitations.

II

Belief and Acceptance. An issue that needs to be considered immediately is what exactly entitlement would be a warrant to *do*. It doesn't just go without saying that it would be warrant to *believe* the proposition in question—there are issues about how 'belief' should be understood. One reason why it is easy to overlook the lacuna in the sceptical arguments is because it can seem impossible to understand how it can be rational to believe a proposition for which one has *absolutely no evidence*, whether empirical or *a priori*. That a warrant to believe that *someone else* is not currently undergoing a sustained lucid dream would have to be evidence-based seems absolutely compelling; how can it make a difference if the subject involved is oneself? Likewise, that it takes evidence to provide warrant for believing a particular (type-II) proposition about the material world seems incontestable—how can it make a difference if one simply escalates the generality of what is believed (up to a type-III proposition)? The idea of a non-evidential warrant to *believe* a proposition can easily impress as a kind of conceptual solecism.

I do not myself know whether the notion of belief *is* actually so tightly evidentially controlled as to underwrite that impression. But at this stage of our discussion, I think the best tactic with the point is to grant it and see where that leads. Let's accordingly concede that entitlement will be best conceived as something other than a kind of warrant to believe. What else could it be? What is required is that there is a mode, or modes, of *acceptance* of a proposition which can be rational but which are not tantamount to believing it in the conceded central sense of 'belief'.

It is plausible that we do have a notion—in fact a variety of notions—of this kind. We register such modes of acceptance in our ordinary thought and talk when we speak of someone as, in a particular situation, *acting on the assumption* that P—as, for example, when one's manner of driving a car may be structured by the assumption that every other motorist one comes across is a dangerous fool—or as *taking it for granted* that P, as when the protagonists in a court of law are required to take it for granted that the prisoner is innocent until proved guilty, no matter what they actually believe on the matter—or as *trusting implicitly* that P, as perhaps in the matter of the reliability of travel directions or the time of day from strangers. In the same ilk, van Fraassen[7] famously proposed a distinction between acceptance of an

7. van Fraassen [1980].

empirical theory and believing it to be true, arguing that evidence of a theory's empirical adequacy justifies one in doing no more than the former. Here I do not think it does justice to his intent if we equate acceptance of a theory with the very belief that it's empirically adequate—accepting a theory is rather a further thing which believing it to be empirically adequate is supposed to justify one in doing. What it justifies one in doing is, roughly, behaving in all—or very many—respects as one would do if one believed the theory to be true.

As a first approximation, then, we may propose the notion of acceptance of a proposition as a more general attitude than belief, including belief as a sub-case, which comes apart from belief in cases where one is warranted in acting on the assumption that P or taking it for granted that P or trusting that P for reasons that do not bear on the likely truth of P. Of course one may—sometimes irrationally—also believe P in such cases, in the sense implicit in a conviction that one knows that P. Successful sceptical arguments may then embarrass such convictions. The aim of the unified strategy, however, will be to show that such scepticism may prove to carry no challenge, nevertheless, to the corresponding *acceptances* and that warrant to accept—rather than to believe—cornerstone propositions may be enough to block the sceptical paradoxes that attend arguments to the effect there is no such thing as getting evidence to believe them.

I'll have plenty more to say about the notion of acceptance in what follows, and we will eventually converge on one particular kind of acceptance as the most germane to the purposes of the unified strategy. But to conclude this section, let me quickly respond to a fairly immediate concern about the strategy.[8] How exactly does it promise to shore up the possibility of justified belief in type-II propositions? We are proposing to concede, after all, that we may indeed have no (evidentially) *justified belief* in type-III propositions—that maybe we can point to no cognitive accomplishment of which the effect is a reason to take it that they are more likely to be true than not—but countering that we may nevertheless be rationally entitled to accept them. But if standard closure principles govern justified belief, then the counter comes too late to do any good. Standard closure principles will have it

8. Urged on me by Stephen Schiffer.

that justified belief in a type-III proposition will be a necessary condition for justified belief in anything one knows to entail it. To surrender the former will therefore be to surrender justified belief in type-II propositions more or less across the board. Maybe an entitlement to accept them nonetheless can be salvaged. But the idea was to use entitlement to save justification, not to replace it.

The observation is well made. It teaches that a proponent of the unified strategy must indeed impose some qualification on standardly accepted closure principles. In particular, it cannot be that evidentially justified belief is closed under (known/justifiably believed) entailment. That is not so remarkable a concession once one notices that evidential relations themselves are not so closed.[9] But if we let 'warrant' disjunctively cover both evidential justification *and* entitlement, it can still be that warrant, inclusively so understood, obeys closure principles suitable to do justice to our strong intuitive conviction that 'justification'— pre-theoretically understood—should do so.

The specific concern about closure should be distinguished from a more general concern it illustrates: that once we admit mere entitled acceptances into the role of cornerstones, we are bound to risk 'leaching', as it were—an upwards seepage of mere entitlement into areas of belief which we prize as genuinely knowledgeable or justified. I'll come back to this more general concern towards the end.

III

Strategic Entitlement. One initially promising-looking direction is illustrated by Reichenbach's famous work on the problem of induction.[10] Imagine Crusoe starving hungry on his desert island and totally unsuccessful in his attempts to find any animal or marine food sources. There are, however, plenty of luridly coloured fruits, of various kinds, all strange to him and none, so far as he can see, being eaten by any of the small number of

9. Which I take to be the minimal lesson of the kind of purported counterexample to closure of knowledge, or justification, originally pressed by Dretske [1970]. Whether or not I am justified in believing that the celebrated stripy animals are zebras but not in believing that they are not mules cleverly disguised as zebras, I unquestionably have the evidence of my eyes for the first and not for the second.

10. See especially Reichenbach [1938], §38.

seabirds that occasionally visit the island (there seem to be no avian land species there). In these circumstances, Crusoe may quite understandably feel that he has absolutely no reason to believe that any of the fruits are safe for consumption, much less nutritious. Nevertheless it's clear, assuming an interest in survival, that he is warranted in eating the fruit. Eating the fruit is, in game theoretical parlance, a *dominant* strategy. If the fruit is edible, he survives by eating it and will not otherwise do so; if the fruit is inedible, eating it will do him no good and may do him some harm—but the worst harm that it may do will be no worse (anyway, let's suppose he so views matters) than the harm of starvation. In all relevant possible futures, the mooted course of action either works out better than all alternatives or no worse than any alternative.[11]

The outlined reasoning justifies a course of *action* that would also be justified by (evidence for the) belief that the fruit is edible. As remarked, though, there is in the circumstances described no evidence for that belief. However in order for the Reichenbachian train of thought to serve the present purpose—that of assisting the unified strategy—something *attitudinal* has to be elicitable from it. In particular, we want to disclose reason to *accept* type-III propositions even if the possibility of obtaining evidence for them is allowed to be foreclosed by the sceptical argument. So

11. Here are three of Reichenbach's own examples:

A blind man who has lost his way in the mountains feels a trail with his stick. He does not know where the path will lead him, or whether it may take him so close to the edge of a precipice that he will be plunged into the abyss. Yet he follows the path, groping his way step by step; for if there is any possibility of getting out of the wilderness, it is by feeling his way along the path (Reichenbach [1949], p. 482).

The man who makes inductive inferences may be compared to a fisherman who casts a net into an unknown part of the ocean—he does not know whether he will catch fish, but he knows that if he wants to catch fish he has to cast his net. Every inductive prediction is like casting a net into the ocean of the happenings of nature; we don't know whether we shall have a good catch, but we try, at least, and try by the help of the best means available (Reichenbach [1968], pp. 245–6).

An example will show the logical structure of our reasoning. A man may be suffering from a grave disease; the physician tells us: 'I do not know whether an operation will save the man. But if there *is* any remedy, it is an operation.' In such a case, the operation would be justified. Of course, it would be better to know that the operation will save the man; but, if we do not know this, the knowledge formulated in the statement of the physician is a sufficient justification. If we cannot realise the sufficient conditions of success, we shall at least realise the necessary conditions of success. If we were able to show that the inductive inference is a necessary condition of success, it would be justified; such a proof would satisfy any demands which may be raised about the justification of induction (Reichenbach [1938] p. 349).

what, if any, attitudinal pay-off is there from the game-theoretic style of reasoning? Is there, on any natural understanding, a warrant provided for Crusoe's *accepting* that the fruit is edible, and should we think of him as implicitly doing so when he goes ahead and eats the fruit?

It's certainly open to us to fix such a use of the word, of course. Acceptance will stand in the appropriate generic relationship to belief just provided we regard an agent as accepting a proposition in all cases where she acts in a way which, given other aspects of her attitudinal set, would be rationally explained by her believing that proposition. So on this proposal, Crusoe, if persuaded to eat the fruits by the (cogent) reasoning outlined, thereby (warrantedly) accepts that the strange fruits are nutritious. And in general, the things one accepts will be the things one behaves—at least to a certain extent[12]—as if one believed. In cases when the explanation of that behaviour is strategic, as in Crusoe's situation, rather than attributable to an agent's actually having evidence for the belief in question, we may then speak of a *mere* acceptance.

That's a possible linguistic proposal. But the resulting use of 'acceptance' may seem forced and psychologically artificial. Consider this example.[13] You've just passed through airport security when an insurance company representative approaches you saying that, as a promotion, his company is offering free travel and accident insurance to every hundredth passenger entering the departures lounge, the only cost being that you leave him your postal address for further promotions. Suppose you are indifferent to that cost or even mildly interested to learn what the company has to offer. It then seems manifestly rational to accept the free policy, by reasoning directly analogous to Crusoe's. If the plane doesn't crash, you'll suffer no harm; and if it does crash, it will have been in your interest—in the extended sense in which one has an interest in the welfare of one's heirs after one's death—to have had the policy. Accepting the offer is therefore a dominant play. But it seems very strange to say that you thereby also accept—even if you do not believe—that the plane is going to crash, or even that you are acting on that assumption. No interesting attitudinal state would seem to be entrained.

---

12. More needs to be said about to what extent—see below.
13. Due to Stephen Schiffer.

There are however two salient differences between the examples. First,[14] whereas you doubtless expect to complete your journey safely, Crusoe has no particular reason to expect that the fruit is *in*edible. If he had, it might still be rational for him to behave in just the same way—eating the fruit might still represent his only chance, though now, subjectively speaking, a reduced one. But then, as in the airport insurance case, it would also seem intuitively wrong to speak of him as *accepting* that the fruit was edible. Second, the airport example does not actually involve what it was proposed that acceptance should minimally involve, viz. the agent's acting in a way which, given other aspects of his attitudinal set, would be rationally explained by his believing the proposition. On natural assumptions, what would be rationally explained by your believing the plane is going to crash would be, not your acceptance of an offer of free insurance, but your refusing to board the plane.

Two revisions to the proposal are thus invited: first, that acceptance that P should require *absence of disbelief* that P: agents can be properly said to accept a proposition only when it is rationally *available* to them; that is, is consistent with what they believe. And second, acceptance of a proposition should require that an agent really does act in *all* respects as if they believed the proposition in question, and not merely in some restricted salient set of respects.

In fact, the second revision entails the first. If I actually disbelieve P, then that fact is inevitably going to impact on the explanation of various things I do, or would be willing to do; so my behaviour will necessarily not be in *all* respects as if I believed P. But the second revision is also too strong as formulated. For if the notion of acceptance is to be well conceived, there had better—of course—be *some* operational differences between an agent who (rationally) merely accepts a given proposition and one who (perhaps irrationally) believes it. And there will. If Crusoe believes the fruit is edible, then his mood, for example, as he eats it is likely to be very different from how it will be if he merely accepts that it is edible in the strategic kind of sense proposed. The matter needs a much more nuanced discussion than I have space to attempt here but the relevant basic point is

14. Observed in discussion by Mauricio Suarez.

that the explanatory parallels between belief and mere acceptance will be restricted to their role as *reasons* for further thought and actions. Ordinary intentional psychological thought routinely involves a number of other—non-rationalising—kinds of explanation. There are many kinds of response—emotions, attitudes and actions—which it views as characteristic or expressive of a given psychological state without being *rationalised* by it. The constitutive requirement on an agent's acceptance that P should be that she (be disposed to) accept the consequences of P and to behave, in so far as she behaves rationally, just in ways that would be practical-syllogistically *rationalised* by her actual desires and other beliefs/acceptances if in addition she were also to believe that P. Note that the second revision, appropriately qualified in this direction, is still going to be strong enough to entail the first.

There is much more to say but let's take stock. There *is* an attitude which can naturally be associated with (some instances of) Reichenbachian reasoning: roughly, that of *committing oneself to act on a certain assumption*. That is certainly an attitude to the content of the assumption in question. Of course the scope of the commitment can be qualified—it may apply just to action for one specific goal in one specific context—and it's duration can be relatively ephemeral. Crusoe's commitment will endure just so long as he needs nutrition and no other possible way of getting it but eating the fruit obtains. What the Reichenbachian thought provides us with is one relatively clear paradigm of how such a commitment can be rational for reasons which do not impinge on the likelihood of the truth of the assumption in question. But it will seem more natural to describe such a rational commitment as involving an attitude of *acceptance* to the extent that its rationality generalises across a variety of situations and contexts and, in the limit, across situations and contexts in general. Beliefs of course can change. But so long as I have it that someone believes something, then *ceteris paribus* that piece of information goes into the explanatory machinery to which I may appeal in rationalising his actions in *any* context. 'Acceptance' will be most naturally reserved for an attitude with a similarly wide explanatory potential.

The foregoing illustrates the general point that, so long as it is insisted that rational belief is *per se* belief supported by evidence, the unified strategy must ultimately rest on a developed philosophical psychology of an attitudinal state, or states, of acceptance which are belief-like, and capable of underwriting belief, yet contrast with belief. Very roughly, if we think of 'belief', in its core uses, as denoting a normatively constrained and normatively constraining state—a state identified by its 'in-' and 'out-rules', as it were: something *essentially rationally controlled* by evidence and *essentially rationally committal* to thought and action—then the general idea I am canvassing is that it will be necessary, in trying to make something of the notion of rational entitlement, to think in terms of attitudinal states which share much of the second ingredient—the element and style of commitments involved—with belief, but *not the first*. Of course it will do no harm to call states of both kinds 'beliefs'. But then the sceptical point—that certain of our cornerstone 'beliefs' seem to be essentially uncontrolled by any proper accumulation of evidence—will no longer carry an automatic critical impact. The question will be whether these 'beliefs' are properly viewed as subject to such controls in the first place or whether they are not instead examples of a species of attitudinal acceptance whose rationality, when it is rational, may be grounded differently.

Here in any case, to round off this section, is a first proposal about entitlement:

An agent X is *contextually strategically entitled* to accept P just in case

(i) X has no sufficient reason to believe that P is untrue; and
(ii) in the particular context and for its characteristic purposes, it is a dominant strategy for X to act—as far as the achievement of those purposes is concerned—as if he had a justified belief that P.

So then

A thinker X is *absolutely strategically entitled* to accept P just in case

(i) X has no sufficient reason to believe that P is untrue; and
(ii) in all contexts, it is a dominant strategy for X to act exactly as if he had a justified belief that P.

In these terms, the Reichenbachian contention about induction may be viewed as being that an acceptance of the Uniformity Thesis is an absolute strategic entitlement, and that we are accordingly justified in basic inductive inference in contexts in general. By contrast, Crusoe is merely contextually entitled to accept that the island fruits are edible. And the airline insurance example involves no, even merely contextual, strategic entitlement.

IV

How Much Can Strategic Entitlement Do? How far might strategic entitlement, roughly so characterised, go towards executing the unified strategy?

Let's review the core thought as it concerns induction. We can represent it like this:

(a) We need, if we are to lead even secure, let alone happy and valuable lives, to be able to form reliable (conditional) expectations about the future—about what will happen (if so-and-so is the case.)

(b) (i) If the Uniformity Thesis holds, inductive methods will be the most effective way of arriving at the true generalisations and theories which will support such reliable expectations.

(ii) If the Uniformity Thesis fails, no methods will do any better than induction as a means for arriving at reliable expectations.

Therefore

(c) The use of inductive methods is a dominant strategy for arriving at reliable expectations.

(d) We have no reason to believe that the Uniformity Thesis fails.

Therefore

(e) We are absolutely strategically entitled to accept the Uniformity Thesis and, hence, to accept that the world is inductively amenable.

If this reasoning is accepted, it immediately provides a modest fire-wall around inductive scepticism. Sure, it doesn't give us the right to say that we *know* that nature will be continuingly inductively amenable. Indeed it appears to provide no reason for the subjective confidence which we undoubtedly repose in inductive method—someone who grasps and acts on the strategic reasoning could quite consistently, it seems, be as pessimistic about induction as you like. (However, I will return to qualify this, and the qualification will be important.) Still, what primarily seems disconcerting about the sceptical argument is the apparent implication that there is no rational basis for preferring the methodology of empirical science to divination of entrails or the tarot pack. Reichenbach complains about Hume that

> he is not alarmed by his discovery; he does not realise that, if there is no escape from the dilemma pointed out by him, science might as well not be continued—there is no use for a system of predictions if it is nothing but a ridiculous self-delusion ... if there is no justification for the inductive inference, the working procedure of science sinks to the level of a game ... [15]

If the reasoning to (e) above is effective, then—in perfect accord with the unified strategy—it pre-empts this depressing prospect. Maybe we do not know that Nature is Uniform and have no genuine evidence for the likelihood of its continuing inductive amenability. But if the argument succeeds, we are absolutely strategically entitled to accept that things will so continue. The methodology of empirical science will have a rational authority, at least insofar as it rests on simple inductive inference, which divination of entrails and readings of the tarot pack cannot match. [16]

I won't here consider further whether (any version of) the Reichenbachian argument should indeed be accepted. [17] One obvious point of vulnerability is claim (b)(ii): worlds in which Uniformity fails, one might suppose, would come in all sorts of chaotic varieties—how can we be sure, *a priori*, that there are

15. Reichenbach [1938], p. 346.
16. This much is not yet a response to the 'leaching' problem highlighted at the conclusion of Section II above.
17. The argument has of course been roundly criticised. But perhaps the most major concern about it is its seeming inability to address Goodman's 'New Riddle' (Goodman [1955]). Even if inductive generalisation of sampled evidence is a dominant strategy, that gives one no guidance about the proper description (green emeralds or grue emeralds?) of the pattern displayed by the sample.

none in which some non-inductive method of belief formation might not be predictively more successful?[18] Our interest now, however, is in the question, with what degree of success we might expect to be able to wield the emergent notion of strategic entitlement against I-II-III scepticism in general—granted, for the sake of argument, that it may prove to carry some clout against inductive scepticism in the fashion Reichenbach hoped.

Is there any possibility that we might make out an absolute strategic entitlement to accept the type-III propositions earlier reviewed? Consider the case of perception and the material world. *Prima facie* it's straightforward to generate an analogue of the reasoning from (a) to (e). Thus:

> (a)* It is of paramount importance to us to find our way around the world, make use of its resources, avoid danger, and so on. If we are to do these things, we need to be able to form reliable beliefs about the locations and dispositions of material objects.
>
> (b)* (i) If the world is generally open to our perceptual faculties, ordinary observation will be the most effective way of forming such beliefs.
>
> (ii) If the world is not generally open to our perceptual faculties, no other capacities that we possess will fare any better.

Therefore

> (c)* Reliance on ordinary observation is a dominant strategy for arriving at reliable beliefs about the location and dispositions of material objects.
>
> (d)* We have no reason to believe that the world is not generally open to our perceptual faculties.

Therefore

> (e)* We are absolutely strategically entitled to accept that the world is generally open to our perceptual faculties.

And that, if allowed, would certainly be a finding worth having. But it's clear, on reflection, that it comes short as a response to material world scepticism—in both Cartesian and I-II-III

---

18. But *can* Uniformity fail altogether? Some of the relevant mathematical issues here are usefully outlined in A. W. Sudbury [1972].

varieties—even in the restricted (non conviction-justifying) way in which (e) responds to inductive scepticism. It comes short as a response to Cartesian scepticism because an entitlement to accept that the world is generally open to our perceptual faculties *when they are engaged* seems to sit quite comfortably alongside the worry that, right now, those faculties are not engaged—that right now I am suffering a persistent lucid dream, or that I am (since yesterday, say) a brain-in-a-vat. And it comes short as a response to I-II-III scepticism about the material world because more is needed, according to that form of scepticism, to facilitate the inference from the relevant kind of type-I proposition to the relevant kind of type-II proposition than is provided by the entitlement which the reasoning actually promises to provide.

To see the last point, reflect that in order justifiably to move from a claim of type-I, concerning how things currently seem according to my experience, to a claim of type-II, concerning characteristics of local material objects, we require, according to the sceptical argument, the collateral information that:

> There is a material world, broadly in keeping with the way in which sense experience represents it.

This embeds two components: the *ontology* of the material world, and the *methodology* of reliance on sense-perception as a source of belief about it. And the Reichenbachian routine, (a)*–(e)*, bears in effect only on the second. Once it is granted that there is a material world at all, we get a strategic entitlement—if the routine succeeds—to take it that it is, broadly, open to our perceptual capacities. But the reasoning simply helps itself to the ontological component—that there is an external material world at all—from the start; it is a presupposition of its premise, (a)*. No strategic entitlement issues to accept that there is a material world: only, if there is one, to accept that our sense experience yields broadly reliable representations of it. We may foresee a similar short-coming in the attempt to address I-II-III scepticism concerning other minds and the past by versions of the same routine.

Why doesn't the Reichenbachian reasoning fall short in a similar way (again, I am not taking a stand on whether it falls short in other ways) as a response to inductive scepticism? Because inductive scepticism, though an instance if I-II-III scepticism, precisely differs from the other examples in targeting the *second* component—the methodological component—in the collateral information which it claims is necessary if the relevant form of ampliative inference is to be justified. It is not in doubt—in the standard dialectic with the inductive sceptic—that there is indeed a (spatio-temporally) extended tract of reality going beyond hitherto observed regularities. The question is: what vindicates inductive method as a way of forming beliefs about that tract of reality? And the Reichenbachian answer, crudely, is that either it works (as well as or) better than anything else or nothing works at all. What the reasoning from (a)* to (e)* makes plausible is that a *methodological* scepticism about perception would be as tractable by such considerations as inductive scepticism is (if that is so tractable at all). Likewise for a methodological scepticism about reliance on others' manifest behaviour and physical condition as a guide to their mental states, or reliance on memory as a guide to the past. But scepticism about the material world, other minds and the past is classically not methodological but ontological. And for this ontological scepticism, it appears, entitlement of strategy promises no cure. If the unified strategy can offer a cure, it will be by means of a different medicine.

V

Entitlement of Cognitive Project. A second, rather different species of entitlement is suggested by one tendency in Wittgenstein's remarks *On Certainty*. Here are two illustrative passages:

> 163. ... We check the story of Napoleon, but not whether all the reports about him are based on sense-deception, forgery and the like. For whenever we test anything, we are already presupposing something that is not tested...

Compare:

> 337. One cannot make experiments if there are not some things that one does not doubt. But that does not mean that one takes certain presuppositions on trust. When I write a letter and post it, I take it for granted that it will arrive—I expect this.
>
> If I make an experiment I do not doubt the existence of the apparatus before my eyes. I have plenty of doubts, but not *that*. If I do a calculation I believe, without any doubts, that the figures on the paper aren't switching of their own accord, and I also trust my memory the whole time, and trust it without reservation.

To take it that one has acquired a justification for a particular proposition by the appropriate exercise of certain appropriate cognitive capacities—perception, introspection, memory, or intellection, for instance—always involves various kinds of presupposition. These presuppositions will include the proper functioning of the relevant cognitive capacities, the suitability of the occasion and circumstances for their effective function, and indeed the integrity of the very concepts involved in the formulation of the issue in question. I take Wittgenstein's point in these admittedly not unequivocal passages to be that this is essential: one *cannot but* take certain such things for granted (though I am not sure how we should interpret his implied contrast between taking for granted and 'taking on trust'. More about trust shortly.)

That is not to deny that, if one chose, one could investigate (at least some of) the presuppositions involved in a particular case. I might go and have my eyesight checked, for example. But the point is that in proceeding to such an investigation, one would then be forced to make further presuppositions of the same general kinds (for instance, that my eyes are functioning properly now, when I read the oculist's report, perhaps with my new glasses on.) Wherever I get in position to claim justification for a proposition, I do so courtesy of specific presuppositions—about my own powers, and the prevailing circumstances, and my understanding of the issues involved—for which I will have no specific, earned evidence. This is a necessary truth. I may, in any particular case, set about gathering such evidence in turn—and *that* investigation may go badly, defeating the presuppositions that I originally made. But whether it does or doesn't go badly, it will have its own so far unfounded[19] presuppositions. Again: whenever claimable cognitive achievement takes place, it does so in a context of *specific* presuppositions which are not themselves an expression of any cognitive achievement to date.[20]

19. —*unbegründet* (*On Certainty* §253).

20. It's natural to rejoin that one may have inductive grounds for confidence in the present sound functioning of one's perceptual faculties. But in that case one relies on the evidence for the induction—on the *previous* sound functioning of one's perceptual faculties. So was that independently checked in a large number of cases? And even if so, is not one in any case now relying, without specific evidence, on one's memory of the outcome of the checks?

These presuppositions are not just one more kind of Wittgen-steinian 'hinge' proposition as that term has come generally to be understood. Hinges, broadly speaking, are *standing certainties*, exportable from context to context. Whereas the present range of cases are particular to the investigative occasion: they are propositions like that my eyes are functioning properly *now*, that the things that I am *currently* perceiving have not been extensively disguised so as to conceal their true nature, etc.

A natural first reaction is that if this is right—if all claimable cognitive achievement rests on specific, ungrounded presupposi-tions—then we just have the materials for a new—third form of—sceptical paradox. The key thought in the new paradox would be a generalisation of part of the Cartesian sceptical routine about dreaming. Plausibly, our confidence in the things which we take ourselves to have verified in a particular context can rationally be no stronger than our confidence in the kind of context-specific presuppositions just remarked. Suppose I set myself to count the books on one of the shelves in my office and arrive at the answer, 26. Then the warrant thereby acquired for that answer can rationally be regarded as no stronger than the grounds I have for confidence that I counted correctly, that my senses and memory were accordingly functioning properly, that the books themselves were stable during the count and were not spontaneously popping into and out of existence unnoticed by me, etc. Yet I will have done nothing—we may suppose—to justify my confidence in all these specific presuppositions. So how have I achieved any genuine warrant at all?

Here is a possible line of reply. If there is *no such thing as* a process of warrant acquisition for each of whose specific presuppositions warrant has already been earned, it should not be reckoned to be part of the proper concept of an acquired warrant that it somehow aspire to this—incoherent—ideal. Rather, we should view each and every cognitive project as irreducibly involving elements of adventure—I have, as it were, to *take a risk* on the reliability of my senses, the conduciveness of the circumstances, etc., much as I take a risk on the continuing reliability of the steering, and the stability of the road surface every time I ride my bicycle. For as soon as I grant that I ought—ideally—to check the presuppositions of a project, even in a context in which there is no particular reason for concern about them, then I should agree *pari passu* that I ought in turn to check the presuppositions of the check—which is one more project after all—and so on indefinitely, unless at some point I can foresee arriving at presuppositions all of which are somehow safer than those of the initial project. If not, then there will be no principled stopping point to the process of checking: the quest for security will be endless, and therefore useless. And if that is the situation, then the right response—the reply will continue— is not to conclude that the acquisition of genuine warrant is impossible, but rather to insist that it does not require this elusive kind of security. Rather, warrant is acquired whenever investigation is undertaken in a *fully responsible* manner, and what the paradox shows is that full epistemic responsibility cannot, *per impossibile*, involve an investigation of every presupposition whose falsity would defeat the claim to have acquired a warrant. (Suggestion: the correct principle is not that any acquired warrant is no stronger than the weakest of one's independently acquired reasons to accept each of its presuppositions. It is, rather, that it is no stronger than the warrant for any of the presuppositions about which there is some *specific antecedent reason* to entertain a misgiving.)

This line of reply concedes that the best sceptical arguments have something to teach us—that the limits of justification they bring out are genuine and essential—but then replies that, just for that reason, cognitive achievement must be reckoned to take place *within such limits*. The attempt to surpass them would result not in an increase in rigour or solidity but merely in cognitive paralysis.

Let me try to harness these ideas to a definite proposal about entitlement. First (to tidy up a bit) a definition: let us say that

> P is a *presupposition* of a particular cognitive project if to doubt P (in advance) would rationally commit one to doubting the significance or competence of the project.

Then the relevant kind of entitlement—an entitlement of cognitive project—may be proposed to be any presupposition of a cognitive project meeting the following additional two conditions:

(i) We have no sufficient reason to believe that P is untrue and

(ii) The attempt to justify P would involve further presuppositions in turn of no more secure a prior standing ... and so on
without limit; so that someone pursuing the relevant enquiry
who accepted that there is nevertheless an onus to justify P
would implicitly undertake a commitment to an infinite
regress of justificatory projects, each concerned to vindicate
the presuppositions of its predecessor.

No doubt that will stand refinement, but the general *motif* is
clear enough. If a cognitive project is indispensable, or anyway
sufficiently valuable to us—in particular, if its failure would at
least be no worse than the costs of not executing it, and its success
would be better—and if the attempt to vindicate (some of) its
presuppositions would raise presuppositions of its own of no
more secure an antecedent status, and so on *ad infinitum*, then we
are entitled to—may help ourselves to, take for granted—the
original presuppositions without specific evidence in their favour.
More generally, wherever we need to carry through a type of
project, or anyway cannot lose and may gain by doing so, and
where we cannot satisfy ourselves that the presuppositions of a
successful execution are met except at the cost of making further
presuppositions whose status is no more secure, we should—are
rationally entitled to—just go ahead and trust that the former are
met.

I said 'trust that' and not merely 'act on the assumption that'.
Here is the place to register a very important gloss on the
understanding of 'acceptance' needed by the unified strategy.
Earlier, in discussion of the Reichenbachian approach, it was
suggested that the kind of acceptance which is motivated by an
(absolute) strategic entitlement would be consistent with agnosticism, even pessimism about the truth of the supposition in
question. That, of course, if correct, limits the power of strategic
entitlement as a response to inductive scepticism, since there is no
question but that ordinary inductive thought involves, more than
a strategic acceptance of the inductive amenability of the world,
an implicit trust in it. Do we do better in this respect with
entitlement of cognitive project? Is it an entitlement to *trust*?

Suppose it is less. In that case, to appreciate my entitlement to
accept that my sensory apparatus, for example, is right now

generally sound will be fully consistent with my taking an agnostic or sceptical view about the matter. But seems impossible to square agnosticism, say, about that with a conviction of the truth of the ordinary day-to-day things I routinely take myself to verify by perceptual means. I cannot *rationally* form the belief that it is currently blowing a gale and snowing outside on the basis of my present visual and auditory experience while being simultaneously agnostic, let alone sceptical, about the credentials of that experience. Sure, I can decide what beliefs it would be *appropriate* to form on the assumption that my sensory apparatus is currently sound, but I will not, if rational, be able to form those beliefs while I am open-minded—so unpersuaded—whether it *is* sound. To choose to act on an assumption is—extensionally—to choose to act in ways that would be rationalised by believing it. But this chosen range of action cannot, for a rational subject, extend to the formation of the beliefs that would be appropriate if, more, one trusted that the assumption was true. Since believing in general is not purely voluntary but is controlled by reasoning and evidence, it is not a rational option for someone who is sceptical or agnostic about the pedigree of the relevant evidence, or the character of the reasoning involved.

So much is indeed implicit in the very characterisation I gave of a presupposition of a cognitive project: something doubt about which would rationally commit one to doubting the significance or competence of the project. Since one will not (rationally) believe anything on the evidence afforded by carrying through a project of whose significance or competence one is unpersuaded, it follows immediately that if acceptance of such a presupposition is to be capable of underwriting rational belief in the things to which execution of the project leads, it has to be an attitude which *excludes doubt*. If there is entitlement of cognitive project, it has to be an entitlement not merely to act on the assumption that suitable presuppositions hold good, but to place trust in their doing so.

The same, indeed, must hold for absolute strategic entitlement too. More carefully, it must hold for absolute strategic entitlement to any supposition which is to underwrite a policy of *belief formation* (rather than merely non-doxastic forms of action). In particular, if a strategic acceptance of the Uniformity of Nature is to ground specific inductively formed *expectations*—contrast:

working hypotheses—then that acceptance cannot be exhausted by the decision merely to act on the assumption of Uniformity in all contexts. For again, free action on an assumption will—in a rational subject who is uncommitted to its truth—inevitably stop short of the formation of the specific beliefs which holding it to be true would mandate. So our discussion of Reichenbach and strategic entitlement needs a crucial amendment. If there is a strategic entitlement to a policy of forming beliefs inductively, it must be an entitlement to *trust* that the world is so constituted that such a policy will, by and large, often enough, be successful. A strategic entitlement to accept the Uniformity of Nature and Crusoe's strategic entitlement to accept that the island fruits are edible differ in just that respect.

This is the point of convergence I promised in Section II. Acceptance, for the purposes of the unified strategy, is—or has to involve—*trust*. 'Warrant for nothing' is entitlement to trust. It is in the nature of trust that it gets by with little or no evidence. That is exactly how it contrasts with belief proper, and it is not *per se* irrational on account of the contrast. Entitlement is rational trust.

VI

How Much Can Entitlement of Cognitive Project Do? We already touched on one striking prospective capture when we noted that the presuppositions of a given cognitive project will character-istically include the proper functioning of the cognitive capacities which need to be engaged in pursuing it, the suitability of the attendant circumstances for their effective function, and indeed the integrity of the very concepts involved in the formulation of the project to hand. Since this goes for any cognitive project, there are bound to be presuppositions falling within these same three broad categories which occur at the next level up—if one were to set out to confirm the presuppositions of the original project—and so on indefinitely. So, while the details need thinking through, there seems every prospect that some presuppositions of at least these three kinds will meet the defining conditions on entitlement of cognitive project. It would follow in particular—provided the very idea of entitlement of project is in good standing—that in all circumstance where there is no specific reason to think otherwise, we are each of us entitled to take it, without special investigative work, that our basic cognitive faculties are functioning properly in circumstances broadly conducive to their successful operation. If so, that immediately empowers us to dismiss the various scenarios of cognitive dislocation and disablement—dreams, sustained hallucination, envatment and so on—which are the stock-in-trade of Cartesian scepticism. That, for instance, I am not right now dreaming is a presupposition in the sense defined of any cognitive project involving perceptual interaction with the world, and a presupposition, moreover, which I have, right now, no reason to suppose unsatisfied and of which any effective investigation by me would involve the same presupposition over again. That indeed was the triumphant thrust of the sceptical routine we reviewed at the start: that there is no evidentially justifying the claim that I am not right now dreaming. But under the aegis of entitlement of cognitive project, that routine is tamed to issue in the benign conclusion that I am rationally entitled to take the falsity of the dreaming hypothesis on trust in any broadly empirical cognitive project; so the Cartesian sceptical argument, which depends on my having no good reason to discount it, is nipped in the bud.

This is a good result, it goes without saying, only if it is selective—only if the entitlements generated turn out to be cornerstones of our actual ways of thinking about and investigating the world and do not extend to all manner of (what we would regard as) bizarre and irrational prejudices. As a test case, suppose I undertake a project is to predict the winners in tomorrow's card at Newmarket by rolling a pair of dice for each runner in the afternoon's races and seeing which get the highest scores. Clearly it is a presupposition of this project that the method in question has some effectiveness. What prevents that presupposition becoming an entitlement?

The obvious answer is that clause (i) is unsatisfied—there is every reason to doubt that the method in question is effective. But that is not the fundamental point. The fundamental point is that (as we know) it would be straightforward to gather no end of empirical evidence to discredit the dice-rolling method. And this would not be possible if the various presuppositions of such evidence-gathering in turn were of 'no more secure a prior standing' than the dice-rolling method. If they were of no more secure a prior standing, we'd have to admit to a stand-off and suspend judgement. So the very discreditability of the method entails that clause (ii) is unsatisfied.

A doubt now comes into focus, however. There is no entitlement to trust in the dice-rolling method because it is a method for assessing statements which allow of independent assessment by more basic means, whose reliability is of more secure prior standing. What of a case where that feature is missing? Suppose I postulate a tract of reality—it might be the realm of non-actual possible worlds as conceived by Lewis— which is spatio-temporally insulated from the domain of our usual empirical knowledge, and a special faculty—as it may be, our non-inferential 'modal intuition'—whose operation is supposed to allow us to gather knowledge about it. Do I have an entitlement of cognitive project to trust the (alleged) faculty on any particular occasion? If not, why not? After all, I have—in the nature of the case, since I cannot compare its deliverances with the facts, independently ascertained—no reason to believe that it is unreliable (so long as its prompting are consistent); and any attempt to check on its functioning will presumably perforce involve further modal intuition, 'of no more secure a prior standing'. But do we want Lewis's views about the nature of modality—making no judgement about their independent merit—to turn out to be a matter of rational entitlement in any case? If not, what blocks them doing so?

The example highlights something vital about the limitations of this genre of entitlement. It may very well prove to be the case that a trust in the reliability of basic modal intuition—in our primitive, non-inferential impressions of modal validity and invalidity—turns out to be a matter of entitlement of cognitive project. What is not an entitlement—or not this kind of entitlement anyway—is the specific Lewisian metaphysics, or *any* specific metaphysics, of the nature of modal reality, any specific conception of the kinds of states of affairs which make modal claims true or false. We may prove to be entitled to trust, in any particular cognitive project involving modal judgement, that those of our faculties which are essentially involved in such judgement are functioning properly in circumstances broadly conducive to their effective function. But we are not thereby entitled to any particular conception of the nature of modal facts.

The point, generalised, is that entitlement of cognitive project fares no better than strategic entitlement as a response to I-II-III scepticism in general, and falls short in a similar way. Type-III propositions—that there is a material world, that there are other minds, that the world has an extended history—are indeed presuppositions of our enquiries in the sense defined. But they are not entitlements of cognitive project as characterised, since they fail to meet condition (ii). The problem with type-III propositions is not that—like 'my visual system is functioning properly on this occasion'—to accept that there is an onus to justify them in any particular context in which they are presuppositional would—plausibly—be to accept an infinite regress of similar justificatory obligations. Rather, it is that, failing some independent response to the sceptical argument, one has no idea how to justify them at all. Entitlement of cognitive project does not, any more than strategic entitlement, extend to matters of ontology. Once granted a certain conception of certain of our cognitive powers and the nature of their sphere of operation, we may be able to appeal to this kind of entitlement to make a case that, for the purposes of any particular enquiry of the relevant kind, we are entitled to take it on trust that those powers are functioning effectively in conducive circumstances. But if so, this congenial finding comes within a context in which the broad nature of the powers in question and the character of their subject matter to which they are sensitive is not in question. Once those matters do come into question, it is hard to see that anything so far said promises much in the way of answers.

VII

Entitlement of Rational Deliberation. Strategic entitlement and entitlement of cognitive project both allow that it is rational to place trust, without evidence, in two kinds of presupposition of pure *enquiry*—those whose acceptance generates a dominant policy in relation to the goals of (a particular kind of) enquiry, and those which believing the results of an enquiry rationally requires us not to doubt, yet which are beyond vindication by evidence except at the cost of further presuppositions of the same kind (or more generally, further presuppositions which are no more secure). In contrast, the third genre of entitlement to be canvassed here is anchored in the constitutive requirements of rational *action*.

The generic thought is that since rational agency is nothing we can opt out of, we are entitled to place trust in whatever (we have no evidence against and which) needs to be true if rational decision-making is to be feasible and effective. More carefully, say that P is a *general presupposition* of rational deliberation just in case it may be recognised *a priori* that a soundly based—justified and correct—decision on the respective merits of alternative courses of action open in a particular context is possible only if P holds good in that context—so that an agent who found herself in possession of reason to regard P as failing in a particular deliberative context would be bound to regard herself as—if only temporarily—incapacitated from rational decision-making. The proposal is, then, that an agent has an entitlement to place trust in any of the general presuppositions of rational deliberation which she has no reason to regard as failing in her particular deliberative context.

She is so entitled because the need to take decisions will, time and again, trump whatever may be the limited possibilities—especially in the light of sceptical argument—for gathering positive evidence that the general presuppositions hold good in the particular context, and because—as a rational agent—her decisions have to be informed by *reasoned beliefs* about what is for the best. Since such beliefs will be possible for her only in a context in which she has trust that what she knows to be necessary conditions for their being soundly arrived at are met, only a thinker who has such trust can be a rational agent.

Two such species of necessary conditions, hence entitlements, are worth remarking. Deliberating what to do involves consideration of alternatives, in the light of one's wishes and aims. So one general presupposition of rational deliberation is that one has sufficient self-knowledge to identify those of one's wishes and aims which are relevant to the decision at hand. Psychological self-knowledge, to that limited extent, is an entitlement of rational deliberation.

A second example emerges from the observation that sound assessment of alternative courses of action requires, *inter alia*, knowing or justifiably believing a range of (open subjunctive) conditionals which variously define what may be expected to occur if such-and-such a direction is pursued. And such knowledge inevitably involves reviewing what support is provided for them by various relevant kinds of known generalisation: it is reasonable to believe that if I were to perform an action of such-and-such a kind, such-and-such a situation would (probably) result because it always (or usually) does, or because, although there is no established pattern, there is theoretical reason, backed by other generalisations, for that expectation. In general, ordinary rational deliberation is possible only for someone who rationally believes in certain relevant empirical generalisations. And it is well grounded only when suitable such generalisations are true.

Consider then the proposition that nature displays sufficiently many inductively and abductively ascertainable regularities to make the prosecution of those methods worthwhile. We have no reason to disbelieve this. And if it is not true, then we lose the means necessary to select the subjunctive conditionals that are needed in practical deliberation, and practical deliberation itself becomes paralysed. By the proposed notion of entitlement, we are therefore in position rationally to accept that nature displays sufficiently many inductively/abductively ascertainable regularities to make the prosecution of those methods worthwhile. But that is enough to ensure the rationality of employing those methods.

In more detail:

> We cannot function effectively as deliberative agents unless we presuppose that there is a wealth of correct subjunctive conditionals.
>
> Subjunctive conditionals are correct in virtue of nomic regularities.
>
> So we cannot function effectively as deliberative agents unless we presuppose that there are sufficient nomic regularities to sustain a wealth of correct subjunctive conditionals.

Since there is no reason to doubt that there is such a sufficiency of nomic regularities, the supposition that there are is accordingly an entitlement by the proposal. But now suppose it may also be shown that

> If a nomic regularity obtains and there are accessible grounds for believing in it at all, then here are broadly inductive, or abductive grounds for doing so—grounds that belong with the methodology of the developed empirical sciences.

Nomic regularities which make an observable difference, in other words, are symptomatised by the availability of scientific evidence that they obtain. It would follow that, in the context of our need to select correct subjunctive conditionals, and hence to find true regularities to sustain them, there is a better type of ground to rely on than the broadly scientific—say an *M-ground*—only if two conditions are met: first, that it likewise follows from the obtaining of a nomic regularity that, if warrantedly believable at all, there will be M-grounds for believing it; and second, that there is less chance of *rogue* M-grounds—M-grounds which indicate a nomic regularity where there is none—than of rogue inductive or abductive grounds. But we know of no such type of ground.

And that, it would seem, is enough. Under the rubric proposed, we have an entitlement of rational deliberation to trust that there are many nomic regularities. Any nomic regularity that has an effect on the observable is symptomatised by the availability of inductive or less direct empirical evidence. We know of no more reliable symptom. So reliance on inductive and abductive methods is the best we can knowledgeably do in pursuit of purposes which are essential to rational agency itself, and thus unavoidable.

This attempt to capture induction as an entitlement is somewhat distant from the strategic route. In particular, there is no need for the lemma that inductive inference is a dominant strategy. The essential thought is merely, that the truth of the Uniformity Thesis is a general presupposition of rational deliberation and that, absent evidence to doubt it and knowing of no superior way in general to gain access to the regularities in whose existence we are thereby entitled to trust, it is rational to rely on inductive and abductive methods in doing so.

VIII

Entitlements of Substance? If, as just argued, entitlement of rational deliberation can be made to cover inductive and abductive inference, then it ought to allow extension to an acceptance of (records concerning) a substantial past. For it is the past that offers the evidence which those methods require. So at least in context of rational deliberation, material is promised to address I-II-III scepticism in two of the originally troublesome areas—empirical generalisations and statements concerning the past. But we still have the problem that has beset us throughout: the prospects of making out that our acceptance of an external material world and the existence of other minds are entitlements seem no better in this context than they transpired to be under the aegis of entitlement of strategy and of cognitive project. Maybe some subtle philosophy can disclose otherwise but it is no obvious presupposition of rational deliberation to conceive of the stuff of the world as matter or to acknowledge the existence of minds besides one's own. Can these—our most fundamental conceptions of the substance of the world—be made out to be matters of entitlement? I have no definite argument to offer for either answer, but must be content merely to indicate a direction by which a (partial) answer might be found.

As I stressed earlier, we may avoid particular versions of the I-II-III argument by arguing for a rejection of the justificational architecture which it presupposes—with perceptual claims, perhaps, in pole position for the attempt. But if this is to be a *globally* successful tactic, then we will have to do nothing less than so fashion our thinking that it *nowhere* traffics in propositions related as type-I propositions and type-II propositions. *None* of the thoughts we think must be such that their truth-makers are beyond our direct cognition, so that we are forced to rely on finite and accessible putative *symptoms* of their obtaining.

Could there be such a way of thinking? Earlier, it was suggested that there could not; that an unavoidable and unacceptable casualty of any such scheme of thought would be the thinker's conception of her own *cognitive locality*—the idea of a range of states of affairs and events existing beyond the bounds of her own direct awareness. Globally to avoid the justificational architecture presupposed by I-II-III scepticism would be to forgo all conception of oneself as having position in a world extending, perhaps infinitely, beyond one's cognitive horizon. In particular, it would be to surrender all conception of our own specific situation within a broader objective world extending *spatially and temporally* beyond us. However it is, of course, a real and crucial question—not to be addressed dogmatically—whether there could be any coherent such system of thought.

I shall not here try to develop an argument that there could not. Certainly, all *our* actual thought and activity is organised under the aegis of a distinction between states of affairs accessible to us at our own cognitive station and others that lie beyond, and it is difficult to form any clear concept of how things might be otherwise. There is however a well-known train of thought, popularly understood as Kantian and given body by Strawson's classic discussion in Chapter 2 of *Individuals* and the memorable critique of Strawson by Gareth Evans,[21] which argues, in effect, that cognitive locality goes with the very idea of our experience as being of an *objective* world, of a reality that stands independent of it. More specifically, it is only via a conception of the possibility of states of affairs and processes occurring *un*perceived that sense can be given to the idea that experience informs us of a reality not of its making. But that conception calls in turn for a conception of a way, or ways, in which states of affairs and processes can elude the awareness of a thinker, which—according to the Kantian train of thought— in turn necessarily involves some *dimension* of variation of locality—the idea of a situation obtaining, in the most abstract sense, *elsewhere*—and hence a conception of that dimension of variation. And now *that* conception in turn arguably demands some notion of the make-up—substance—of a state of affairs suitable to allow it to be situated 'elsewhere'.

Of course, that is all—to put the matter kindly—somewhat promissory. And it impresses as ambitious to hope that our specific conceptions of space (and time) and matter might somehow precipitate themselves out of this direction of enquiry as transcendentally imposed by the very idea of objective experience. But something less specific might: it does not seem altogether fanciful that a developed (Kantian or Strawsonian) metaphysics might teach us that to operate any scheme of thought rich enough to recognise objective experience—rich enough to allow for experience of states of affairs whose existence is constitutively independent of experience—must involve a grasp of the idea of particular states, events and processes existing outside the thinker's cognitive locality, and hence some concep-tion of dimension(s) of locality and an appropriately co-

21. P. F Strawson [1959] and Gareth Evans [1980].

ordinated conception of substance. If so, then the mere conception of ourselves as capable of experience *of* a world cannot escape *some* conception of substance: of the nature of what fundamentally constitutes the kinds of states of affairs that can be situated 'elsewhere'. Assuming that conceiving of experience as objective is somehow independently mandated—of course, that raises further major issues—a somewhat minimal notion of entitlement of substance might then emerge: since some conception of one's cognitive locality and of the substance of states of affairs that are elsewhere is essential to any objective conception of experience—and since (suppose) so conceiving of experience is independently warranted or unavoidable—a thinker is entitled to the basic ontology involved in an otherwise coherent conception of what kind of thing might obtain at other localities.

Notice that this still falls short of requiring a *specific* ontology. Unless there are independent objections to any other ways of realising the general shape—or unless there are no such other ways— it merely gives us a *permission* for matter and space. And it says, so far, nothing about mind.

IX

Concluding Reflections. Let me review the main lines of the prospectus I've tried to motivate and highlight some of the matters that remain for further work.

'Warrant for nothing' is a nice phrase, but is entitlement—at least in the guise that has emerged—happily captioned by it? After all, there has been no suggestion that one is justified, by default and without evidence for their truth, in holding to certain *beliefs*. Rather, the proposal is that the idea of entitlement is best approached in terms of a more generic kind of propositional attitude—the kind of attitude signalled, at least in certain kinds of use, by the phrases 'acting on the assumption that', 'taking it for granted that' and 'trusting that'. We can think of both belief and other attitudes of this kind as sub-species of a more general notion of *acceptance*, unified by analogies and overlap in what they respectively require of a rational agent who, in one or another way, accepts a given proposition. I have not here tried to fill out the detail of the analogies and overlap.

I have suggested that the relevant mode of acceptance for the purposes of the unified strategy is trust. It is in the nature of trust that it may be placed, without stigma, in things for which one has no evidence. But it is not *per se* 'for nothing' if that is understood as 'normatively unconstrained'. Trusting without evidence can still be rational or not. Entitlements are *warrants to trust*, supported in the kinds of ways we have been reviewing. The basic respect in which 'warrant for nothing' is apt as a caption for entitlement is that recognising the rationality of trusting that P need involve none of the work—empirical or *a priori*—that would have to go into the accumulation, perhaps *per impossibile*, of evidence for believing P. Counting both entitlements and evidential justifications as types of warrant, then, entitlement is not, maybe, a warrant costing nothing at all but it is at least a warrant costing nothing of the kind that would be involved in getting evidence for the truth of the proposition in question.

That said, though, there is a further element in the way the caption is naturally understood. The question arises whether, in order to enjoy an entitlement to a particular proposition, one has *oneself* to accomplish the demonstration that there is such warrant—to recognise oneself that the case is one where trust is rational. In normal circumstances, and putting to one side special issues concerning testimony, a thinker's knowing or justifiably believing something requires that she herself have evidence for it sufficient to constitute knowledge or justified belief. By contrast we do not, at least in a wide class of cases, demand that before a thinker can justifiably infer in accordance with a principle of inference, she must herself have accomplished a justification for the use of that rule. At least in cases where a valid pattern of inference demands no special training but is followed by the 'light of natural reason', we will naturally credit a thinker with warrant to proceed as she does, even if she has given no explicit thought to that way of proceeding and would not have the slightest idea how to answer if a request for justification was made. If entitlement stands comparison in this matter with justified belief rather than warranted inference, then—in the present state of our understanding of these issues—no-one yet has ever had much in the way of entitlements. Roll on the day when we get these things straightened out, and can at last get some entitlement to our cornerstones, fend off scepticism and start accumulating some knowledge! Clearly this is yet another issue for further attention, but entitlement had better prove to be 'for nothing' in this additional sense too—had better be comparable to rights of basic inference, as it were—if any but a few philosophers are to benefit from a vindication of the notion. The matter is deep and the comparison with basic logic suggestive.

I have outlined a case for three kinds of entitlement—strategic entitlements, entitlements of cognitive project, and entitlements of rational deliberation—and have gestured, in the most promissory and indefinite way, at the possibility of—and need for—a fourth, entitlement of substance. Entitlement of cognitive project seems to promise well in addressing the challenge of Cartesian scepticism, or any variety of scepticism that works by trying to dislodge a cornerstone of our intellectual or cognitive competence. Entitlements of strategy, and of rational delibera-tion, promise to be of use in addressing the challenge of inductive—and, more generally, methodological—scepticism, and also scepticism concerning the reliability of the various kinds of cognitive faculty that enter into the ways we form beliefs about subject matters of all kinds—*provided* we are granted an unchallenged conception of such subject matters. But as far as I have been able to see, these three kinds of entitlement fall short of the materials needed for a complete execution of the unified strategy. Humean—I-II-III—scepticism about the material world, and about other minds, *does* challenge our conception of the kinds of subject matter which, at the most general categorical level, the world puts up for our consideration. An entitlement of substance—an entitlement to have a view about the most basic categories of stuff and thing the world contains—is what it would take to close this gap. But we have glimpsed the merest outline of a recipe for the beginnings of a case there are any such entitlements.

The situation has to raise a concern about the ability of the unified strategy to fend off an unwelcome pluralism. It is, to be sure, an essential feature of the notion of entitlement that it is a matter of *rational* trust—and that's sufficient safeguard, for all but the most thoroughgoing sceptic about rationality, that not just any old trustings will do. But the point remains: if the most favourable light that can be cast on our acceptance of a material world, or other minds, consists in argument that our very rationality means we have to have *some* such commitments—for instance, that any system of rational objective thought has to incorporate *some* conception of the kind of stuff that inhabits other cognitive localities—then we seem to have no claim to the objective correctness of the most fundamental categories of substance that we actually employ. More, there will be no obstacle in principle to the idea of alternative, equally valid ways of conceiving the substance of the world, either involving substitutions for our categories, or their augmentation in, as many would feel, bizarre and unmotivated ways. What are the barriers to an entitlement to wood spirits, ectoplasm, gods and a plethora of existing but non-actual spatio-temporally unrelated concrete possible worlds?[22]

That's a concern about whether entitlement can reach far enough to meet our needs. But there are also concerns about its potency even where it does reach. In general, it has to be recognised that the unified strategy can at most deliver a *sceptical solution*—so will disappoint those who are disappointed with sceptical solutions in general. Sceptical solutions concede the thrust of the sceptical arguments they respond to. Kripke's sceptical solution, for instance, concedes that meaning and its cognates are shown to be non-factual by the famous (putatively Wittgensteinian) sceptical argument. The unified strategy likewise concedes the basic point of the sceptical arguments to which it reacts, namely that we do indeed have no claim to know,[23] in any sense involving possession of evidence for their likely truth, that certain cornerstones of what we take to be procedures yielding knowledge and justified belief hold good. It then attempts to provide an accommodation with this concession, arguing that there is nevertheless no irrationality, or capriciousness, in our proceeding in the ways we do—that we are warranted in so proceeding but warranted in a different way. That is, of course, a very important claim if it is true. But there is no disguising the fact that the exercise comes as one of damage limitation. That will disappoint those who hanker after a demonstration that there was all along, actually, no real damage to limit—that the

---

22. The last is no mere rhetorical flourish. Lewis's ontology stands to (most of) ours as an ontology of other minds stands to solipsism.

23. Note: have no *claim* to know, not: do *not* know.

sceptical arguments involve *mistakes*. Good luck to all philosophers who quest for such a demonstration.[24]

A more specific concern about potency is what I earlier termed the 'leaching' problem. The general picture is that the cornerstones which sceptical doubt assails are to be held in place as things one may warrantedly trust without evidence. Thus at the foundation of all our cognitive procedures lie things we merely implicitly trust and take for granted, even though their being entitlements ensures that it is not irrational to do so. But in that case, what prevents this 'merely taken for granted' character from leaching upwards from the foundations, as it were like rising damp, to contaminate the products of genuine cognitive investigation? If a cognitively earned warrant—say my visual warrant for thinking that there is a human hand in front of my face right now—is achieved subject to a mere entitled acceptance that there is a material world at all, then why am I not likewise merely entitled to accept that there is a hand in front of my face, rather than knowing or fully justifiably believing that there is?

The short answer is that there is leaching, but that it is at one remove and can be lived with. In general, to be entitled to trust that, for example, my eyes are right now functioning effectively enough in conditions broadly conducive to visual recognition of local situations and objects is to be entitled to claim that my vision is right now a source of reliable information about the local perceptible environment and is hence at the service of the gathering

---

24. Stephen Schiffer (see e.g. Schiffer [2003], pp. 68–9, and Schiffer [forthcoming]) usefully distinguishes between 'happy face' and 'unhappy face' solutions to paradoxes. Happy face solutions consist, broadly in the disclosure of mistakes in the premises or reasoning of the paradox. But in the general run of philosophical paradoxes, Schiffer counsels us to ready for the possibility that there is no solution of this kind, that the only way out will be via conceptual revision. There is then a further division: *weak* unhappy face solutions propose conceptual revisions that are broadly conservative of the purposes and utility of the paradox-generating concepts; but in other cases—where only a *strong* unhappy face solution is possible—each of the possible paradox-preempting revisions will involve significant loss.

The general form of solution to the paradoxes of scepticism pursued by the unified strategy rather straddles the boundary between happy face and weak unhappy face. One can treat the sceptical arguments as involving a mistaken conflation of evidential justification and warrant—as overlooking the possibility of rational entitlement. Or one can see the invocation of entitlement as, in effect, a form of conceptual revision—extension—of our conception of the range of ways in which acceptance of a proposition can be justified. But in any case, the proposal does not wear the happiest of faces—that would only belong to a solution which somehow faulted the sceptical reasoning as applied to evidence.

of perceptual knowledge. To be entitled to trust that other humans have mental states whose character may be accurately discerned by applying our normal interpretative criteria to the things they say and do is to be entitled to trust that other minds can be known in standard ways. And to be entitled to trust in the soundness of a basic inferential apparatus—to anticipate a discussion of the status of fundamental rules of inference on which I have not here embarked[25]—is to be entitled to regard its correct deployment as serving the generation of proofs and hence, since what is proved is known, to be entitled to claim knowledge of the products of reasoning in accordance with it. In general, the effect of conceding that we have mere entitlements for cornerstones is not uniformly to supplant evidential cognitive achievements—knowledge and justified belief—with mere entitlements right across the board but to qualify our claims to *higher order* cognitive achievement. I am right now in possession of a plethora of perceptual knowledge concerning occurrences around me. That is a claim which, if the unified strategy delivers as hoped, I will be rationally entitled to make. But in order to be able to *know* that it is true, I need (this is a closure step, of course) to be able to know the presuppositions of its truth, some of which—we are taking it—sceptical argument has put beyond evidence. So scepticism demands the surrender of higher order knowledge—the claim to know that we know. But entitlement, in the best case, promises to save the warrantability nevertheless of the first order claim to know. And maybe that is enough to be going on with.

   Dissatisfaction may remain.[26] Let C be any cornerstone which sceptical argument persuades us is beyond evidence and let P be any ordinary, non-basic belief in the region of enquiry for which C is a cornerstone which, in line with the train of thought we just ran through, we are supposedly entitled to regard as knowledge-able nonetheless. Let warrant include both evidence and entitlement, and assume that, although closure across (known) logical consequence is qualified for evidential justification (as suggested at the end of Section I), it holds for warrant. Then the

25. For an initiation of discussion of the part entitlement may play in the epistemology of basic logic, see my [forthcoming].

26. The following train of thought is a version of an objection put to me by Sebastiano Moruzzi.

leaching problem, in a sharper formulation, is that the following trio of claims may all seem to be warranted:

First, if we run a risk in accepting C, then we run a risk in accepting P.

This seems merely to articulate an immediate implication of C's being a cornerstone for the class of beliefs typified by P.

Second, we do run a risk in accepting C.

—after all, entitled as we may be, the fact has not gone away that we have no evidence for C.

Third, P is known.

—a claim we are warranted (entitled) in making, by hypothesis. But now it appears that we must be warranted in claiming both that P is known and that we run a risk in accepting it. And that seems, near enough, a contradiction. A major part of the point of the concept of knowledge is that it is meant to mark a state in which belief is *safe*, in which it is risk-free. If it does not do that, what is the content of the claim to have knowledge that P?

The reply I am making in behalf of the unified strategy, transposed to this form of the leaching worry, is that what is wrong is not the third claim but the (consequent of the) first. What necessarily inherits the risk we run in trusting C without evidence is not our belief that P—for we may in fact have reliable evidence for P—but our belief that we have reliable evidence for it. To be sure, to *claim* to know P is indeed to promise that it is safe to accept P. However, that promise is not automatically worthless, or inappropriate, if the claim to know is not itself knowledgeable. It will still have every point if enough has been done to ensure that all that remains to put the knowledge claim at risk is the possible failure of conditions in which everybody, speaker and audience, (rationally) trusts.

One final matter. The discussion has proceeded with no mention of the opposition between *internalist* and *externalist* views of knowledge and justification. But its spirit, it may seem, has been very much internalist: entitlements, it appears, in contrast with any broadly externalist conception of warrant, are essentially recognisable by means of traditionally internalist resources—*a priori* reflection and self-knowledge—and are generally independent of the character of our actual cognitive situation in the wider world[27]—indeed, are designed to be so. Anyone who thinks that the paradoxes of scepticism are best solved, or dissolved, by proper emphasis on the external character of knowledge, or genuine warrant, is therefore likely to be impatient with the present project. If knowledge, and justification, are essentially *environmental*—are constituted by (perhaps reflectively inscrutable) contingencies of our cognitive powers and the way they enable us to interact with the external world—then no mere sceptical paradox, developed in the armchair, can show that we have no knowledgeable or justified beliefs. So why bother trying to make out entitlements?

Fully to address this reservation would need a complex and extensive discussion. But one immediate observation is that what is put in doubt by sceptical argument is—of course—not our *possession* of any knowledge or justified belief—not if knowledgeability, or justification, are conceived as constituted in aspects of the external situation in which we come to a belief. (How indeed could armchair ruminations show anything about that?) What is put in doubt is rather our right to *claim* knowledge and justified belief. It is this which the project of making out entitlements tries to address and which, on what seems to me to be a correct assumption, externalism is impotent to address.

That assumption is that epistemic values are subject to a division broadly similar to one within moral values. While some meta-ethical views—classical utilitarianism, for instance—can be seen as driven by a sort of moral monism, it is intuitively plausible is that there are at least two quite different kinds of virtue which an action may possess or lack: virtue of consequence (utility), and virtue of provenance—of conscience, or integrity—relating to the attitudinal states of the agent that determined her choice to act in that particular way. The two types of virtue are not, of course, independent—good conscience requires that one reckon with the foreseeable consequences of one's actions—and there seems no reason to expect that one should generally trump the other, still less to expect reducibility in either direction. I want to endorse a broadly analogous distinction in the ethics of belief: that we should allow a comparable kind of division between considerations of *intellectual integrity* and considerations to do

---

27. This claim would need qualification to allow for entitlements of substance.

with the *situational provenance* and other potentially fortunate or unfortunate aspects of the circumstances of a particular belief (for instance, its being the product of a reliable—truth-conducive—belief-forming mechanism). Both categories of virtue are important—indeed, I would argue, indispensable. So those philosophers who have done so have been right to lay stress on notions of knowledge, or justification, which emphasise the second. But, again, there is no reason to expect either type of virtue to reduce to, or trump, the other.

Descartes' project in the *Meditations* was one of harmonisation of his beliefs with the requirements of rational conscience and its timeless appeal is testimony to the deep entrenchment of virtues of intellectual integrity in our cognitive lives. The *right to claim* knowledge, as challenged by scepticism, is something to be understood in terms of—and to be settled by—canons of intellectual integrity. The paradoxes of scepticism are paradoxes for the attempt at a systematic respect of those canons. They cannot be addressed by a position which allows that in the end thoroughgoing intellectual integrity is unobtainable, that all we can hope for is fortunate cognitive situation. When good conscience fails, there are still, indeed, other good—circumstantial—qualities which our beliefs may have. But what is wanted is good conscience for the claim that this possibility is realised on the grand scale we customarily assume.[28]

28. Versions of some of these ideas were presented in my NYU seminars on Scepticism in Spring 2002, and later in that year at a departmental colloquium at the University of Bristol, at the European Summer School in Analytical Philosophy held in Paris and at the Birkbeck Philosophy Society. They also featured prominently in a series of three seminars given at the University of Bologna in January 2004. My thanks to all who participated in those discussions, which generated innumerable improvements. I have also been greatly helped by the comments of my colleagues— Roy Cook, Philip Ebert, Nikolaj Jang Pedersen, Agustin Rayo, Marcus Rossberg, and Robbie Williams—in the Arché AHRB project on Foundations for Classical Mathematics, who have patiently allowed several of our weekly project seminars to be diverted onto this material, trusting in its eventual relevance to the issue of fundamental *a priori* knowledge. My thanks to Annalisa Coliva, Duncan Pritchard, Stephen Schiffer, and Tim Williamson for helpful comments on an earlier draft. I am especially grateful to David Enoch and Joshua Schechter who have been working independently [Enoch and Schechter, unpublished manuscript] on a generalised development of the broadly Reichenbachian direction, focused on the justification of belief-forming methods, and who each provided me with extensive constructive criticisms and comparisons with their own approach. I hope to take up the comparisons on another occasion. Most of the research for the paper was conducted during my tenure of a Leverhulme Research Professorship and I once again gratefully acknowledge the support of the Leverhulme Trust.

References

Burge, T., 1993, 'Content Preservation', *The Philosophical Review* 102, pp. 457–88.

Enoch, D. and Schechter, J., 'How Are Basic Belief-Forming Methods Justified?' Unpublished TS.

Evans, G., 1980, 'Things Without the Mind', in Zak van Straaten, ed., *Philosophical Subjects: Essays Presented to P. F. Strawson* (Oxford: Clarendon Press) pp. 76–116.

Goodman, N., 1995, *Fact, Fiction, and Forecast* (Cambridge, Mass.: Harvard University Press).

Hume, D. *An Enquiry Concerning Human Understanding* (ed. L. A. Selby-Bigge).

McDowell, J., 1994, *Mind and World* (Cambridge, Mass.: Harvard University Press).

Putnam, H., 1994, 'Sense, Nonsense and the Senses: An Enquiry Into the Powers of the Human Mind', *Journal of Philosophy* 91, pp. 445–517.

Reichenbach, H., 1938, *Experience and Prediction* (Chicago: University of Chicago Press).

Reichenbach, H., 1949, *The Theory of Probability*, 2nd edition tr. E. H. Hutten and M. Reichenbach, (Berkeley: University of California Press).

Reichenbach, H., 1968, *The Rise of Scientific Philosophy*, Berkeley and Los Angeles: University of California Press).

Schiffer, S., 2003, *The Things We Mean* (Oxford: Clarendon Press)

————'Skepticism and the Vagaries of Justified Belief', *Philosophical Studies*, forthcoming.

Strawson, P. F., 1959 *Individuals: An Essay in Descriptive Metaphysics* (London: Methuen).

Sudbury, A. W., 1973 'Could There Exist a World Which Obeyed No Scientific Laws?' in *The British Journal for the Philosophy of Science* 24, pp. 39–40.

van Fraassen, Bas. C., 1980, *The Scientific Image* (Oxford: Clarendon Press).

Wittgenstein, L., 1969, *On Certainty* (Oxford: Basil Blackwell).

Wright, C., 1985, 'Facts and Certainty', Henriette Hertz Philosophical Lecture for the British Academy, December 1985, in *Proceedings of the British Academy* LXXI, pp. 429–72.

Wright, C., 2002, '(Anti)-Sceptics, Simple and Subtle: G. E. Moore and J. McDowell', *Philosophy and Phenomenological Research* LXV, pp. 330–48.

Wright, C., 'Intuition, Entitlement and the Epistemology of Basic Logical Laws', *Dialectica*, forthcoming.

ON EPISTEMIC ENTITLEMENT

by Crispin Wright and Martin Davies

II—*Martin Davies*

EPISTEMIC ENTITLEMENT, WARRANT TRANSMISSION AND EASY KNOWLEDGE

ABSTRACT   Wright's account of sceptical arguments and his use of the idea of epistemic entitlement are reviewed. His notion of non-transmission of epistemic warrant is explained and a concern about his notion of entitlement is developed. An epistemological framework different from Wright's is described and several notions of entitlement are introduced. One of these, negative entitlement, is selected for more detailed comparison with Wright's notion. Thereafter, the paper shows how the two notions of entitlement have contrasting consequences for non-transmission of warrant and how they go naturally with two conceptions of the presuppositions of epistemic projects. Problems for negative entitlement are explained and solutions are proposed.

In the first section of his paper, Crispin Wright distinguishes two kinds of sceptical paradox—the Cartesian and the Humean—which, he suggests, 'capture, in essentials, all that we have to worry about'. Sceptical arguments of both kinds are supposed to show that we lack a warrant for crucial propositions that Wright calls 'cornerstones'. But in each case there is a gap in the argument. The sceptic needs to move from our having no evidential justification to our having no warrant at all. So one strategy for responding to the sceptic is to appeal to a kind of warrant that is not a matter of evidential support—a kind of warrant that 'we do not have to *do any specific evidential work* to earn'. This is the kind of warrant that Wright calls 'entitlement'. The main business of the central sections (III–VIII) of Wright's paper is then to make a start on the major philosophical project of providing a substantive account of our epistemic entitlements. So he considers the prospects for, and the limitations of, strategic entitlements and entitlements of cognitive project, of rational deliberation, and of substance.

In my paper, I focus on structural features of Wright's notion of entitlement. I begin (Section I) with an earlier discussion of

sceptical arguments that covers some of the same ground as the
first section of his paper in this symposium. Then, in Section II, I
turn to the question that Wright addresses in his second section,
namely, the question of what epistemic entitlement is an
entitlement to do (to believe, to accept, or something else). I
suggest that Wright's answer to this question, when taken
together with some ideas about transmission of epistemic
warrant, may impose a strain on our ordinary thinking about
the proper management of our web of belief.

While I do not press that concern about Wright's notion of
entitlement, I go on to describe a different notion, negative
entitlement (Section III). I show how the two notions yield
different answers to questions about transmission of epistemic
warrant and how the negative notion does not impose the just-
mentioned strain on our ordinary thinking about belief (Section
IV). And I connect the two notions of entitlement with two ways of
thinking about the presuppositions of a cognitive or epistemic
project (Section V). In the final two sections, I explain a problem
that is faced by the epistemological framework into which the
notion of negative entitlement naturally fits and then propose a
solution.

I

Two Patterns of Sceptical Argument: Dreaming and I-II-III. In his
British Academy Lecture, 'Facts and Certainty' (1985), Wright
begins from 'two simple patterns of argument which can be
brought to bear upon a variety of large regions of discourse so as
to generate what seem to be genuine sceptical paradoxes' (*ibid.*,
p. 430). Arguments that exhibit the first pattern make use of
sceptical possibilities that I am dreaming, that I am a brain in a
vat, or that I am hallucinating. Thus, for example, if the sceptic
can argue for the principle (C) that 'at no time t do I have
sufficient reason to believe that I am not dreaming at t' (*ibid.*,
p. 432) then we seem to be led to the conclusion that perception
does not provide a basis for knowledge or even for reasonable
belief. And the sceptic does appear to be well placed to argue for
that principle, to the extent that neither empirical evidence nor
a priori considerations can furnish me with a reason to believe
that I am not dreaming.

The second pattern of sceptical argument is to be appreciated by 'reflecting on the intuitive inadequacy of G. E. Moore's [1959] "proof" of the existence of the external world' (*ibid.*, p. 434). Moore's argument can be set out as follows:

MOORE (I)   I am having an experience as of one hand [here] and another [here].
MOORE (II)   I have hands.
              If I have hands then an external world exists.

Therefore:

MOORE (III)   An external world exists.

MOORE (I) is a proposition about Moore's experience and, on one conception of perceptual warrant, MOORE (II) is arrived at by inference from this proposition. On another conception, it is the experience itself, rather than a belief about the experience, that provides the defeasible warrant for believing the proposition about hands. But, whichever conception of perceptual warrant is adopted, the key question at this point in Wright's account is whether the support for MOORE (II) is transmitted to MOORE (III) across the *modus ponens* inference in which the conditional premise is supported by an elementary piece of philosophical theorising.

On behalf of the sceptic, Wright (*ibid.*, pp. 435–6) asks us to compare Moore's argument with the following:

ELECTION (I)   Jones has just written an 'X' on that piece of paper.
ELECTION (II)   Jones has just voted.
                If Jones has just voted then an election is taking place.

Therefore:

ELECTION (III) An election is taking place.

Here, the evidence summarised in ELECTION (I) provides defeasible support for ELECTION (II); and this premise, together with the conditional premise that is warranted by a conceptual connection between voting and elections, clearly entails ELECTION (III).

Given this relationship between ELECTION (II) and ELECTION (III), we might expect that empirical evidence against

ELECTION (III) would count against ELECTION (II) by going into the scales on the opposite side from the evidence summarised in ELECTION (I). In particular, we might expect that evidence that there is no election taking place would leave intact the status of Jones's writing an 'X' on the paper as evidence supporting the belief that Jones has just voted. It would simply outweigh that evidence. But, Wright stresses, this is not, in general, the correct picture (*ibid.*, p. 436):

> Imagine ... that you live in a society which holds electoral 'drills' as often as we hold fire drills, so that the scene you witness of itself provides no clue whether a genuine election is going on or not. In that case, unless you have further information, the knowledge that Jones has placed an 'X' on what looks like a ballot paper has no tendency whatever to support the claim that he has just voted.

In a situation where I have reason to believe that what I am watching is a drill rather than an election, the support ordinarily provided for ELECTION (II) by ELECTION (I) is not outweighed but removed.[1] So, Wright says (*ibid.*, p. 436):

> The evidential support afforded by [ELECTION (I)] for [ELECTION (II)] is itself conditional on the *prior* reasonableness of accepting [ELECTION (III)] ... Knowledge of the first does not begin to provide support for the second unless it is *antecedently* reasonable to accept the third.

The imagined sceptic then says that Moore's argument is relevantly similar (*ibid.*, p. 437):

---

1. We are here in the vicinity of John Pollock's (1974) distinction between rebutting and undercutting defeaters. Wright does not commit himself to any specific analysis of the distinction between outweighing and removing evidential support, but that there is some such distinction is intuitively very plausible and I shall follow Wright in presuming upon it.

When Wright speaks of the scene 'provid[ing] no clue whether a genuine election is going on or not' should we think of this as the background information making it rational to assign equal probabilities to the genuine election possibility and the election drill possibility? For if that were the situation, then the probability of the election possibility given Jones's writing an 'X' would be 0.5 (supposing that Jones would write an 'X' only if there were either a genuine election or a drill). The probability of Jones's having just voted given Jones's having just written an 'X' would also be about 0.5 and, presumably, significantly higher than its prior probability. So it would be difficult to maintain that Jones's writing an 'X' 'has no tendency whatever to support the claim that he has just voted'. The main point is that Jones's writing an 'X' does nothing to support the claim that he has just voted against the claim that he has just taken part in an election drill.

Once the hypothesis is seriously entertained that it is as likely as not, for all I know, that there is no material world as ordinarily conceived, my experience will lose all tendency to corroborate the particular propositions about the material world which I normally take to be certain.

As a result (*ibid.*; emphasis added): 'Only if Moore *already* has grounds for [MOORE (III)] does [MOORE (I)] tend to support [MOORE (II)].'

The sceptic's point is that ELECTION (III) cannot be supported by inference from ELECTION (II) when this is supported in turn by evidence of the kind described in ELECTION (I). Similarly, MOORE (III) cannot be supported by inference from particular claims like MOORE (II) when these are supported in turn by evidence of the kind described in MOORE (I), that is, by the evidence provided by putatively perceptual experiences. According to the sceptic, independent and antecedent support for ELECTION (III) and MOORE (III) is what is needed. But while independent evidence in support of ELECTION (III) might be gathered, there is no prospect of such support for MOORE (III). If this pattern of sceptical argument is accepted, then, as Wright says (*ibid.*, p. 438),

We seem bound to recognize that all our evidential commerce is founded upon assumptions for which we have no reason whatever, can get no reason whatever, and which may yet involve the very grossest misrepresentation of reality.

Of course, Wright himself is by no means committed to the sceptical conclusion. The question, though, is how to avoid it. In the second half of 'Facts and Certainty', he notes that we could escape the sceptical bind 'if it could be reasonable to accept a group III proposition *without reason*; that is, without evidence' (*ibid.*, p. 459). This leads Wright to consider the possibility that there are propositions that lie outside the domain of *cognitive achievement*. These propositions would not be known in a narrow sense; but they might still be known in a more inclusive sense. As Wittgenstein says in *On Certainty* (1969), 357–9:

357. One might say: ' "I know" expresses *comfortable* certainty, not the certainty that is still struggling.'

358. Now I would like to regard this certainty, not as something akin to hastiness or superficiality, but as a form of life ...

359.   But that means I want to conceive it as something that lies beyond being
        justified; as it were, as something animal.

Wright actually explores the idea that these propositions lie
outside the domain of cognitive or epistemic achievement because
they lie outside the domain of truth-evaluability—they are *not
fact-stating*. But it seems that the general structure of Wright's
proposal as involving narrower and more inclusive notions of
knowledge or warrant could be retained even if we were not to go
so far as to deny the fact-stating status of the propositions to
which only the more inclusive notion ('comfortable certainty')
applied. We might distinguish between a narrower notion of
knowledge or warrant that is an *achievement* and a more inclusive
notion that embraces assumptions that we are epistemically
entitled to make. As Wright says at the very end of the paper
(1985, p. 471; second emphasis added):

> If ... the concept of reasonable belief ... embraces *certainty* in
> Wittgenstein's more inclusive sense, then the argument for C [the
> principle mentioned in the first paragraph of this section] fails: it does
> not follow from the impossibility of my *achieving* cognition that I am
> not dreaming at t that I cannot be legitimately certain that I am not.

Before turning from Wright's 1985 lecture to his paper in the
present symposium, I want to draw attention to one aspect of
his account of the sceptic's arguments. In the discussion of both
the (ELECTION) argument and the (MOORE) argument,
Wright's sceptic appears to take a small but important step.
From the agreed point that if it were antecedently reasonable to
reject the type-III proposition then the putative support for the
type-II proposition would be removed, the sceptic moves to the
apparently different claim that it is only if it is antecedently
reasonable to *accept* the type-III proposition that the type-II
proposition is really supported. Wright himself does not dispute
this latter claim. His appeal to the idea of epistemic entitlement
is intended as a way of providing the antecedent warrant that
the sceptic demands. But we could dispute the claim and, in
what follows, I consider epistemological accounts that do
dispute it.

II

Cornerstones, Entitlement, and Non-Transmission of Warrant. In his paper in this symposium, Wright returns to the two kinds of sceptical paradox, organising his discussion around the notion of a proposition being a *cornerstone* for a given region of thought. If we were to lack warrant for the cornerstone proposition then we could not rationally claim to have warrant for any belief in the region.[2] In line with the first pattern of sceptical argument, the negation of the dreaming hypothesis, or of the brain-in-a-vat hypothesis, is taken to be a cornerstone for a large class of beliefs including, we may suppose, many perceptually based beliefs.[3] In line with the second pattern of sceptical argument, type-III propositions are taken to be cornerstones for corresponding regions of type-II beliefs.

As in the earlier account, it is allowed that the project of assembling evidential support for the cornerstone would be futile. In the case of the first pattern (p. 169): 'So it appears that my acquiring a warrant by empirical means for the proposition that I am not now dreaming requires that I *already have* a warrant for that same proposition. So I cannot ever acquire such a warrant (for the first time).' In the case of the second pattern (p. 171): 'So, again, there is a vicious circle.' The sceptical conclusion threatens. But, as before, there appears to be a way out of the sceptical bind (pp. 174–5):

> Suppose there is a type of rational warrant which one does not have to *do any specific evidential work* to earn ... Call it *entitlement*. If I am entitled to accept P, then my doing so is beyond rational reproach even though I can point to no cognitive accomplishment in my life ... whose upshot could reasonably be contended to be that I had come to know that P, or had succeeded in getting evidence justifying P.

This appeal to antecedent entitlement—entitlement to our cornerstones—is the beginning of the *unified strategy* for responding to both patterns of sceptical argument.

2. We should note that, in the definition of a cornerstone, Wright says that from a lack of warrant for the cornerstone proposition it would follow that one *could not rationally claim* warrant for any belief in the region—not that one *would not have* warrant for any belief in the region. At the outset, he is not explicit about the significance that he attaches to the distinction; but it looms large in the concluding section of his paper.

3. Wright, 1985, p. 431.

We should ask, as Wright does in the second section of his paper, what the nature of this entitlement is. What is it an entitlement *to do*? It is initially introduced as an entitlement to 'accept' a proposition P, and Wright goes on to suggest that it is *not* a non-evidential warrant to *believe* a proposition P but something like a warrant to act on the assumption that P, take it for granted that P, or trust that P (pp. 175–6). Later, he settles on the idea that entitlement is rational trust (p. 194). So the overall picture is that, against the background of our rational trust that the type-III proposition is true, the type-II proposition is supported by evidence and we have a warrant to believe it.

Someone might query whether something *less* than an antecedent warrant to *believe* the type-III proposition can really secure this favourable outcome for the type-II proposition. Wright addresses this question in the concluding section of his paper.[4] But suppose, for the moment, that we do indeed have a warrant to believe the type-II proposition. Then a second question arises. Given that the type-II proposition obviously entails the type-III proposition, do we end up with a warrant to believe the type-III proposition as well? Does the I-II-III argument serve to transform the lead of rational trust into the gold of justified belief? In order to address this question, we need first to sketch Wright's ideas about non-transmission of epistemic warrant—going back, once again, to his 1985 lecture.

Within his discussion of the second pattern of sceptical argument—the I-II-III pattern—Wright introduces the idea of non-transmission of epistemic warrant in the specific form of non-transmission of evidential support (1985, pp. 436–7):

> It simply is not true that whenever evidence supports a hypothesis, it will also support each proposition which follows from it. The important class of exceptions illustrated are cases where the support offered to the hypothesis is conditional upon its being independently reasonable to accept one in particular of its consequences.

So, for example, it may be that the evidence described in ELECTION (I) supports ELECTION (II). But this support is not transmitted to ELECTION (III) because (at least according to Wright's sceptic) the support offered for ELECTION (II) is

---

4. See his discussion of the 'leaching' problem, pp. 207–9.

already conditional upon its being antecedently reasonable to accept ELECTION (III). Similarly, even if the evidence described in MOORE (I) were to support MOORE (II), this support would not be transmitted to MOORE (III). For the support offered for MOORE (II) would be conditional upon its being (*per impossibile*, according to the sceptic) antecedently reasonable to accept MOORE (III).

This suggests a first shot at a general principle limiting transmission of epistemic warrant[5]—something along the following lines:

Non-transmission of warrant
Epistemic warrant is not transmitted from the premises of a valid argument to its conclusion if the putative support offered for one of the premises is conditional on its being antecedently and independently reasonable to accept the conclusion.[6]

In his new paper, the issue of non-transmission arises again when Wright says (p. 172):

Type-III propositions cannot be warranted by transmission of evidence provided by type-I propositions for type-II propositions across a type-II to type-III entailment—rather it's only if one already has warrant for the type-III proposition that any type-II propositions can be justified in the first place.

The point here is not that evidential support cannot be transmitted across the type-II to type-III entailment because, given the sceptical argument, there is no evidential support for the type-II proposition in the first place. Rather, even supposing that there is evidential support for the type-II proposition and that there is some kind of antecedent warrant, perhaps entitlement, for the type-III proposition (since it is a cornerstone), the evidential support for the type-II proposition still cannot be transmitted to the type-III proposition. It provides no additional support for the type-III proposition. As Wright puts it in another recent paper, the I-II-III arguments are not *cogent* (2003, p. 57):

---

5. See also Wright 2000, 2002, 2003.
6. We can allow that the putative warrant for believing the premise of an argument might be provided by some further warranted belief or by something other than a belief such as, for example, a perceptual experience.

[A cogent argument] is an argument, roughly, whereby someone could/ should be moved to rational conviction of the truth of its conclusion— a case where it is possible to *learn* of the truth of the conclusion by getting warrant for the premises and then reasoning to it by the steps involved in the argument in question. Thus a valid argument with warranted premises cannot be cogent if the route to warrant for its premises goes—of necessity, or under the particular constraints of a given epistemic context—via a prior warrant for its conclusion. Such arguments, as we like to say, 'beg the question'.

Say that a particular warrant, w, *transmits* across a valid argument just in case the argument is cogent when w is the warrant for its premises.

With this much about non-transmission of warrant by way of background, we can return to the question whether, at the end of a I-II-III argument, the entailed type-III proposition ends up with any more warrant than it started out with—whether, by following through a I-II-III argument, we can perform a kind of epistemic alchemy. It seems to me that the principles governing transmission of warrant dictate a negative answer to this question. The direction of the inferential step from type-II to type-III is opposite to the direction in the space of warrants—for, according to Wright, the warrant for the type-III proposition is *antecedent* to the warrant for the type-II proposition. But this negative answer, taken together with the idea that we do indeed have a warrant to believe the type-II proposition, seems to impose some strain on our ordinary thinking about the proper management of our web of belief.

Ordinarily, we think that, if I review some of my beliefs, $P_1, \ldots, P_n$, and notice a valid argument from those premises to Q then I should adopt the belief Q or, if other considerations argue against Q, then I should reconsider my beliefs $P_1, \ldots, P_n$. If there are warrants for me to believe $P_1, \ldots, P_n$ then, if I also believe Q, I shall again believe something for which there is a warrant. I shall think the thing that is the thing to think. But there is a distinction between believing something that is, as it happens, the thing to think and believing something *because* it is the thing to think. If I believe $P_1, \ldots, P_n$ because there are warrants for doing so, then I do well doxastically. If I start out believing $P_1, \ldots, P_n$ because there are warrants for doing so, and I go on to believe Q precisely because it follows from those premises, once again I do well doxastically.

These familiar thoughts suggest that, given the obvious entailment in the I-II-III argument, if we believe the type-II proposition that is supported by the evidence described in the type-I proposition, then we should also believe the type-III proposition that is the argument's conclusion. If considerations about non-transmission argue for going no further than the antecedent trust in the type-III proposition then we should reconsider whether belief is the proper attitude towards the type-II proposition. At the end of the second section of his paper, Wright offers a quick response to what is, I think, nearly enough this concern. But the response does not quite address head-on the question whether, if we start out with rational trust and then consider the I-II-III argument, we should, in the end, believe the type-III proposition.[7]

I am not committed to the view that this concern poses a serious threat to Wright's account of epistemic entitlement. But I shall go on to describe a different notion of entitlement for which the concern does not arise.

7. The concern is attributed to Stephen Schiffer; p. 177, n. 8. The response has two components. One is that closure principles for specific kinds of warrant are liable to be subject to restrictions. Wright's example is evidential warrant; an even more obvious case is non-inferential warrant. The other component is that warrant, construed inclusively so as to encompass both evidential justification and entitlement, is subject to less restricted, or even unrestricted, closure principles.

One way of responding to the concern would be to allow that entitlement is, after all, entitlement to believe. With just that change, Moore's argument, for example, would remain a case of non-transmission of warrant. But despite the non-transmission, there would be closure of warrant to believe. We would have a warrant for believing the type-II proposition; and at the conclusion of the argument we would still have what we had at the outset, namely, a warrant for believing the type-III proposition. The warrants would be of different types. The first would be an achieved evidential warrant; the second would be a warrant of entitlement. But we should not expect unrestricted closure for specific kinds of warrant.

A more radical way of responding to the concern about the proper attitude that should be taken towards type-III propositions would be to regard those propositions as being outside the domain of our ordinary thinking about doing well doxastically. Lying outside the domain of cognitive achievement, those propositions would also be 'outside the domain of what may be known, reasonably believed, or doubted' (1985, pp. 470–1). So, even if belief were the proper attitude towards a type-II proposition, belief could not be the proper attitude towards the entailed type-III proposition.

III

The Structure of Entitlement. As I noted at the end of Section I, there is a striking feature of Wright's appeal to entitlement as a way of escaping the sceptical bind. He does not challenge the sceptic's claim that, in order to have a warrant for the belief that there is, say, a computer in front of me, I need an antecedent warrant for ruling out the dreaming hypothesis, the brain-in-a-vat hypothesis, and so on (the first pattern of sceptical argument). Nor does he challenge the sceptic's claim that, in order to have a warrant for believing a type-II proposition such as the proposition that I have hands, I need an antecedent warrant for believing (or at least for trusting in the truth of) a type-III proposition such as the proposition that an external world exists (the second pattern of sceptical argument). The appeal to entitlement is supposed to make good the accepted need for an antecedent warrant—despite the fact that there seems to be no way to earn such a warrant.

An alternative strategy would be to challenge the sceptic's claim. We could deny that, in general, we need all these antecedent warrants. We could do this, even while allowing that both my warrant for believing that there is a computer in front of me and my warrant for believing that I have hands are defeasible. We could allow that there are propositions that are rather like cornerstones in that a warranted doubt about such a proposition defeats a putative warrant for any belief in the corresponding region. Furthermore, we could allow that, for such a cornerstone-like proposition P, even an unwarranted doubt about P would make it impossible for one rationally to avail oneself of a warrant for any belief in the corresponding region.[8] But a cornerstone-like proposition is not yet a cornerstone. According to the alternative strategy, as according to Wright's strategy, doubt about P would be epistemically damaging. But the alternative strategy would not, in general, allow that, in order to avoid epistemic damage, we need a

---

8. Here we have a distinction between the conditions for having a warrant and the conditions for rationally claiming (or rationally availing oneself of) a warrant. Someone with an unwarranted doubt about a cornerstone-like proposition P may still have an undefeated warrant for believing that he has hands, for example. But he cannot rationally combine that doubt with a claim to have such a warrant.

positive warrant—earned or unearned—for some attitude towards P that excludes doubt. For there may be no doubt and no reason to doubt even though doubt is not excluded by a competing attitude towards the proposition P. Indeed, someone might have no doubt about P and no reason to doubt P without even being able to grasp the proposition P.[9]

This, in barest outline, is the strategy that James Pryor (2000, 2004) adopts in the case of the justification of perceptual beliefs. Pryor develops an argument on behalf of the sceptic and ends with (2000, p. 532):

> [The sceptic about perceptual justification] says that if you're to be justified in believing that things are as they perceptually seem to you, you need to have antecedent reason to believe that you're not in certain sceptical scenarios.

But while Wright grants the sceptic this point, Pryor disputes it (*ibid.*):

> According to the dogmatist [about perceptual justification], when you have an experience as of *p*'s being the case, you have a kind of justification for believing *p* that does not presuppose or rest on any other evidence or justification you may have. To be justified in believing *p*, you do *not* need to have the antecedent justification the sceptic demands.

Pryor does not make explicit use of any notion of entitlement and he certainly has no need for the idea that one is entitled to adopt some attitude towards the propositions for which the sceptic demands antecedent warrant—that there is an external world, that one is not dreaming, or that one's perceptual apparatus is working properly. But we could introduce a notion of entitlement into the dogmatist account in one of at least two ways.

First, since warranted doubt about one's perceptual apparatus would defeat the warrant for a perceptual belief and even

9. We should note, once again, that Wright's definition of a cornerstone has it that without a warrant for a cornerstone proposition one cannot *rationally claim* to have a warrant for any belief in the region. On the alternative conception, as presumably on Wright's conception, the requirements for rationally claiming a warrant are stricter than the requirements for having a warrant. But, on the alternative conception, in the absence of doubt (warranted or unwarranted) about a cornerstone-like proposition, one can both have a warrant, and rationally claim to have a warrant, for believing that one has hands, for example.

unwarranted doubt would prevent one from availing oneself of that warrant, we could say that one has an entitlement not to doubt, not to call in question, or not to bother about, various things—unless there is some reason to doubt. This would be an entitlement *not to adopt the attitude of doubt* where Wright has an entitlement *to adopt the attitude of trust.* If entitlement is introduced into the dogmatist account in this first way, then it is a *negative* notion that operates at the *same* point—the cornerstone or cornerstone-like proposition—as does Wright's positive notion. It is this notion of negative entitlement that I shall compare with Wright's notion in the sections that follow.[10]

Second, while the sceptic says that we have no warrant for our perceptual beliefs without an antecedent warrant for a cornerstone proposition, we could say that one has an entitlement to one's perceptual beliefs provided only that there is no warrant for doubt about the cornerstone-like proposition. If entitlement is introduced into the dogmatist account in this second way, then it is a *positive* notion; indeed, it is a more positive notion than Wright's since it is entitlement *to adopt the attitude of belief* rather than just entitlement *to adopt the attitude of trust.* But it operates at a *different* point from Wright's notion. Roughly, it applies to type-II propositions rather than type-III propositions.

It is this second notion of entitlement that we find in the work of Tyler Burge. He says, for example (1993, pp. 458–9):

> The distinction between justification and entitlement is this: Although both have positive force in rationally supporting a propositional

10. The difference between negative entitlement and Wright's notion of entitlement is not adequately captured by the distinction between not adopting the attitude of doubt and adopting the attitude of trust. Indeed, it might be said that this latter distinction marks no significant difference in cases where the question whether ones's perceptual apparatus is working properly is allowed to arise. For, if one is entitled not to adopt the attitude of doubt and the question arises then, presumably, one should adopt some such attitude as belief or trust. The difference between negative entitlement and Wright's notion must be understood, rather, against the background of the difference between two epistemological frameworks. The dogmatist disputes the sceptic's demand and says that, in the absence of any reason to doubt that one's peceptual apparatus is working properly, a perceptual experience itself provides an epistemically adequate warrant for belief. This warranted perceptual belief may then figure in inferential warrants for other beliefs such as the belief that an external world exists or the belief that one's perceptual apparatus is working properly. The difference between the two epistemological frameworks is, in large part, a difference over the proper justificatory order. See below, especially Sections VI and VII. (I am indebted, here and elsewhere, to discussion with Paul Horwich.)

attitude or cognitive practice, and in constituting an epistemic right to it, entitlements are epistemic rights or warrants that need not be understood by or even accessible to the subject. We are entitled to rely, other things equal, on perception, memory, deductive and inductive reasoning, and on—I will claim—the word of others. The unsophisticated are entitled to rely on their perceptual beliefs. Philosophers may articulate these entitlements. But being entitled does not require being able to justify reliance on these resources, or even to conceive such a justification.

This passage might suggest a third way to introduce entitlement into the dogmatist account. Perhaps we could introduce a notion of entitlement *to rely on* various cognitive capacities or faculties. We could say that one is entitled to rely on the proper operation of one's perceptual apparatus unless there is some reason to think that it is not working properly. This does not, so far, sound like an entitlement to adopt any attitude towards a proposition. But, of course, reliance on one's perceptual apparatus would play a role in one's doing something, just as reliance on the proper operation of a power drill might play a role in one's putting together a piece of furniture. In particular, we should say that one is entitled to rely on the proper operation of one's perceptual apparatus *in forming beliefs* about one's perceptible environment. So, the third notion of entitlement is, after all, closely involved with the adoption of attitudes, in particular, with the formation of beliefs. Indeed, Burge says (2003a, p. 531): 'An epistemic entitlement to rely on a perceptual state or a perceptual system just *is* an entitlement to hold appropriately associated perceptual beliefs.'

IV

Unearned Assumptions and Negative Entitlement. If the third notion of entitlement is not really separate from the second notion, then we only need to consider two notions of entitlement that might be introduced into the dogmatist account. One is the negative notion of entitlement not to doubt, not to call in question, or not to bother about, Wright's type-III propositions—unless there is a reason to doubt. The other is the notion that Burge uses: entitlement is a species of warrant for beliefs, and it applies to Wright's type-II propositions. Each notion is legitimate—though, of course, if both are in play then we need to mark the difference terminologically. But it is vital that the negative notion of entitlement not to call cornerstone-like propositions in question should be distinguished from Wright's own notion of an unearned warrant to assume, whether this is to believe or to trust, that cornerstone propositions are true. As we shall see at the end of this section, these two notions have quite different consequences for non-transmission of warrant.

Consider again the argument (ELECTION). We are asked to imagine 'that you live in a society which holds electoral "drills" as often as we hold fire drills, so that the scene you witness of itself provides no clue whether a genuine election is going on or not' (Wright, 1985, p. 436). It is plausible that, if I lived in such a society, then the evidence of Jones writing an 'X' on what looked like a ballot paper would not constitute a warrant for my believing that Jones had just voted. From that starting point, I would need additional information, some positive reason to think that this was not a drill but a genuine election, before that evidence could provide a warrant for believing that Jones had just voted. In short, I would need to earn the assumption that an election is taking place [ELECTION (III)].

But there is another kind of case. Suppose that I live in a society where there are elections every few years and no election drills, nor even rumours of election drills. In this case it is not nearly as plausible that the evidence of Jones writing an 'X' on what looks like a ballot paper could not constitute a warrant for believing that Jones had just voted unless I had an antecedent positive reason for ruling out the election drill possibility.[11]

It might be suggested that we can acknowledge the importance of the difference between these two cases even while agreeing that, in both, the evidence constitutes a warrant only against the background of an assumption that this is a genuine election and not just a drill. For, it might be said, the important distinction is between an assumption that is earned and an assumption that is unearned—perhaps a default assumption. In the first case, the

---

11. As described, the two cases differ in whether or not there really are election drills. If there is an intuitive difference between the cases just as described, then presumably this reflects some externalist element in our conception of warrant. But we can take it that, in the first case, I have a belief—indeed, a warranted belief—that what looks like an election is quite likely to be an election drill. In the second case, I have no such belief and no warrant for such a belief.

background assumption has to be earned. I need to do something substantive to rule out the election drill possibility. In the second case, it might be said, the same background assumption is unearned. I just assume, or take it for granted, that an election, rather than a drill, is taking place. And I have the epistemic right to take this for granted in the absence of any reason to doubt that an election is taking place or to think that it might just be a drill. I have a warrant for my assumption even though I have undertaken no 'specific evidential work' to earn that warrant.[12]

This is Wright's notion of entitlement and, whether or not he would make use of it in this particular case, the notion surely holds some appeal. It promises, not only some relief from the sceptic's challenge, but also a fairly plausible account of the way in which, when there are no election drills nor even rumours of drills, the evidence of Jones writing an 'X' on what looks like a ballot paper could provide a warrant for believing that Jones had just voted.

However, it is not clear that, in every case where earning the right to a background assumption is intuitively not required, we should postulate an unearned or default background assumption. A thinker to whom we would, on this proposal, credit a default background assumption may not have any such assumption in mind. Even in a situation where there are regular elections and no drills, I might not have in mind any assumption to the effect that this is a genuine election and not an election drill. I might not even have the concept of an election drill.

In the case of a perceptual warrant, a thinker may simply *take* the deliverances of perceptual experience as veridical, without having in mind the assumption *that* the deliverances of perceptual experience are veridical. Certainly a thinker need not have in mind any assumptions about lighting conditions being normal, about perceptual apparatus working properly, or about not being the envatted victim of a powerful but deceptive scientist. A thinker could have a perceptual warrant for a belief while lacking

---

12. This account would, of course, face the question why, in the absence of empirical investigation, the assumption that a genuine election is taking place enjoys default status, not only descriptively—this is what I do assume—but normatively—this is what I have the epistemic right to assume. This question would have to be answered by a substantive philosophical account of our epistemic entitlements, of the kind offered by Wright in his paper. (This is not to say that Wright himself is committed to our having an entitlement to the assumption that a genuine election is taking place.)

the intellectual resources even to formulate such assumptions. As Burge (1993, 2003a, 2003b) argues, retaining the notion of an assumption—a kind of propositional attitude—in all such cases is an over-intellectualisation of the epistemological situation.

Consistently with Burge's or Pryor's account of the epistemological situation, and using Burge's notion of entitlement, we could say that the thinker is entitled to his perceptual belief that he has hands and that he is entitled to rely on the proper operation of his perceptual apparatus. Switching to the negative notion of entitlement, we could add that the thinker is entitled not to bother about, nor even to consider, the possibility that his perceptual apparatus might not be operating properly. But we must not slide from this to the idea that, since the thinker does not doubt that his perceptual apparatus is operating properly, he *assumes* this. For the thinker need not be capable of adopting any attitudes towards that proposition.

We might say that the negative notion of entitlement not to doubt a type-III proposition takes account of the Wittgensteinian idea that we are dealing here with 'something animal' (*OC*, 359) more fully than does Wright's notion of entitlement to trust that the proposition is true. But however that may be, there is a clear difference between the two notions in respect of their consequences for transmission of warrant.

If, as Wright does, we accept the sceptic's claim that we need an antecedent warrant for adopting some propositional attitude towards type-III propositions, then Moore's argument, for example, is a case of non-transmission of warrant. The argument involves a vicious circularity. Warrant is not transmitted from MOORE (II) to MOORE (III) because the putative support offered for MOORE (II) by the experience described in MOORE (I) is conditional on its being antecedently reasonable to accept MOORE (III). Thus, as we saw towards the end of Section II, if the antecedent warrant— entitlement—to accept MOORE (III) is an entitlement to trust, rather than an entitlement to believe, then it seems that the inference from MOORE (II) to MOORE (III) cannot provide a warrant for believing MOORE (III). And this is so, even if we do have a warrant for believing MOORE (II).

But suppose that, with Burge and Pryor, we say that there is no need for an antecedent warrant—not even for an antecedent unearned warrant. Suppose we say that the evidence described in a type-I proposition by itself supports the type-II proposition. Then there is no vicious circularity. The direction of the inferential step coincides with the direction in the space of warrants and the I-II-III argument could be a route to a first warrant for believing that there is an external world [MOORE (III)]. In short, if we reject the sceptic's claim and employ only the negative notion of entitlement for type-III propositions, then Moore's argument is *not* a case of transmission-failure.[13] It is for this reason that I said, at the end of Section II, that for the alternative notion of entitlement—negative entitlement—the concern about whether following through a I-II-III argument can yield a warrant to believe the type-III proposition does not arise.

In Sections VI and VII, we shall return to the consequences of the two notions of entitlement—Wright's notion and the negative notion—for issues about warrant transmission. But first, I want to connect that difference with the idea of the presuppositions of a cognitive or epistemic project.

V

Presuppositions and Entitlements of Cognitive Project. When, in Section 5 of his paper, Wright turns to entitlements of cognitive project, he says (p. 189):

> To take it that one has acquired a justification for a particular proposition by the appropriate exercise of appropriate cognitive capacities—perception, introspection, memory, or intellection, for instance—always involves various kinds of presupposition. These presuppositions will include the proper functioning of the relevant cognitive capacities, the suitability of the occasion and circumstances for their effective function, and indeed the integrity of the very concepts involved in the formulation of the issue in question.

A presupposition of a cognitive project is defined as a proposition P for which to doubt P (in advance) 'would rationally commit one to doubting the significance or competence of the project' (p. 193).

13. See Pryor, 2004.

Some presuppositions have the feature that, although it would be possible to undertake an investigation as to their truth or falsity, an attempt to provide evidence of their truth would involve a further cognitive project with its own presuppositions 'of no more secure a prior standing', and an attempt to provide evidence of the truth of these presuppositions in turn would involve yet a further cognitive project, and so on. In short, a presupposition P may have the feature that to accept 'an onus to justify P' would be to 'undertake a commitment to an infinite regress of justificatory projects' (p. 192). The key idea about entitlements of project is that such a presupposition is an entitlement provided only that (p. 191): 'We have no sufficient reason to believe that P is untrue.' And to say that a presupposition is an entitlement is to say that 'we should—are rationally entitled to—just go ahead and trust' that the presupposition is met (p. 192).

According to the definition of a presupposition, doubt about the presuppositions of an epistemic project would be epistemically damaging. It is consistent with the definition to suppose that warranted doubt, or a warrant for doubt, about a presupposition would defeat any putative warrant that an epistemic project might yield and that even unwarranted doubt would make it impossible for one rationally to avail oneself of any warrant that the project might yield. So, rational pursuit of an epistemic project requires negative entitlement to the project's presuppositions. But Wright's account of entitlements of cognitive project goes beyond this. For it suggests that, in order rationally to carry out an epistemic project, and in order rationally to take oneself to have arrived at a reason to believe a particular conclusion, one needs to adopt an attitude—trust— towards the presuppositions of that project. So, do we need to assume, trust, or believe that the presuppositions of our epistemic projects are true? Or is it enough that we should not doubt those presuppositions or call them into question? Do we need entitlement as Wright conceives it or only negative entitlement?

In earlier work,[14] I have considered the presuppositions of epistemic projects in the context of arguments about self-knowl-

14. Davies, 1998, 2000, 2003a, 2003b.

edge and externalism about content.[15] I have been particularly concerned with the presupposition that there is such a proposition to think as the purported proposition that formulates the issue on which the project is focused. I take it that this is encompassed in one of the presuppositions that Wright mentions, namely, the presupposition of 'the integrity of the very concepts involved in the formulation of the issue in question'.

In his seminal contribution to the topic of externalism and self-knowledge, Burge says (1988, pp. 653–4):

> Among the conditions that determine the contents of first-order empirical thoughts are some that can be known only by empirical means. To think of something as water, for example, one must be in some causal relation to water—or at least in some causal relation to other particular substances that enable one to theorize accurately about water ... To know that such conditions obtain, one must rely on empirical methods. To know that water exists, or that what one is touching is water, one cannot circumvent empirical procedures. But to *think* that water is a liquid, one need not *know* the complex conditions that must obtain if one is to think that thought.

In order to think that water is wet, and even to know that I am thinking that water is wet, I do not need to know anything of externalist philosophical theory, and I do not need to know that the conditions required by that theory actually obtain. This, in essence, is why there seems to be a problem with combining self-knowledge and externalism. For it seems that self-knowledge and philosophical theorising together provide a route to too-easy knowledge that certain environmental conditions obtain (McKinsey, 1991).

Burge also says (1988, p. 653; emphasis added): 'It is uncontroversial that the conditions for thinking a certain thought must be *presupposed* in the thinking.' In my view, this is the heart of the solution to the apparent problem posed by self-knowledge and externalism.[16] But my present concern is with two different ways of interpreting Burge's remark about presupposition.

---

15. See, for example, Davies (1998, p. 354): 'In any given epistemic project, some propositions will have a presuppositional status. Suppose that the focus of the project P is the proposition A, and that the investigation is carried out using method N. Then within P it is presupposed, for example, that A is a hypothesis that can be coherently entertained (can be believed, doubted, confirmed, disconfirmed); and it is also presupposed that N is a method that can yield knowledge, at least with respect to A.'

16. See especially Davies, 2003b.

On one possible interpretation—*not* the one that Burge intends—Burge is saying that, in thinking that *I am thinking that water is wet*, I assume that various conditions on the world around me are met. I do not need to earn an antecedent positive warrant for the assumption; rather, I am entitled to make the assumption. According to this first interpretation, Burge's account of authoritative self-knowledge makes use of something like Wright's notion of entitlement to empirical background assumptions.

This appeal to unearned assumptions seems once again to over-intellectualise the epistemological situation. For it is not especially plausible that, just in thinking that *I am thinking that water is wet*, I assume that some particular environmental conditions E obtain. In response to this worry it might be said that, for a thinker who has not engaged in any philosophical theorising, the assumption is just that there is such a proposition to think as that *I am thinking that water is wet*. Perhaps it is only philosophical theorising that leads me from this basic assumption to the further assumption that environmental conditions E obtain. But even the basic assumption seems too sophisticated to be required of every thinker who enjoys authoritative self-knowledge. So, although the notion of an unearned assumption will surely have some application in epistemological theory, it is better to interpret Burge in a different way. He is not saying that I assume—or trust or believe—that the requirements for thought actually obtain. Rather, he is saying that I rely on the obtaining of the requirements for thought rather as I rely on the reliability of perceptual mechanisms in normal conditions. I rely on these things even though they may be beyond my conceiving.

In fact, in response to a recent paper of mine (Davies, 2003b), Burge himself is explicit about this (2003b, p. 264):[17]

> I do *not* assimilate this notion of presupposition to a notion of assumption by the individual ... In order to think that water is wet, an individual need not have the concepts necessary to assume that the

---

17. I say (Davies, 2003b, p. 117–8): 'Perhaps there is a distinction to be drawn between assumptions and presuppositions. But, on the face of it, Burge is allowing that in thinking that water is wet, or in thinking that I am thinking that water is wet, I presuppose or assume that the conditions necessary for me to think that thought do obtain.' In response, Burge says (2003b, p. 264): 'I do *not* assimilate this notion of presupposition to a notion of assumption by the individual, as Davies conjectures.'

relevant conditions for thinking the thought are in place. A child can think that water is wet without having the concepts *condition, environment, causal relation between environment and individual subject, normal,* and so on. I did not intend presupposition to be a propositional attitude. It is an impersonal relation between the thinking and actual principles or conditions governing its possibility.

Such a presupposition plays no epistemic role in justifying ... an individual's authoritative self-knowledge.

While Burge is particularly concerned with self-knowledge, the point applies more generally. If I am to be warranted in believing a proposition Q then I must be able to think or entertain that proposition. The requirements for thinking the thought are presupposed in the thinking. This does not mean that, in order to be warranted in believing Q, I must have either an earned or an unearned warrant for assuming that those presupposed conditions C are met. But still, a warranted belief that the conditions C are *not* met would defeat the warrant for Q. And even an unwarranted belief that those conditions are not met would make it impossible for me rationally to avail myself of the warrant for Q.[18]

If this is right then, at least in the case of one of the presuppositions of an epistemic project, it is just negative entitlement that is required.

VI

The Problem of Easy Knowledge. The title of Wright's paper implicitly suggests that one problem that an account of entitlement might face is that it should make knowledge or warrant too easy. Indeed, this problem arises for the dogmatist epistemology of perceptual beliefs into which the negative notion of entitlement fits so naturally. I explain the problem in this section and then, in the next section, propose a solution.

Stewart Cohen (2002) raises a problem for epistemological views that seek to avoid a particular sceptical challenge by allowing what he calls 'basic knowledge'. The sceptical challenge

18. If I am to have a warrant for believing Q then I must not have a warranted doubt about whether the presupposed conditions C are met. If I am rationally to claim to have a warrant for believing Q then I must not have a doubt—warranted or not—that the conditions C are met.

is similar to the one that Wright (1985) develops from his reflections on the intuitive inadequacy of Moore's argument.[19] In Cohen's exposition, it is posed by 'the problem of the criterion' (2002, p. 309):

> A natural intuition (pretheoretically anyway) is that a potential knowledge source, e.g., sense perception, can not deliver knowledge unless we know the source is reliable. But surely our knowledge that sense perception is reliable will be based on knowledge we have about the workings of the world. And surely that knowledge will be acquired, in part, by sense perception. So it looks as if we are in the impossible situation of needing sensory knowledge prior to acquiring it ... Scepticism threatens.

One way to avoid the challenge is to deny the following problematic principle (*ibid.*):

> KR   A potential knowledge source K can yield knowledge for S, only if S knows K is reliable.

To deny that principle (KR) and accept that a belief source, such as sense perception, 'can deliver knowledge prior to one's knowing that the source is reliable' is to allow *basic knowledge* (*ibid.*, p. 310). But, Cohen argues (ibid., p. 311): 'Once we allow for basic knowledge, we can acquire reliability knowledge very easily—in fact, all too easily, from an intuitive perspective ... We can call this "The Problem of Easy Knowledge".'

Cohen's first instance of the problem of easy knowledge arises from the following example (*ibid.*, pp. 312–3):

> TABLE (I)   I am having an experience as of this table being red.
> TABLE (II)   This table is red.
>   If this table is red then it is not the case that this table is white but illuminated by red lights.
>
> Therefore:
>
> TABLE (III)   It is not the case that this table is white but illuminated by red lights.

According to someone who allows for basic knowledge, my warrant for believing TABLE (II) is constituted by the visual

---

19. It is also similar to the argument that Pryor develops on behalf of the sceptic in Section 2 of 'The Skeptic and the Dogmatist' (2000). See Pryor (2004) for his way of responding to Cohen's (2002) problem of easy knowledge.

experience described in TABLE (I), provided only that I do not have any reason to doubt that the lighting conditions are normal or that my perceptual apparatus is working properly. In particular, my warrant for believing TABLE (II) does not depend on my having any antecedent warrant for believing TABLE (III). I have a simple *a priori* warrant for believing the conditional premise; and it is straightforward to perform the *modus ponens* inference. But, as Cohen says (*ibid.*, p. 313), 'It seems very implausible to say that I could in this way come to know that I'm not seeing a white table illuminated by red lights.'

Wright (2003, pp. 60–63) discusses this same example—though with a wall instead of a table. His view, like Cohen's, is that one could not, just by looking at a surface, acquire a warrant for believing that it is not illuminated by red lights. And, according to Wright, the principles governing transmission of warrant have the desired result that the evidential warrant for TABLE (II) is not transmitted to TABLE (III) (*ibid.*, p. 61):

> While you have—no doubt quite justifiably—taken it for granted that the conditions were generally suitable for the acquisition of reliable information by causal-perceptual means, it would be absurd to pretend that you had *gained a reason for thinking so* ... just by dint of the fact that those specific possibilities [such as deceptive lighting] are logically excluded by the beliefs which, courtesy of your background assumption, you have now confirmed.

The warrant for TABLE (II) is not transmitted to TABLE (III) because it only counts as a warrant in the first place because of my antecedent warrant for assuming, or taking for granted, TABLE (III).

However, suppose that, as against Wright's view, there is no need for an antecedent warrant—not even an antecedent unearned warrant—for assuming, trusting, or believing that TABLE (III) is true. Suppose that the evidence described in TABLE (I) by itself supports TABLE (II). Then, not only do I have an evidential warrant for believing TABLE (II), but also, by following through the *modus ponens* argument, I can gain— perhaps for the first time—a warrant for believing TABLE (III). When the evidence described in TABLE (I) is the warrant for TABLE (II), the argument from TABLE (II) and the conditional premise to TABLE (III) is *cogent* and the principle limiting transmission of epistemic warrant (Section I) is not triggered. So the epistemological view that goes naturally with the notion of negative entitlement faces the problem of easy knowledge in a way that Wright's view does not.

Cohen's second instance of the problem of easy knowledge arises from the thought that, once basic perceptual knowledge is allowed, we have an easy—too easy—route to knowledge that perceptual experience is reliable, or at least to a battery of evidence that seems to support the hypothesis that perceptual experience is reliable. Cohen calls this form of the problem of easy knowledge 'the Problem of Easy Evidence' (*ibid.*, pp. 317–8).

Consider the following argument (*ibid.*, p. 318):

EVIDENCE (0)   I am having an experience as of this table being red.
EVIDENCE (1)   This table is red.
EVIDENCE (2)   This table visually appears to be red.

Therefore:

EVIDENCE (3)   On this occasion, at least, my colour vision operated correctly.

As before, I have a perceptual warrant for believing EVIDENCE (1), constituted by the visual experience described in EVIDENCE (0). Furthermore, I have a first-personal warrant for believing EVIDENCE (2). From EVIDENCE (1) and EVIDENCE (2), it follows that the table is the way it visually appears to be. But, according to Cohen, it is implausible that I could in this way come to know that, at least on this occasion, my colour vision operated correctly or that I could in this kind of way amass evidence to support the claim that my colour vision is generally reliable.

VII

Limiting the Rational Deployment of Warrants. If we adopt the notion of negative entitlement and the epistemological framework into which it naturally fits, then Moore's argument turns out not to be an example of transmission-failure (Section IV). Furthermore, as we have just seen, looking at a table turns out to be a way of gaining a warrant for believing, first, that it is not a white table illuminated by red lights and, second, that one's colour vision is operating correctly. Earlier, we noted that, if warrant is transmitted from premises to conclusion in Moore's argument, then a concern (developed towards the end of Section II) does not arise. That is a good result. But there is also a cost. For if Moore's argument is not an example of transmission-failure then we need something else to say about why it is unsatisfying as a response to the sceptic.

That is one problem for negative entitlement; and Cohen's problem of easy knowledge is another. Both problems have the same source, namely, the shift from Wright's notion of entitlement and his acceptance of the sceptic's demand to the negative notion of entitlement and rejection of the sceptic's demand. For, once that shift is made, the (MOORE) argument, and the (TABLE) and (EVIDENCE) arguments, no longer trigger the principle that limits transmission of warrant as Wright defines that notion. Thus in the case of the (EVIDENCE) argument, for example, Wright will claim that the experience described in EVIDENCE (0) counts as a warrant for believing EVIDENCE (1) only because we have an antecedent warrant—entitlement—for assuming the truth of the conclusion EVIDENCE (3). But, after the shift, we have to deny this. In this section, I want to sketch an idea that offers an alternative response to the problems posed by transmission of epistemic warrant in these arguments.

If we replace Wright's notion of entitlement to trust with the purely negative notion, then we deny that a lack of positive warrant for a cornerstone-like proposition P is, by itself, epistemically damaging. But warranted doubt about P is still damaging. For it defeats or removes a putative warrant for any belief in the corresponding region. And if that is so then even an unwarranted doubt is damaging to our pursuit of epistemic projects. For a doubt about P rationally commits one to not availing oneself of a warrant for any belief in the corresponding region.[20]

20. Pryor (2004) draws a distinction between 'what you have *justification* for believing, and what you are *rationally committed to believing*, given the beliefs and doubts you in fact already have'. He then says (*ibid.*): 'Suppose you suspect that your colour vision might not be working properly. This doubt is in fact unjustified, but you have not realized that. In any case, I'm inclined to say that your doubt would make it irrational for you to form any beliefs about colour, on the basis of your visual experiences. Even though your experiences might very well be giving you justification for those beliefs.'

If this much is right then we can, it seems to me, take one further step. For suppose that we undertake an epistemic project whose conduct is conditioned by an initial supposition that P is, or may very well be, false. Suppose, in short, that the conduct of the project is conditioned by suppositional doubt about P. Then, within the context of that project it is not possible rationally to avail oneself of those warrants that would, in reality, be defeated by a warranted doubt about P.

Now there is a kind of epistemic project whose conduct is conditioned by suppositional doubt, namely, the project of *settling the question* whether a particular proposition is true. As I understand this idea, the epistemic project of settling a question begins with my regarding that question as open *pro tem*. By this, I do not mean that I work myself into a state of really doubting that the proposition is true. When I begin by regarding a question as open, I suppose, for the purposes of the project, that the proposition is, or may very well be, false. This initial supposition then conditions my conduct of the project. In particular, it conditions my rational deployment of epistemic warrants as I try to answer—to settle—the question that I have begun by regarding as open. If I try to settle the question whether or not some cornerstone-like proposition P is true then I begin by suppositionally doubting that P is true and my conduct of the question-settling project is conditioned by that suppositional doubt. But then, within the context of that project, I cannot rationally avail myself of a warrant for any belief in the corresponding region. So, in particular, I cannot deploy those warrants to settle the question in favour of P. This is so even though in reality—outside the context of the question-settling project—I do have warrants for those beliefs. And it is so whether in reality I have a positive entitlement to assume P (as on Wright's account) or just a negative entitlement not to call P into question (as on the alternative account).

To see how a suppositional doubt conditions the conduct of a question-settling project, imagine that I undertake the project of settling the question whether or not there is an external world as ordinarily conceived—whether instead, perhaps, I am the envatted victim of a powerful but deceptive scientist. In particular, imagine that I attempt to settle that question in favour of an external world by deploying the warrants that I have for believing the premises of Moore's argument. I begin the project by regarding the question of the truth of the conclusion of Moore's argument as open *pro tem*. So my conduct of the question-settling project is conditioned by the initial supposition that Moore's conclusion is, or may very well be, false.

As the sceptic points out, if I really believed what I now suppose—if I really doubted Moore's conclusion—then I could not rationally regard my experience as constituting a warrant for believing MOORE (1). Just so, within the context of a project whose conduct is conditioned by the suppositional doubt, I cannot rationally avail myself of the warrant for believing MOORE (1). In short, I cannot settle the question whether or not the conclusion of Moore's argument is true—and, in particular, cannot settle it in favour of Moore's conclusion—by deploying the epistemic warrants that I have for believing the premises.

The idea of the epistemic project of settling a question offers— I hope—an alternative response to the problems posed by transmission of epistemic warrant. In a fuller treatment, this idea would be set against the background of a distinction between two kinds of epistemic project—deciding what to believe and settling a question—and two notions of transmission of epistemic warrant. The two kinds of epistemic project correspond to two dialectical purposes of arguing that Frank Jackson calls the teasing-out purpose and the convincing purpose.[21] Principles limiting the two kinds of transmission of warrant correspond to limitations on arguments that can be effectively propounded for each of the two purposes and so to two notions of how an argument can beg the question. But all of that is for another paper.[22] Here, I only want to indicate how the idea of settling a question gives us something to say about the intuitive inadequacy of Moore's argument and about Cohen's problem of easy knowledge.

In the concluding section of his paper, Wright says (p. 206):

> In general, it has to be recognised that the unified strategy can at most deliver a *sceptical solution* ... The unified strategy ... concedes the basic point of the sceptical arguments to which it reacts, namely that we do indeed have no claim to know, in any sense involving possession

21. Jackson, 1987, Chapter 6.
22. 'Two Purposes of Arguing and Two Epistemic Projects', forthcoming.

of evidence for their likely truth, that certain cornerstones of what we take to be procedures yielding knowledge and justified belief hold good.

In the alternative epistemological framework that I have been exploring, the warrants for the premises of Moore's argument provide us with a reason to believe the conclusion. Warrant is transmitted, in Wright's sense: MOORE (III) is what we should believe. But we cannot rationally avail ourselves of the warrant for MOORE (II) within the epistemic project of settling the question whether or not MOORE (III) is true—even though, in reality, it is an epistemically adequate warrant. This is the point at which we concede something to the sceptic. Moore's argument furnishes a warrant, but not a question-settling warrant, for MOORE (III).[23]

Turning now to the first of Cohen's two examples of the problem of easy knowledge, we can say that it is implausible that I could *settle the question* whether or not the table is white but illuminated by red lights by deploying my warrants for believing TABLE (II) and the conditional premise. But the unwanted result is not a consequence of allowing basic knowledge. Suppose that I were to doubt the truth of the conclusion TABLE (III). Suppose that I were to believe that this is, or may very well be, a white table illuminated by red lights; in short, that the lighting is, or may very well be, deceptive. This belief—this doubt—would rationally commit me to not availing myself of the perceptual warrant for believing TABLE (II). Just so, if I were to begin an epistemic project by suppositionally doubting TABLE (III) then, within the context of that project, I could not rationally avail myself of the perceptual warrant for believing TABLE (II). I have an epistemically adequate warrant for believing TABLE (II) and warrant is transmitted, in Wright's sense: TABLE (III) is what I should believe. But I cannot deploy my warrant for TABLE (II) in order to settle the question whether or not TABLE (III) is true.

Finally, the situation is similar with the second of Cohen's examples. If I were to doubt the truth of EVIDENCE (3) then I

---

23. It remains to connect this point with Wright's distinction between knowing and having a *claim* to know (p. 206, n. 23).

could not rationally take my visual experience as of the table being red as providing any support at all for EVIDENCE (1). Just so, in the context of the project of settling the question whether or not EVIDENCE (3) is true, I cannot rationally avail myself of the perceptual warrant for EVIDENCE (1).

VIII

Conclusion. Wright accepts the sceptic's demand that there should be antecedent epistemic warrants for the propositions that Wright calls 'cornerstones' and for the presuppositions of cognitive and epistemic projects. Epistemic entitlement, as Wright conceives it, is a kind of epistemic warrant, though not a warrant that is earned.

In this paper, I have been exploring the prospects for a different notion of entitlement—I have called it 'negative entitlement'. This is not a kind of epistemic warrant, for negative entitlement is not an entitlement to assume, trust, or believe any proposition. Since we can scarcely hope to earn an antecedent warrant for Wright's cornerstone propositions, and since it is not coherent to aim to earn a warrant for the presuppositions of every epistemic project in which we engage, negative entitlement fits naturally into an epistemological framework in which the sceptic's demand is disputed. Thus, for example, negative entitlement goes naturally with the dogmatist account of perceptual justification that Pryor favours.

If the sceptic's demand is accepted then there are examples of non-transmission of epistemic warrant, as Wright defines that notion. These examples include Moore's argument and the two problematic arguments that Cohen considers. So we have a ready account of the intuitive inadequacy of Moore's argument as a response to the sceptic; and we avoid Cohen's problem of easy knowledge. But if the sceptic's demand is disputed then Moore's argument is not an example of transmission-failure and neither are Cohen's two arguments. So we need to find something else to say about why Moore's argument is unsatisfying; and we need a solution to the problem of easy knowledge. I have tried to meet these needs by appealing to the idea that, even where warrant is transmitted from the premises to the conclusion of an argument, still it may not be possible rationally to deploy the warrants for the premises in order to settle the question whether or not the conclusion is true.

I have defended negative entitlement and the epistemological framework into which it fits by responding to the objections that arise out of the differences from Wright's account over warrant transmission. But I have been relatively cautious in arguing for negative entitlement and against Wright's notion. Still less have I ventured any substantive account of our epistemic entitlements as Wright does in the central sections of his paper. At the outset, I contrasted epistemic entitlement with epistemic achievement. But while entitlement is not itself an epistemic achievement, under-standing the nature and source of entitlement would certainly be an epistemological achievement of some magnitude.[24]

REFERENCES

Burge, T., 1988, Individualism and Self-Knowledge. *Journal of Philosophy*, 85, pp. 649–63.

Burge, T., 1993, Content Preservation. *Philosophical Review*, 102, pp. 457–88.

Burge, T., 2003a Perceptual Entitlement. *Philosophy and Phenomenological Research*, 67 pp. 503–48.

Burge, T., 2003b, Reply to Martin Davies. In M. J. Frápolli and E. Romero (eds.), *Meaning, Basic Self-Knowledge, and Mind: Essays on Tyler Burge* (Stanford: CSLI Publications) pp. 250–7.

Cohen, S., 2002, Basic Knowledge and the Problem of Easy Knowledge. *Philosophy and Phenomenological Research*, 65, pp. 309–29.

Davies, M., 1998, Externalism, Architecturalism, and Epistemic Warrant. In C. Wright, B.C. Smith and C. Macdonald (eds.), *Knowing Our Own Minds* (Oxford: Oxford University Press) pp. 321–61.

Davies, M., 2000, Externalism and Armchair Knowledge. In P. Boghossian and C. Peacocke (eds.), *New Essays on the A Priori* (Oxford: Oxford University Press) pp. 384–414.

Davies, M., 2003a, The Problem of Armchair Knowledge. In S. Nuccetelli (ed.), *New Essays on Semantic Externalism and Self-Knowledge* (Cambridge, MA: MIT Press) pp. 23–55.

Davies, M., 2003b, Externalism, Self-Knowledge and Transmission of Warrant. In M.J. Frápolli and E. Romero (eds.), *Meaning, Basic Self-Knowledge, and Mind: Essays on Tyler Burge* (Stanford: CSLI Publications) pp. 105–130.

Jackson, F., 1987, *Conditionals* (Oxford: Blackwell Publishers).

McKinsey, M., 1991, Anti-Individualism and Privileged Access. *Analysis*, 51, pp. 9–16.

24. My first thoughts about warrant transmission and about transmission-failure were prompted by reading Crispin Wright's British Academy Lecture. I have continued to learn from that lecture and from Wright's subsequent writings on the topic. I am much indebted to Tyler Burge and Jim Pryor—to their writings on epistemology and, in recent years, to conversations with each of them. Special thanks to Mark Greenberg for comments and conversations over many years and for his detailed comments on a penultimate draft.

Moore, G. E., 1959, Proof of an External World. In *Philosophical Papers* (London: Allen and Unwin) pp. 127–50.

Pollock, J., 1974, *Knowledge and Justification* (Princeton, NJ: Princeton University Press).

Pryor, J., 2000, The Skeptic and the Dogmatist. *Noûs*, 34, pp. 517–49.

Pryor, J., 2004, Is Moore's Argument an Example of Transmission-Failure? *Philosophical Perspectives*, 18.

Wittgenstein, L., 1969, *On Certainty* (Oxford: Basil Blackwell).

Wright, C., 1985, Facts and Certainty. *Proceedings of the British Academy*, 71, pp. 429–72.

Wright, C., 2000, Cogency and Question-Begging: Some Reflections on McKinsey's Paradox and Putnam's Proof. *Philosophical Issues*, 10, pp. 140–63.

Wright, C., 2002, (Anti-)sceptics Simple and Subtle: G. E. Moore and John McDowell. *Philosophy and Phenomenological Research*, 65, pp. 331–49.

Wright, C., 2003, Some Reflections on the Acquisition of Warrant by Inference. In S. Nuccetelli (ed.), *New Essays on Semantic Externalism and Self-Knowledge* (Cambridge, MA: MIT Press) pp. 57–77.